Tenth Edition

Essentials of Illinois School Finance

A Guide to Techniques, Issues, and Resources

James B. Fritts - Author
Ann Williams - Senior Editor

IASB Illinois Association of School Boards
Lighting the Way to Excellence in School Governance

ISBN 978-880331-42-2

Copyright © 2024 by the Illinois Association of School Boards. All rights reserved.

This work may not be reproduced in any manner, in whole or in part, by itself or as part of a derivative work, nor may it be stored in any information storage and retrieval system, without the express written permission of the Illinois Association of School Boards.

Cover art: Matt Schultz/Getty Images

Disclaimer: The contents of this publication are designed to provide helpful information on the subject matter covered. Federal, state, and local financing sources, provisions, and requirements vary and often change, and it is the responsibility of the user to modify the contents accordingly. The publication excludes some provisions and procedures that are unique to Chicago Public School District 299. Neither the author nor the Illinois Association of School Boards can in any way assure that the contents will be used for the purposes intended and accordingly neither assumes any responsibility for their use.

About the Tenth Edition

Illinois school officials who rely on this book for help in navigating the complex issues involved in school finance owe thanks to author James B. Fritts, Ph.D., and senior editor Ann Williams, Ed.D. for their work to keep the book as current and accurate as possible.

This Tenth Edition retains and updates information on the basic principles and operations of Illinois school financial management. It describes the rationale for and the workings of the state's Evidence-Based Funding formula and the prospects it brings for improvement in the equity and adequacy of Illinois school funding. Part One presents key information about Illinois school finance, emphasizing budgeting and management of revenues. Part Two addresses the budgeting and management of expenditures and describes ways to assess a district's overall financial health. Part Three describes the school board's financial responsibilities and how the board can fulfill its leadership responsibilities for the school district's financial health. An appendix identifies resources that enable the reader to locate additional information.

All editions of this book have reflected the wisdom and insights of instructors in school administration and finance, state officials, school administrative staff, and school board members.

About the Author and Senior Editor

James B. Fritts earned a bachelor's degree in history at Swarthmore College, a master's degree in education at the University of Pennsylvania, and a doctor of philosophy in educational administration at Northwestern University. He has 35 years' experience in public schools as a teacher and administrator. Thirty years were spent in Skokie District 68 in several administrative capacities, including assistant superintendent for business.

Fritts also taught graduate courses in educational administration and finance at Loyola University Chicago, and currently teaches at Northeastern Illinois University. He is a frequent presenter at conferences and workshops of the Illinois Association of School Business Officials and the Illinois Association of School Boards. He is a senior associate of Hazard, Young, Attea and Associates, where he specializes in administrative selection, organizational studies, and financial planning.

This work has been updated in 2023 with assistance by senior editor Ann Williams, SFO, CSBO, Ed.D., who is Deputy Superintendent for Operations and Treasurer for Elgin-based School District U-46, the second-largest school district in Illinois. As a leader in the school business profession, she serves on the Illinois State Board of Education's Professional Review Panel which oversees the Evidence-Based Funding model for Illinois public schools.

With more than 20 years' experience in finance and operations, Williams is also an adjunct professor, teaching courses in finance, collective bargaining, and human resources. She has trained Illinois school board members on fiscal accountability. Williams received her bachelor's degree from Northern Illinois University, a master's degree from DePaul University, and her Ed.D. from Roosevelt University.

Contents

Part One — Securing, Budgeting, and Managing Revenue

1. The Illinois System of Public School Funding 3
2. Categories for Revenue Budgeting and Accounting 6
3. The Property Tax Cycle 10
4. Determining Property Tax Revenue 26
5. Personal Property Replacement Tax Revenue 38
6. Evidence-Based State Funding 39
7. State Categorical Funding 48
8. Federal and Other Grant Revenue 51
9. Local Funding Sources 57
10. Projecting Revenue 64
11. Borrowing Options 69
12. Revenue Management and Control 76
13. Calling a Finance Referendum 79

Part Two — Budgeting and Managing Expenditures

14. The Structure and Development of the Expenditure Budget 83
15. Budgeting Calendars and Communications 90
16. Budgeting the Elementary School 94
17. Budgeting the Secondary School 102
18. Budgeting and Managing Non-Instructional Costs 106
19. Expenditure Management and Control 118
20. Long-Term Expenditure Projections 123
21. Looking at the Big Picture 125
22. Looking Ahead 130

Part Three — Financial Responsibilities

23. Financial Responsibilities of the School Board 133
24. The Essential Role of School Board Financial Policy 135
25. The Board's Financial Duties and Calendar 139
26. The Financial Responsibilities of the Superintendent 146

Appendix

A / Resources and Acknowledgements 149
B / Bibliography 152
C / Index of Tables and Figures 155
Index 158

Foreword

By Kimberly Small, J.D.,
Executive Director, Illinois Association of School Boards

Essentials of Illinois School Finance was first published in 2002 as a tool for school business officials, superintendents, and other administrators with budgeting responsibilities. For the Illinois Association of School Boards, it serves as an excellent resource for members because subsequent editions add material on the financial responsibilities of school boards. Details help school board members understand what is involved in the financial management work of administrative staff and their responsibility as a member of the governing board.

Illinois' public schools face unprecedented financial challenges requiring administrators to hone their skills in managing school finances. Cuts to school funding tested the trust between boards of education and school leaders as districts struggled with difficult decisions about programming and personnel. In 2017 historic education funding reform — Evidence-Based Funding — required significant changes to portions of this book.

More recently, the COVID-19 pandemic presented new fiscal and operational challenges that stretch beyond the 2019-2020 and 2020-2021 academic years. This edition discusses effects of the pandemic on revenue sources and managing costs. Boards of education play an important role in the financial oversight of how schools are distributing new sources of relief funds.

Schools are now faced with deeper and more critical challenges to address school safety and security. This edition discusses costs associated with security upgrades and offers some cost-saving measures to help districts budget.

In addition to explaining revenue (Part One) and expenditures (Part Two), this book describes means by which the school board can fulfill its leadership responsibilities for the school district's financial health. In Part Three, *Chapter 24* describes the function of board policy and illustrates how discussion of a policy on financial health underlies short- and long-term budget planning. *Chapter 25* outlines the board's legal duties with respect to finance and the annual calendar of required actions on the budget, tax levy, annual financial report, and other matters. *Chapter 26* summarizes the financial responsibilities of the superintendent and the administrator responsible for the business functions.

It is essential to recognize that the financial responsibilities of the board of education differ markedly from those of the administrative staff. Although the detailed guidance contained in this book will help the board member understand what is involved, financial management is staff work, not board work.

Part One

1 / The Illinois System of Public School Funding

How Illinois Funds its Schools

January 2023 dawned with the expectation of improvement in the equity and adequacy of Illinois' school funding system. Healthy tax collections were projected to fund an increased General Fund budget for Fiscal Year 2024, which began in July 2023. In May, the State Board of Education approved a P-12 Education budget of $10.3 billion.

For many years, the state has ranked at the bottom in national rankings of school funding equity. By FY 2018, Illinois had fallen to 42nd place in funding equity while ranking only in the average range in adequacy. According to the National Center for Educational Statistics (NCES), the local share of Illinois school funding in FY 2018 was 55%. The state's share was only 39% while the federal share was 6%. (See *Figure 1*.)

Under the state's current funding formula, a child's education depends on the property tax wealth of the school district. The higher the local share of funding, the lower the state's allocation will be for that district. While Illinois' adequacy ranking (measured in regionally adjusted average dollars spent per pupil) was about $85 below average, the $10,488 spread between the districts with the highest and lowest per-pupil expenditures was the third widest among the states.

Proponents of school finance reform suggest that Illinois' funding dilemma is not that the total funds available to schools is inadequate. Rather the problem is that the available funds are not equitably distributed, and therefore the funding is not spent to its greatest effect. The Evidence-Based Funding (EBF) distribution formula was intended to address both objections. While some progress has been made, the formula will not provide adequate funding to the schools most in need for many years.

Beginning in 2017-2018, the EBF formula consolidated and redirected to the neediest districts several state aid programs with the most significant being General State Aid. Other programs included in the new funding model included supplemental state aid for children from low-income families; grants for English language programs; and the special education grants for personnel, students, and summer school. A district's EBF-distributed funding seeks to close the gap between its local fiscal capacity and the cost of offering an adequate program so that the district can achieve the state's goals for its students.

The district's "adequacy target" is based on student-related and cost variables for teachers, support staff, and non-personnel costs. Adjustments are made for districts in areas of the state with higher or lower than average costs. The formula also

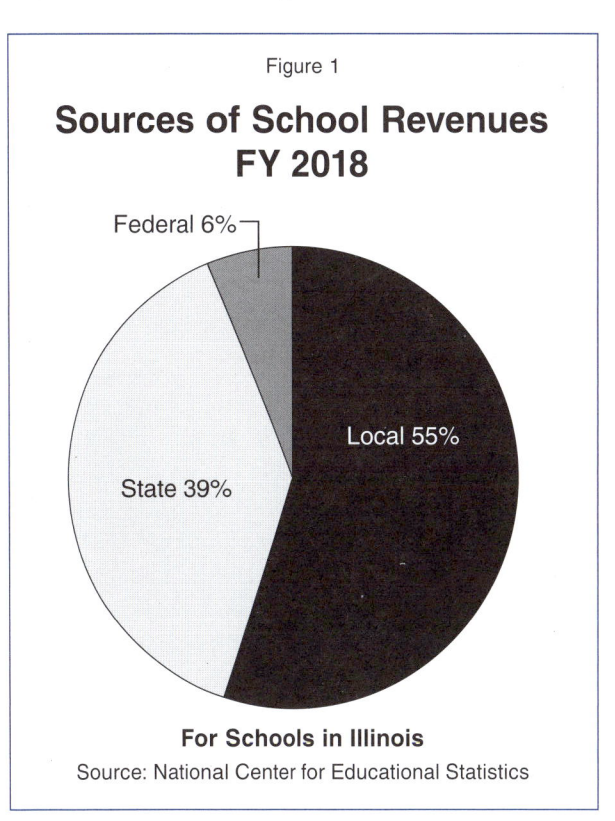

Figure 1

Sources of School Revenues FY 2018

Federal 6%
Local 55%
State 39%

For Schools in Illinois
Source: National Center for Educational Statistics

encourages and provides funding for a district to adopt improvements, based on its students' needs, from a menu of 27 research-supported practices including reduced class sizes, high levels of pupil support services, and intensive, focused professional development.

Districts with the greatest gaps between their "capacity targets" and "adequacy targets" receive most of the annual increases in EBF. Full funding of EBF will require substantial new state contributions at a time of extreme pressures on the state budget and resistance to tax increases. With an initial projected cost of $5 billion to move all districts up to the third tier (of four) in funding, the phase-in period was projected to be approximately 10 years. Inflation and the freeze of the EBF increase for 2020-2021 have upset the projected timeline, which may not reach full funding until well into the 2030s.

Chapter 6 describes the research-based components of the EBF formula and the variables that determine a district's funding and illustrates the calculation of a district's entitlement.

The 2024 State Budget

In May 2023, the General Assembly and Governor approved a General Fund budget calling for an increase in P-12 education funding, but no increase in EBF funding. Appropriations did increase for Early Childhood Education, mandated categorical grants for special education, English language programs and transportation. Details of the categorical grant budget appear in *Chapter 7*.

Non-discretionary expenditures, those for the operations of state government, public safety, and essential human services are expected to consume much of the projected revenue. Individual and corporate income taxes contributed 58% of General Fund revenue in the FY 2023 budget, and sales taxes contribute 20%. (See *Table 1*.) These revenues are vulnerable in a recession, unless income and sales tax rates increase. Other options include increases in corporate tax rates, lottery, gaming, liquor, or various "excise taxes." One bright spot in FY 2023 revenues was higher-than-expected receipts from state taxes on recreational marijuana.

Among the most productive revenue-increasing options would be broadening the sales tax to include services, common in most sales tax states. Increasing the personal income tax through taxation of retirement income and elimination of deductions

Table 1

Fiscal Year 2024 Illinois General Fund Projected Revenues and Expenditures

FY 2024 Forecast General Fund Revenue

Total Revenue $49,944,000,000

Source	$ millions
Individual income taxes	24,659
Corporate income taxes	5,548
Sales taxes	10,415
Utility taxes	721
Lottery	759
Gaming	175
Cannabis	116
All other sources	2,537
Other transfers	1,000
Federal sources	4,014
Total	**$49,944**

FY 2024 Forecast General Fund Expenditures

Total Expenditures $51,800,000,000

Category	$ millions
P-12 Education	10,329
Higher Education	2,470
Environment and Culture	98
Economic Development	323
Public Safety	2,462
Human Services	9,900
Health Care	9,070
Government Services	3,824
Chicago Teacher Pensions	323
Group Health Insurance	1,837
K-12 Education Pensions	6,043
State University Pensions	1,918
State Employee Pensions	1,871
Transfers Out	436
Debt Service	1,596
Unspent Appropriations	(700)
Total	**$51,800**

Source: Illinois Approved Budget, May 26, 2023

and credits have also been proposed. However, an Amendment to the Illinois Constitution to establish graduated income tax rates on higher-income taxpayers did not receive voter approval in the November 2020 election. Some school supporters fear that a property tax freeze or other restrictions may accompany higher income tax rates, and that shifting some of the state's obligation for teacher funding to local districts may also occur to alleviate pressure on the state education budget.

Board members and school leaders should become and remain familiar with the state budget process, the mechanisms of distributing grants to school districts, proposals to restrict access to the local property tax, and shifts of teacher pension obligations to school districts in trade for state tax increases. A goal of this book is to provide insight into these topics in efforts to ensure board members and school leaders are effective advocates for their schools.

2 / Categories for Revenue Budgeting and Accounting

Information in this chapter is intended to guide the user in reading and using the budget form. However, a full treatment of school financial accounting is beyond the scope of this book; balance sheet account codes required for recording transactions and financial reporting are not included. Consult the current accounting manual, forms, and regulations that are available from the Illinois State Board of Education website (www.isbe.net) for additional information.

The Budget as a Legal Document and Revenue Plan

Illinois law requires school districts to prepare a balanced annual budget by designated dates and to include in it specified information on anticipated revenues and expenditures for the coming year. The budget comprises the district's financial plan for the year. A summary section reveals whether the budget is balanced or shows a surplus or a deficit, and projects the changes in the district's balance sheet that will result from the year's operations. If the budget is not balanced, a plan to achieve a balance within three years must be completed and filed with the budget.

Legally, the adoption of the budget provides authority for taxation and for expending money and provides managerial information for use by state and federal agencies and the school district's board of education and administration. The legal calendar for budget adoption is discussed in *Chapter 15*.

Section 23 Illinois Administrative Code, Part 100 (IAC) — previously referred to as the Illinois Program Accounting Manual — specifies the requirements for budgeting and accounting of receipts and expenditures. Districts design their own "chart of accounts" within this framework. The requirements are consistent with federal accounting manuals, updates to Generally Accepted Accounting Principles (GAAP) standards, and changes to various laws. The Administrative Code may be found on the Finance, Budgets, and Funding section of the Illinois State Board of Education (ISBE) website. The IAC assigns numbers to each balance sheet, revenue, and expenditure account. These numbers appear on the state forms used for compiling the annual budget and the end-of-year Annual Financial Report. While districts may prepare displays of their budgets in various formats to facilitate communications with their boards of education, public, and staff, the official budget and accounting system must follow the state revenue categories and numbering system.

The IAC specifies the categories of revenues and the allowable fund assignments for each revenue item. The revenue section of the budget form is a matrix, with the funds defining the columns and the revenue items defining the rows. A white space in a cell indicates that the district can assign all or a portion of that revenue to that particular fund. A shaded space indicates a non-allowable assignment

The official state budget form can be downloaded from the ISBE website as a Microsoft Excel worksheet, allowing one to create or simulate a school budget and follow the changes in the district's financial position that result from increasing or decreasing certain revenue and expenditure items. The form is found on the Finance, Budgets and Funding section of the ISBE website. An excerpt of the revenue section of the budget form appears in *Table 2* on *page 8*.

The budget revenue section details, in more than 100 categories, the various local, state, and federal revenues that schools are eligible to receive. A district will not receive all of these revenues; some items are specific grant programs that benefit only specific

> Effective with Fiscal Year 2021, one form (50-36/50-39) is provided for both the school district budget and the joint agreement budget. Instructions for downloading, completing, and submitting the budget form are contained in "The School District/Joint Agreement Budget Instructions (For New Users)." Search for "Budget Form" on the ISBE website.
>
> Instructions for coding revenue and expenditure transactions and information on balance sheet and summary sections and on borrowing, transfers and other common transactions, are found in *Mechanics of a School District Budget* published by ISBE. The chart of accounts and rules for accounting, budgeting, and financial reporting are found in the Illinois Administrative Code. Links to these resources are found on the ISBE website.
>
> In addition to recording revenues, expenditures, and other budget data, the budget form contains sections on which budget deficits are calculated. If required, the district reports its deficit reduction assumptions and required plans. Other information reports are required on the district's administrative salaries, vendor contracts, and plans to use its Evidence-Based Funding grants (see *Chapter 6*.)

student populations in some districts. The revenue section of the budget is divided into four major groups:
1. Local revenues, such as property taxes, fees, tuition payments, and interest.
2. Flow-through receipts and revenues from one local educational agency to another.
3. Unrestricted state revenues, mainly Evidence-Based Funding aid and restricted grants in support of programs such as special education, bilingual education, and other special purposes.
4. Federal revenues, including special purpose grants and student meal reimbursements. Some grants are received directly from the federal government and others come through the state.

The reader of the budget or accounting report can discern the source of the funds by noting the account number assigned to the item in question. Local revenues are numbered in the 1000 series, flow-through revenues in the 2000s, state revenues in the 3000s, and federal revenues in the 4000s.

Other sources of receipts, such as proceeds from the sale of bonds and property and transfers of funds among accounts, are budgeted and accounted for in a 7000 series, "other financing sources." These transactions are not recorded in the revenue section of the budget but appear in the Budget Summary section at the beginning of the budget document, along with other uses of funds, such as transfers among funds in an 8000 series. Proper accounting treatment of non-recurring transactions is essential to an accurate budget and its interpretation to the board of education, public, bond rating agencies, and other audiences.

Fund Accounting

Each item of revenue must be assigned in the budget to one or more funds and to its designated account. A minimum six-digit account number is used. The first two digits designate the fund. The second four identify the revenue account description (e.g. Designated Purposes Levies, Regular Transportation Fees from Pupils or Parents (In State), Evidence-Based Funding Formula), following the chart of accounts in the IAC.

A "fund" is a division of the budget for specific activities and objectives. Each fund is subject to laws and regulations to assure money in that fund is used for the purposes specified for it in the law and the school district budget. A fund is not the same as a bank account; the district's bank accounts and investments may co-mingle the various funds, though some districts maintain separate bank accounts for each individual fund. The accounting system separates the moneys for the purpose of administering the budget, much as one's personal bank accounts might be divided in the household budget into "funds" for living expenses, vacation, or entertainment.

There are nine major funds listed in the state budget form. While nine funds are established by code, districts may elect to use fewer funds based on their budgetary allocations for each year. As an example, if a district does not have any capital projects planned for a given school year, the district may not include the Capital Project Fund in that year's budget. School districts do not require all of them unless special purpose revenues and expenditures apply to that year's budget. The major funds, their purposes, and the numbers assigned to them for accounting purposes are shown in *Table 3* on *page 9*.

Certain revenues, such as property taxes, are allocated to all of the funds according to tax rates determined by law, actions of the district's board of education, and, in certain instances, by its voters in a referendum. Some forms of state assistance and many locally raised revenues can also be allocated to the various funds, depending on need. Other revenues, such as taxes levied to repay bonded debt and to pay employer

Table 2
ISBE Budget Form

Here is a segment excerpted from the Illinois State Board of Education (ISBE) school district budget form for estimated receipts and revenues. The form is a grid created by arraying the nine funds across the top and listing the individual tax levies and other revenue sources down the side. Forms and instructions may be downloaded from the ISBE website at www.isbe.net.

Description	Acct No.	Educational	Operations & Maintenance	Debt Service	Transportation
RECEIPTS/REVENUE FROM LOCAL SOURCES					
AD VALOREM TAXES LEVIED BY LOCAL EDUCATION AGENCY					
Designated Purposes Levies	1110 - 1120				
Leasing Purposes Levy	1130				
Special Education Purposes Levy	1140				
FICA and Medicare Only Levies	1150				
Area Vocational Construction Purposes Levy	1160				
Summer School Purposes Levy	1170				
Other Tax Levies (Describe & Itemize)	1190				
Total Ad Valorem Taxes Levied by District					
PAYMENTS IN LIEU OF TAXES					
Mobile Home Privilege Tax	1210				
Payments from Local Housing Authority	1220				
Personal Property Replacement Taxes	1230				
Other Payments in Lieu of Taxes (Describe & Itemize)	1290				
Total Payments in Lieu of Taxes					
TUITION					
Regular Tuition from Pupils or Parents (In State)	1311				
Regular Tuition from Other Districts (In State)	1312				
Regular Tuition from Other Sources (In State)	1313				
Regular Tuition from Other Sources (Out of State)	1314				
Summer School Tuition from Pupils or Parents (In State)	1321				
Summer School Tuition from Other Districts (In State)	1322				
Summer School Tuition from Other Sources (In State)	1323				
Summer School Tuition from Other Sources (Out of State)	1324				
CTE Tuition from Pupils or Parents (In State)	1331				
CTE Tuition from Other Districts (In State)	1332				
CTE Tuition from Other Sources (In State)	1333				
CTE Tuition from Other Sources (Out of State)	1334				
Special Education Tuition from Pupils or Parents (In State)	1341				
Special Education Tuition from Other Districts (In State)	1342				
Special Education Tuition from Other Sources (In State)	1343				
Special Education Tuition from Other Sources (Out of State)	1344				
Adult Tuition from Pupils or Parents (In State)	1351				
Adult Tuition from Other Districts (In State)	1352				
Adult Tuition from Other Sources (In State)	1353				
Adult Tuition from Other Sources (Out of State)	1354				
Total Tuition					
TRANSPORTATION FEES					
Regular Transportation Fees from Pupils or Parents (In State)	1411				
Regular Transportation Fees from Other Districts (In State)	1412				
Regular Transportation Fees from Other Sources (In State)	1413				
Regular Transportation Fees from Co-curricular Activities (In State)	1415				

Table 3
Major Funds for Budgeting and Accounting

10	Educational Fund	The largest fund, for instruction-related items
20	Operations & Maintenance Fund	For the upkeep of buildings and grounds
30	Debt Service Fund	Used solely for payments on debt and capital leases
40	Transportation Fund	For costs associated with busing and transportation staff
50	Municipal Retirement/Social Security Fund	For the district's share of required payments
60	Capital Projects Fund	Used for non-recurring projects
70	Working Cash Fund	For funds dedicated to provide a cash reserves
80	Tort	For liability insurance and judgments
90	Fire Prevention and Safety Fund	For eligible, code-required building projects

Please consult the ISBE publication, *Mechanics of a School District Budget*, for an expanded summary of the types of transactions that are to be assigned to the various funds.

shares of Social Security, Medicare, and Municipal Retirement payments, must be allocated to that fund only and cannot be spent for any other purpose. The allowable fund assignments for each revenue item are specified in the IAC and the state budget form.

The Importance of Budgeting Revenues

School districts engage in budgeting activities throughout the school year. A sound revenue premise is essential for making decisions on the programs, personnel, and purchases that will be reflected in the following year's expenditure budget. Information pertinent to estimating the following year's revenues from property taxes, state and federal aid, and other major sources should be gathered regularly, and a first draft of a revenue budget for the following year prepared in the fall. These estimates can be revised over the coming months, as additional information becomes known. While many districts adopt the annual budget earlier in the fiscal year, state statute does not require adoption until September, which allows for more accurate revenue projections.

Long-term revenue projections are an essential element of planning for the future of the school program. Such projections are commonly constructed by "trending forward" the changes that have taken place for the most recent three to five years. A major disruption in one or more revenue sources, especially one of uncertain duration such as occurred in 2020 due to the COVID-19 pandemic, may also require alternative "best-case and worst-case" projections under differing assumptions about property taxes and state and local funding. Adjustments are made to reflect new factors, such as changes in property valuations and state funding. Like the annual revenue budget, projections should be frequently updated and shared with the board of education, so long-term planning can take place based on the latest information on available resources. *Chapter 10* explains the process for budgeting and projecting the major sources of revenues.

To understand your district's dependence on local revenues, especially property taxes, as compared with state and federal revenue sources, read the revenue pages of your district's budget. Locate the lines showing the local, state, federal, and total revenue for each fund and for all funds. For each fund, calculate the percentage of fund revenues from local, state, and federal sources. Make the same calculation for the total revenue budget. How does the revenue breakdown compare to current Illinois averages? (See *Chapter 1*.) This information is useful in telling the community about how its schools are funded.

3 / The Property Tax Cycle

This chapter describes the Illinois property tax system and how schools gain access to their main source of revenue. It identifies the officers and agencies that are responsible for each event in the cycle, and the timetable of events that determine a school district's property tax revenue. It then discusses the assessment procedures for the different types of property that comprise the tax base of Illinois school districts. Finally, it describes those actions which the board of education must take each year to secure property tax revenue, concluding with the tax levy filed each December.

Special thanks to Ares Dalianis, Partner of Franczek P.C. of Chicago for contributions to this chapter. Additional contributors are listed in the bibliography (Appendix B).

School districts can exert less control over revenues than expenditures. Therefore, it is important that superintendents, business managers, and board members understand the points of control that do exist for each revenue source. In the case of property taxes, these necessary understandings include the calculation of tax revenue needs and levies; the critical decisions, steps, and deadlines for board levy actions; and awareness of the measures that the district can take in response to assessment appeals, tax objections, tax increment financing districts, and other economic development incentives.

Overview of the Property Tax Cycle

The property tax cycle has two major parts. The first is assessment, in which township, county, and state officials and agencies participate. It produces the total equalized assessed valuation (EAV) of the school district, also known as the property tax base. The second part of the cycle converts the tax base into revenue. It begins with the board of education's annual tax revenue request (called the levy). The county clerk, working from the EAV and the levy, calculates the school district's total tax rate and property tax billings (called the extension). Finally, the county treasurer prepares and mails the tax bills and handles the collection of taxes and distribution of payments to schools and other government units. *Figure 2* on *page 12* identifies the role of each official and agency in the cycle.

Each year begins a new property tax cycle. For reasons going back to the Great Depression, Illinois property taxes are paid one year in arrears. Therefore, the cycle for the 2022 tax year will generate revenues to be received during the 2023 calendar year. Money from the levy filed in December will begin flowing to the schools towards the end of the 2022-23 school year and continue through the summer and fall of calendar year 2023, during the 2023-24 school year. Because the cycles for more than one year are underway at any given time, it is important to understand which tax year is involved in the various steps of the cycle as they impact the school district. The steps are summarized by season in the box on *page 19*.

The Assessment Process

Property assessment is an unpopular, difficult, and somewhat subjective process involving several layers of government. Assessment is primarily a township and county function, performed by elected officials. Their work is then reviewed at both the county and state levels to achieve the level and uniformity required by law and the Illinois Constitution. By law, property is to be assessed at one-third of its fair market value. The Illinois Constitution, in Article IX, Section 4, makes an exception for counties with a population greater than 200,000 that have approved a classification ordinance setting levels of assessment other than 33.33%. To date, only Cook County has availed itself of this exception. The Cook County Real Property Assessment

Glossary of Terms

Illinois property tax administration uses some specialized terminology. Key terms are defined here:

Appeal: A process by which a property owner or taxing agency requests an adjustment of an assessment.

Assessment: The process of valuing real property for tax purposes.

Assessed valuation: The taxable value placed on the property by the local assessor.

Collection: Receipt of property owners' payments by the county treasurer.

Distribution: Payments of tax receipts by the county treasurer to schools and other units of local government.

Equalization: Adjustments to local assessed valuations to bring about an overall assessment for a township or county equal to one-third of fair market value.

Equalized assessed valuation (EAV): A property's valuation after county and state equalization are performed. The term is applied to both individual properties and the total property within a school district or unit of government. For farm acreage and buildings and coal rights, the final assessed valuation is also the equalized value.

Extension: The process by which the county clerk calculates a government agency's tax rate. The total extension is the product of the agency's EAV multiplied by its calculated tax rate, and is equal to the total property tax billings on the agency's behalf. For revenue budgeting, it should be adjusted to allow for taxes that will be delayed or not collected, and for possible refunds.

Levy: The amount of the school district's need for property taxes for each fund as certified in the board of education's annual levy resolution in December.

Multiplier (also known as the equalization factor): The factor applied to a township or county's total assessed valuation to equalize it to one-third of fair market value, the rate specified in law.

Review: Oversight and adjustment of a local assessor's valuations by a county agency to assure uniformity and conformance with legally specified assessment levels.

Tax base: The total equalized assessed valuation (EAV) of a school district.

Tax cap: Shorthand for the Property Tax Extension Limitation Law (PTELL) which was enacted to control the growth of property tax receipts of schools and some other units of government.

Tax rate: The amount of property taxes extended, expressed as a percentage of equalized assessed valuation (e.g. a rate of 2.50% or .0250 computes to a tax bill of $2.50 per $100 of EAV). There is a separate rate calculation for each fund for which a levy is made and a total rate for the district. The total rate is equal to the total extended taxes divided by the district's EAV.

Tax year: The calendar year in which property is assessed and the levy is made. Taxes are billed, collected, and distributed in the following calendar year.

Classification Ordinance provides that Cook County may establish classes of property, each with its own assessment factor. The assessment process concludes in state equalization, which applies a corrective multiplier to the valuations of each county, including Cook, to bring that county to an average assessment of one-third of fair market value. Farmland, railroads' operating property, mines, and certain pollution control devices are exceptions to local assessment. The Illinois Department of Revenue assesses these properties in those counties where the tax assessors do not. The farmland assessment process is described later in this chapter.

The assessment profession has developed many standardized procedures for determining value. The law requires only that the assessor "view and determine as nearly as practicable" the value of each property. In fact, assessment of most residential property is conducted from secondary information such as building permits, records of home sales, and other indications of market value. Databases, "drive-by" observations, sampling, and statistical techniques are commonly used. Rarely do assessors visit individual residential properties. Building permits and other reports of modifications may trigger a visit and update of the assessor's database on that property.

The fair market value (FMV) of a property is not necessarily the price at which it most recently exchanged hands. FMV is that hypothetical price at which a property will be exchanged when neither buyer nor seller has any compulsion to act, and when there are no special considerations or factors that influence the actual sale tax. For instance, in a home sale between related parties, a short sale or foreclosed property, or other "outside of the market" circumstances that provide advantage to a buyer or seller in determining the price may be considered "non-FMV" by the assessor, and the valuation adjusted to be more uniform with similar properties.

All property except farm property is to be reassessed every four years; a local option exists to reassess more frequently. Properties whose condition has significantly changed, or which have been incorrectly assessed, may be adjusted between countywide reassessments. Countywide general reassessments every four years are the norm. Tax years 2023 and 2027 are scheduled general reassessment years outside Cook County. Cook County assesses north suburban, south

Figure 2

The Tax Cycle Players and What They Do

Assessor – Township or County

Values property for taxation and hears initial appeals

SUPERVISOR OF ASSESSMENT

Makes assessment changes, sends change notices, publishes changes

Sends tentative abstract to Property Tax Administration Bureau at the Illinois Department of Revenue
(Basis for tentative multiplier)

BOARD OF REVIEW

Hears appeals, finalizes assessments, and delivers them to county clerk

Reviews applications for exemption from assessment

COUNTY CLERK

Reports assessments to State Property Tax Administration Bureau
(Basis for final multiplier)

Determines total Equalized Assessed Value for each taxing district, calculates tax rates for each taxing district, and calculates aggregate tax rate for each tax code area

Extends taxes and enters extensions in collectors' books

COUNTY TREASURER

Prepares and mails tax bills

Collects first and second installments and distributes receipts to taxing districts

Prepares delinquent tax list and sends notice to owner

Obtains judgment in court and holds lien sale on real estate

Issues refunds on successful property tax appeals

suburban, and Chicago townships on a rotating three-year schedule.

Assessors are elected officials and are accountable for their performance to the electorate. In counties with less than three million inhabitants, assessors or supervisors of assessment may either be elected or appointed after the county board adopts such an ordinance or a referendum is approved. The level and the uniformity of their assessments will come under the scrutiny of county and state officials. If errors or political pressures lead assessors to value property at less than the required one-third of fair market value, the system is designed to correct for such actions through equalization.

The market and condition of property on January 1 determine its assessed value for that tax year. Thereby, January 1, 2022 was the date of record for determining the fair market value for tax year 2022. The record date is important to consider when projecting the changes in tax revenue arising from new construction and other changes, including increases or decreases in the occupancy of commercial structures. Do not budget the revenue impact of new construction or other property improvements too early. For example, the full tax base impact of the opening of a new hotel in June 2022 will not be reflected until the following assessment record date, January 2023, which begins the next tax year. The assessment for 2022 will be prorated based on the date of issuance of the occupancy permit. The 2023 tax base will reflect the completion of the hotel; but, due to the practice of billing taxes a year in arrears, the hotel will not fully benefit school tax revenues until the late spring and fall of 2024. The delay between the hotel's opening and the full tax revenue increase is over two years (June 2022-fall 2024). Even then, if occupancy is low during the hotel's first year of operation, the owner may have a case for reduction of its assessed valuation and may appeal the valuation for that tax year.

School officials should watch for the annual publication of assessment changes and especially for the complete assessment roll for the school district published in general assessment years. Assessment data for many counties may be found on the county assessor's website. It is useful to select a sample of residential and business properties, especially the 10 or 20 largest ones, and monitor these assessments over the years. Such data will enable one to discern trends in valuation and assessment that will impact future revenues and the distribution of the property tax burden between residential and business taxpayers where large businesses are active in appealing their assessments.

Business Property

Business property assessments follow different procedures than those for residential property. An understanding of these procedures is important to officials in districts with commercial or industrial property. In valuing business property, assessors will consider such factors as construction costs (if the property is newer), assessment and sales data on similar properties, and the property's capitalized income flow. As with residences, uniformity in the application of the value components that determine the assessment of a property is critical. In an appeal, the property owner will submit data seeking to challenge the uniformity of the assessment. A school district claiming underassessment must present data backing its claim.

The capitalized value of an income property is determined by dividing the annual income to its owner by a market interest rate. For example, as more stores occupy a new shopping center and rental income increases, the assessed value of the center should increase also. If it doesn't, contact the assessor and ask why. Valuation can also increase or decrease in inverse proportion to fluctuations in interest rates (the denominator of the capitalization calculation), which measure the value of the revenue generated by the property. Unexpected changes may also be due to owner appeals.

Successful owner appeals before assessments become final do not reduce school revenues but instead produce a shift in the property tax burden to other taxpayers. Until 2021, a school district could not recoup reductions made after taxes were extended and billed. Such refunds are paid out of current or future collections. With the approval of Public Act 102-519 in 2021, Section 18-233 was added to the Property Tax Code allowing taxing districts to 'recapture' property tax revenue lost due to refunds caused from decisions of the Property Tax Appeal Board (PTAB), orders relating to valuation objections from the circuit court, and the issuance of certificates of error. Now, on or before November 15 of each year, the county treasurer must certify to each taxing district the aggregate refunds caused by these three sources from the prior 12-month period. The county clerk will then automatically increase the taxing district's extension to include this recapture amount. The recapture amount is not subject to the limitations of the Property Tax Extension Limitation Law and is not included in the next year's aggregate extension for purposes of calculating the limiting rate. Districts where large appeals have been granted or are pending need to adjust their budgeted tax revenues accordingly. Some have succeeded in negotiating the schedule for refunding tax reductions over a multi-year period. See the *text box* below summarizing taxpayer and school appeal procedures.

If the political benefits and/or potential loss in tax revenue justify the expense, a district may file an underassessment appeal or an objection to an assessment reduction. Such actions can require extensive research and fees for appraisals and attorneys and may involve proceedings before the county board of review, PTAB, or in circuit court. As a start, school officials should monitor the notices from the county board of review of appeals requesting reductions of $100,000 or more in the assessed valuation of any parcel. The law provides for such notice to taxing agencies of assessment appeals to PTAB and, except in Cook County, of valuation appeals filed in circuit court. The school attorney may be able to ferret out such cases and advise the district on what actions it may take.

The COVID-19 pandemic and changes in the retail industry as a result of online competition have contributed to sharp decreases in sales and occupancy of many commercial properties. Many retail chains closed stores that served as anchors of shopping centers and malls depressing traffic and contributing to the demise of smaller stores in the complex. The metrics used in assessing the value of the complexes have changed, and tax revenues to schools and local governments from these particular properties are expected to trend downward in the years following the

Summary of Taxpayer and School Appeal Options, Timelines, and Consequences

At the Board of Review: Having monitored its large property assessments, the district may file an undervaluation appeal within the published timeframe for appeals, and submit evidence from a qualified appraiser. If an increased assessment is granted, the district's overall EAV increases.

Districts are entitled to notices of taxpayer EAV appeals of $100,000 or more and have a very short timeframe for action — not enough to line up an appraisal not yet in hand. In such cases, its role is primarily passive, and expectations for what can be accomplished are limited. The information obtained will help determine the feasibility of further action. A successful taxpayer appeal shifts its tax burden to others.

At PTAB: Districts are entitled to notice of all appeals where the requested reduction in assessment is $100,000 or greater and the school has 60 days to intervene and submit its evidence, taking as active or inactive a role as the case requires. The proceedings take place before an administrative law judge, and may extend beyond the date for tax billing. In that case, any refunds ordered must be paid from current tax collections.

In Circuit Court: The district must uncover tax objection complaints filed in circuit court, for no notice is provided. Intervention in such cases, which can result in substantial refunds, are paid from current collections. Intervention is active, including presentation of evidence.

The courts also hear tax rate objection complaints, which can allege over levies, excessive balance accumulations, misuse in specific funds, or errors in the many steps of the tax levy process. The complainants request reduction or elimination of the offending levies or rates. Attorneys for the objectors often offer to settle the objection prior to a court hearing. Districts receive notice of all tax rate objections filed against them from the circuit clerk and/or the local state's attorney.

Property Tax Exemption Requests: Districts are entitled to notice where requested exemptions will reduce a property's assessed valuation by $100,000 or more. The uses of existing exempt properties should also be monitored, and, where appropriate, the Board of Review asked to deny or revoke a property's exempt status. The courts have recently decided cases involving charitable property tax exemptions for hospitals, upscale retirement complexes, and "open land" recreational property (golf courses).

The hospital exemption is now covered by statute; generally, the hospital is exempt if the value of its charitable care and activities exceeds the amount of its property tax bill. A for-profit continuing care community was denied religious and charitable exemptions by a circuit court. Golf club improvements such as a clubhouse, tennis courts, and swimming facilities were found by a circuit court not to have a "sufficient nexus" to qualify for the lower open-space assessment available to open land designated for preservation.

closings. Hotels and restaurants have shown sharp declines, and office complexes are proving harder to fill as on-site employment decreases and employees work remotely. On the bright side, the values of data centers and warehouse space benefit from the work from home and online shopping trends. Only time will reveal the duration of these trends and the value of the stricken properties for alternative uses such as housing. The U.S. real estate market has proven to be resilient, bouncing back from prior economic dislocations, and we can expect that properties suffering from COVID's impact will be replaced and reimagined in the years to come.

Some districts form coalitions with other schools and taxing agencies, including park and library districts, to work for fair taxation of non-residential property within their districts. Representatives of the coalition monitor appeals and attend hearings. When intervention is deemed necessary, an attorney is employed, and an independent appraisal of the property is secured. The coalition stays with the proceedings through resolution of the appeal by negotiation or hearing and decision. In addition to preventing or mitigating revenue losses, the proactive approach to assessment appeals sends a message to district residents that the schools are working for a fair sharing of the property tax burden.

Farmland and Mineral Assessments

Farmland is reassessed annually by the Illinois Department of Revenue based on its value in agricultural use, rather than its fair market value. Use value assessments are generally lower than market value assessments. Historically, this change occurred after farm values and taxes rose much more rapidly than farm income during periods of development of agricultural land for residential and commercial uses. Farmers thereby became property rich and income poor. Farm homesites and dwellings are assessed at one-third of fair market value. Agricultural buildings are assessed at one-third of their respective contribution to the farm's productivity.

Figure 3 on *page 16* illustrates the Farmland Assessment Process.

The assessed valuation of farm property reflects soil productivity, average land sale values, and farm income over a multi-year period. Multi-year averaging is used to correct for variations that occur when commodity market factors cause farmers to store crops for sale in a future year, or to sell stored crops harvested in a previous year. Because of multi-year averaging of farmland assessments, upward and downward trends in rural districts' assessed values are "locked in" for multi-year periods.

Rural school districts must watch farm income and assessment trends closely to gauge the impact on their future revenues. Due to multi-year averaging calculation of farmland values, cyclical crop prices constitute an upward or downward force on farmland assessments for several years forward.

Additional information on the methodology and current factors of farmland assessments is available from the Illinois Department of Revenue website, www.revenue.state.il.us. Properties containing coal or other mine, or stone or other quarry, are valued at one-third of their fair cash value. Oil, gas, and other minerals, except coal, are assessed separately at one-third of their fair cash value. Coal is assessed at one-third of the coal reserve economic value.

Review, Appeals, and Equalization

The assessment process concludes with the steps of review, appeal, and equalization. It is here that the system corrects for under, over, and non-uniform assessments by local assessors. The county supervisors of assessments and boards of review evaluate the work of assessors and make and publish changes. An appeal process at the Board of Review is available to taxpayers and taxing agencies upon publication of the assessments for a tax year. Property owners and taxing agencies may take their final appeals to the state Property Tax Appeal Board (PTAB) or the circuit court for adjudication. *Figure 4* on *page 17* depicts an overview of the assessment establishment, review and appeals process showing which types of appeals generate refunds and which do not.

The purpose of equalization is not to achieve proper assessments for an individual property in relation to market value or to other similar properties. It is neutral with respect to property tax inequity, preserving it where it already exists. Inequities must be resolved through the review and appeal process. Rather, equalization is performed to assure uniformity within and equity among counties at the statutory assessment level of one-third of fair market value. If such uniformity and equity did not exist, assessors or county boards of review could manipulate assessments to transfer the burden of such regional entities as community colleges to other counties or shift the school funding burden more to the state through the state aid formula. Application of tax rate and bonded indebtedness limits also requires uniform assessment levels.

Figure 3

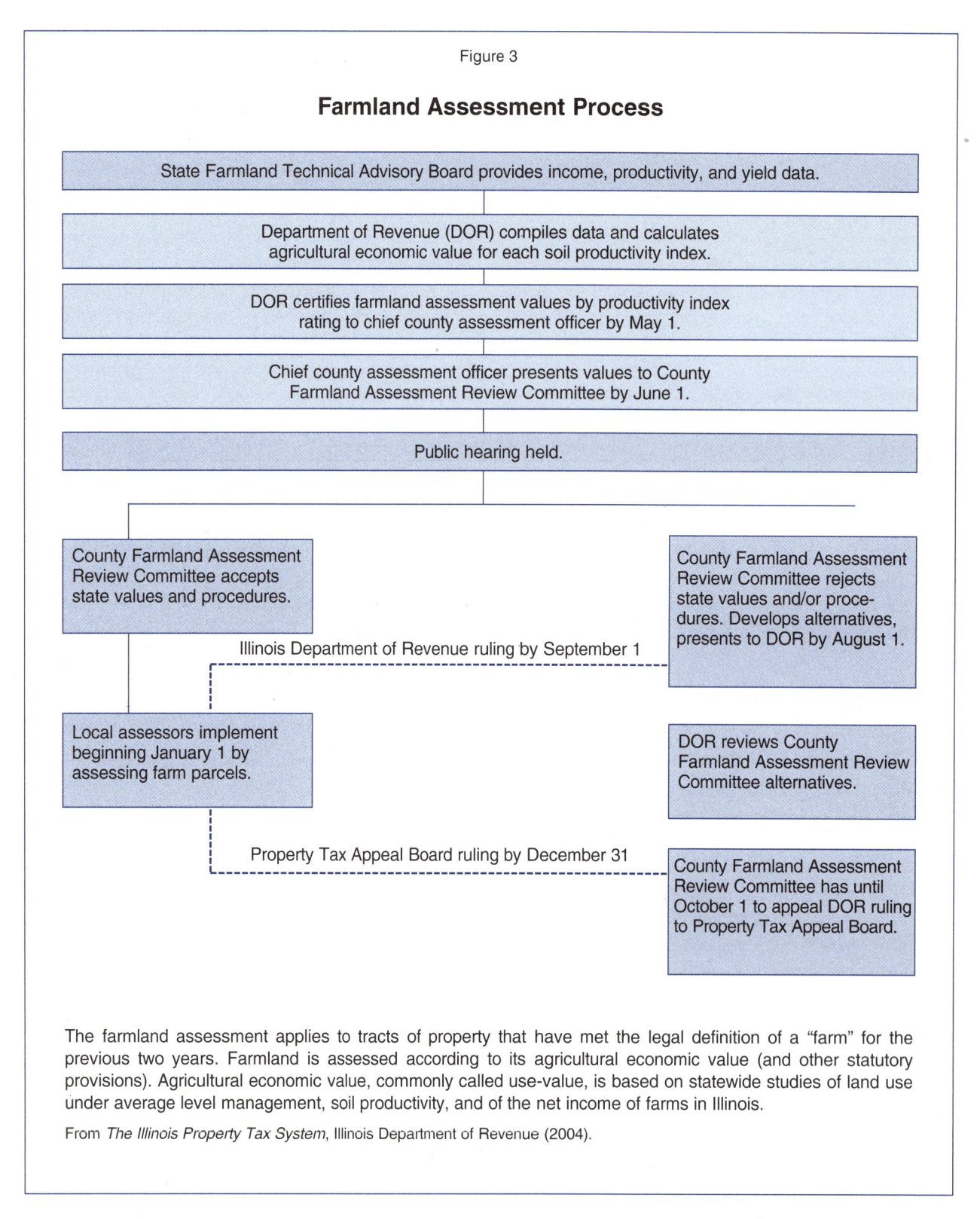

Farmland Assessment Process

- State Farmland Technical Advisory Board provides income, productivity, and yield data.
- Department of Revenue (DOR) compiles data and calculates agricultural economic value for each soil productivity index.
- DOR certifies farmland assessment values by productivity index rating to chief county assessment officer by May 1.
- Chief county assessment officer presents values to County Farmland Assessment Review Committee by June 1.
- Public hearing held.

Branch A:
- County Farmland Assessment Review Committee accepts state values and procedures.
- Local assessors implement beginning January 1 by assessing farm parcels.

Branch B:
- County Farmland Assessment Review Committee rejects state values and/or procedures. Develops alternatives, presents to DOR by August 1.
- DOR reviews County Farmland Assessment Review Committee alternatives.
- County Farmland Assessment Review Committee has until October 1 to appeal DOR ruling to Property Tax Appeal Board.

Illinois Department of Revenue ruling by September 1

Property Tax Appeal Board ruling by December 31

The farmland assessment applies to tracts of property that have met the legal definition of a "farm" for the previous two years. Farmland is assessed according to its agricultural economic value (and other statutory provisions). Agricultural economic value, commonly called use-value, is based on statewide studies of land use under average level management, soil productivity, and of the net income of farms in Illinois.

From *The Illinois Property Tax System*, Illinois Department of Revenue (2004).

Equalization occurs as county and state officials review a sample of assessments versus samples of sales data for each area being equalized. Multi-year rolling averages are used for the comparisons. Outside Cook County, county officials perform initial equalization of each township's assessments. For Cook County, all equalization is done by the state for the county as a whole. A factor called the multiplier is applied first to township assessments (except in Cook, St. Clair, and commission counties) and then to county assessments to bring the area to a median assessment level of one-third of fair market value. For farm acreage and buildings and coal rights, the final assessed valuation is also the equalized valuation.

The multiplier will be less than one if assessments are found to average more than one-third of fair market value. It will equal one if assessments are found to be at the specified level. It will be more than one if they average less. It is wise to monitor trends in township and county multipliers where the district is located. A trend of increases in the multiplier suggests a decrease in local assessment levels. In that case, the schools may be losing tax revenues and the board of education may want to become involved in investigating and challenging assessments of large properties where underassessment is indicated.

Assessments in Cook County

Although state law provides that property is to be assessed at one-third of its fair market value, Cook County has historically applied different assessment formulas for classes of property as permitted under the Illinois Constitution. Cook County assessment factors are determined by the County Board and have been periodically changed over the years, thereby shifting the tax burden back and forth between residential and non-residential property. Since 2009, Cook County assessment levels have remained 10% for residential property and 25% for commercial/industrial property. Those levels of assessment remain in place.

A multiplier of 2.916 was applied by the Illinois Department of Revenue to bring Cook County assessments as a whole to the one-third level for tax year 2019. The high multiplier reflects the fact that all classes of property in the County are assessed at less than the 33% level, averaging 11.43%. The 2019 multiplier was based on a study of a comparison of the actual selling price of individual properties, over a three-year period, with the value placed on of those properties by the County Assessor and adjusted by the Board of Review. Dividing 33.33 by 11.43 produces the multiplier of 2.916. The multiplier is constant for all classes of property except specially assessed properties (e.g., farmland).

A new County Assessor has announced initiatives to increase assessments of commercial and industrial property, which brought about an even higher level of owner appeals. Subsequently, the assessor's office announced reductions in residential assessments, beginning with the south and southwest suburbs, reassessed in 2020. The effects of these changes on taxpayers and taxing agencies, including schools, are difficult to discern due to increased appeals intertwined with pandemic-driven market value decreases. City properties are scheduled for reassessment in 2021, with north and northwest suburbs scheduled for 2021.

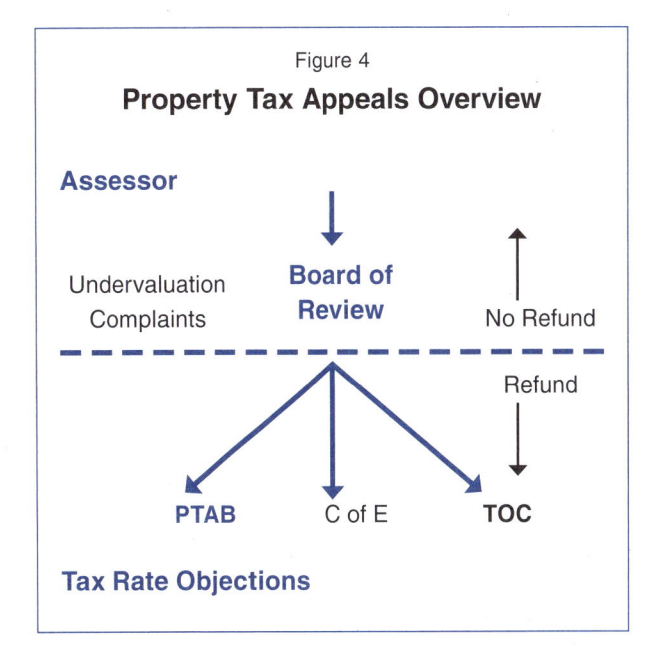

Figure 4
Property Tax Appeals Overview

Assessor
↓
Undervaluation Complaints — Board of Review — No Refund
- -
Refund
PTAB   C of E   TOC
Tax Rate Objections

Problems of the Cycle

With state equalization, the assessment process is complete. The school district's equalized assessed valuation (EAV), or tax base, has been determined for that tax year. Depending on the county, that determination can take nine or more months since the January 1 date of record for assessments. The cycle generally runs longer in Cook County, where the volume of individual properties increases the number of potential appeals at the county and state levels. The result is that EAV is typically set 14 to 16 months following the January 1 date of assessment in Cook County.

Outside of Cook County the specified deadlines for payment of property taxes in two equal installments are June 1 and September 1. In Cook County the first installment is due March 1 in an amount equal to 55% of the previous year's total bill. All adjustments in tax rates and amounts are made in the second installment. In the past, delays in finalizing Cook County valuations and bills commonly resulted in second installment tax collections being delayed into late fall. Local governments thereby lost interest on funds or incurred borrowing costs until the tax money was distributed to them. However, recent tax year calculations and bills were completed on time, with second installment tax payments due August 1.

When the cycle runs late, and final information on the district's equalized assessed valuation is not available, boards must act to establish the tax levy in

November and December without knowledge of what revenue it will actually generate. In such cases, the board may opt to inflate the levy to ensure full revenue from the district's maximum tax rates in the event of an increase in the district's EAV. Public relations problems ensue as taxpayers read notices of such "ballooned levies" along with their property assessment notices, fearing large increases in their tax bills, which may not, in fact, occur. Levy management strategies are discussed in *Chapter 4*.

TIFs and Other Development Incentives

Many municipalities have established Tax Increment Financing (TIF) districts to stimulate the redevelopment of designated areas for commercial or residential uses. The property tax revenue growth (increment) that results from the redevelopment is dedicated to the municipal infrastructure necessary to the development and is therefore not available to schools for up to the 23-year maximum life of the TIF district. The term of a TIF district can be extended by the General Assembly for up to 12 years in some circumstances. It is important for school officials to be informed about proposed TIFs and to participate in the negotiations that establish or extend a TIF district. The extension of a TIF may provide an opportunity for an inter-governmental agreement on the distribution of surplus TIF payments.

Because the TIF freezes the property valuations within the boundaries of the TIF district, it increases the local tax rate and distributes additional tax burden on the rest of the community. Moreover, as a consequence of changes in the real estate market, some TIF districts have experienced declines in revenue, resulting in lower allocations of tax dollars allocated to schools and other taxing agencies. School officials should treat the revenue projections of TIF advocates with this fact in mind and decide accordingly on the position the district should take on a proposed TIF. *Figure 5* illustrates how a TIF district works in terms of where the property tax revenue flows and for how long.

When a TIF is being considered, consult the school attorney to gain an understanding of the legal steps for formation of a TIF district and the issues that can be negotiated with the municipality. School districts are entitled to a seat on the Joint Review Board, which is established to advise the municipality on the administration of a TIF, and to make an advisory recommendation on its formation or rejection. Schools have become increasingly sophisticated in negotiating with municipal officials for a share of TIF-generated

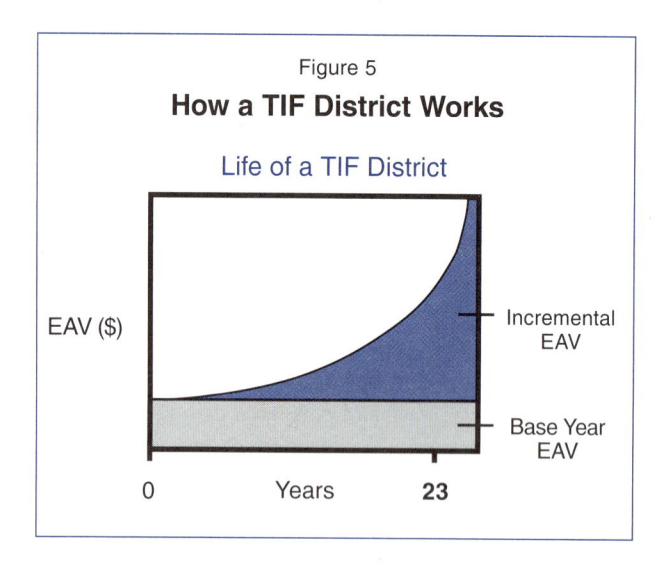

Figure 5
How a TIF District Works

Life of a TIF District

revenue or other concessions. Such negotiations are particularly important when the development involves residential property that will result in additional students attending the schools, when developer payments in lieu of tuition on behalf of students residing in TIF housing can be negotiated. In particular, school business officials must be mindful of the September 30 deadline each year in seeking reimbursement for new students residing within the boundaries of a TIF district. Under the TIF Act, school districts that provide 'reasonable evidence' of students residing within housing units within the TIF district to the local municipality, are entitled to reimbursement based upon a statutory formula.

School officials also need to be aware of the impact of other development incentives, such as abatements and enterprise zones, on their future tax revenues — and to make residents and municipal officials aware of this impact. Property tax bills must now include a list of each TIF in which the property is located and the amount of tax due that is allocable to the TIF district.

Other economic development incentives may impact school tax revenues, and schools may wish to communicate with municipal officials as they are considered. The school attorney can advise on the process by which they are enacted, how they affect revenues, and the extent to which schools may influence or participate in their formation. These incentives include:

- Incentive assessment classifications (Cook County) which reduce the school district's tax base.
- Abatements allow schools and other taxing agencies to reduce the property taxes paid by certain properties, and abatements on specific new construction, renovation, or rehabilitation of specific properties. Schools can say "no" to participation in such abatements. If the school participates, it

will lose tax revenue, but gain the "new property" valuation up front. Abatement agreements should be in writing and reviewed with the county tax extension office. For the most common type of abatement, the abatement is limited to $4 million for all taxing districts combined and a term not to exceed 10 years.
- Redevelopment of blighted areas with additional sales or hotel taxes.
- Special service area allowing additional municipal taxes for special services to that area.
- State initiatives including enterprise zones, investment tax credits, and sales and utility tax exemptions.

Property Tax Exemptions

In addition to challenges to the assessment of a property, taxing district officials will from time to time be confronted with a property owner seeking an exemption from assessment. In these cases, the local school districts are entitled to notice of the exemption request when the exemption would reduce the assessed value of the property by more than $100,000. It is advisable to ask the school district attorney to investigate the exemption request to make sure it is supported by the facts and the law. Districts are entitled to appear and fully participate in the exemption proceedings at the local board of review, before the Illinois Department of Revenue, and in the circuit courts. The general presumption under Illinois law is that all property is subject to taxation and that exemptions should be narrowly construed in favor of taxation.

Keeping Informed and Proactive on Property Tax Matters

Superintendents and business officials should get to know the key people in the offices that administer the various phases of the property tax cycle — especially assessors and the officials in the county clerk's office who compute tax rates and administer the extension process. Attorneys, bond underwriters, and financial advisors can offer assistance in developing levy strategies and projections of future tax revenues and in trying to fathom the mysteries of the property tax system. Property assessment information for many counties can be obtained on the county's website, and data for some counties can be obtained digitally, facilitating the establishment and analysis of a database to track trends on a district's tax base.

A number of sources provide data and perspective that will help school officials with their financial planning and help them create a broader consensus about property taxes within their district.
- General information on the property tax system, including assessment and appeal procedures, is available on the website of the Illinois Department

---

The Seasons of the Property Tax Cycle

In the Spring
- Assessment of property for bills payable in following calendar year.
- Following equalization, County Clerk calculates tax rates based on levies made the previous December. Cook County equalization will not occur until the summer or fall.
- Taxpayers pay first installment of taxes; money is distributed to schools.
- Schools complete budget decisions for the following school year.

In the Summer
- Taxpayers pay their second installment tax bills. Schools receive the remainder of their tax revenues based on the levies made the previous December.
- Schools finalize their revenue budgets.

In the Fall
- County agencies issue assessment notices, hear appeals, and finalize assessments.
- State issues equalization multipliers for some counties; those schools know their tax bases for the coming levy.
- Schools hold hearings, adopt budgets, and begin preliminary work on their following year's budget.
- Schools adopt tentative levies and publish Truth in Taxation notice, if required.

In the Winter
- State equalization continues for counties for which it has not been completed.
- Schools adopt the levy for taxes to be collected the following calendar year, and file it with the County Clerk before the last Tuesday in December.

of Revenue, www.revenue.state.il.us. It has a wealth of data that can be used to compare a district's property tax experience with a wider universe of taxing agencies.
- The websites of county assessment officials vary in the completeness of their data, but it can be extensive. The Cook County Assessor's site, for example, has reports that break down assessments by class of property and list all the properties with assessed values of $1 million or more within each township. The Cook County Clerk's office provides information on Tax Increment Financing (TIF) districts. Districts impacted by current or prospective TIFs require this information to project their tax revenue and manage levies so as to access revenue from expired TIF valuations.
- Nonprofit organizations such as the Civic Federation of Chicago, the Taxpayer's Federation of Illinois, and the Lincoln Institute offer research and perspectives on the property tax system.

The Levy and Extension Process

Boards of education must take action on a legally specified timetable each year to certify the amount of revenue required from local property taxes. The document the board creates and acts on is called the certificate of levy. A tax levy is the amount of money a taxing body requests to be raised from property taxes. When the board considers the amount of the levy, it should look forward to the next school year, since the levy filed in December will produce revenues to be received in the following summer and fall. (The first installment of taxes in Cook County is received in the spring.) Spending the first installment taxes before July, or borrowing against tax revenues before they are distributed to the school district, are legal and common practices borne of necessity. However, they are signs of fiscal weakness. If ever-larger percentages of each year's taxes are spent or borrowed from year to year, the district will soon be facing a financial crisis requiring severe cutbacks or a tax rate referendum to cure.

The certificate of levy is a statement of need for tax revenue. The certificate itself does not generate tax revenue. Tax revenues are a function of the tax base, the levy, and applicable fund rate limits. (See the formula in *Figure 6*) Calculation, billing, collection, and distribution of property tax revenues for each taxing agency are performed by the officials in the county or counties in which the district is located. Those steps are described in *Chapter 4.*

In some parts of the state, new construction, property values, and assessments have been recovering from declines during the Great Recession. Monitoring these trends is essential so that when the amount of the levy and the estimated EAV on which it is based are run through the extension calculations in both tax-capped and non-tax-capped counties, there is no revenue left on the table due to a levy that falls short of the maximum available revenue. Superintendents and business officials who are inexperienced in the mechanics of establishing tax levies and calculating extensions will benefit from consultations with colleagues in professional organizations, the district's financial advisor and auditor, and the tax extension officials in the county clerk's office who will perform the critical calculations.

Figure 6
Tax Revenue Formula

Total Extension	=	Tax Rate	x	Equalized Assessed Valuation
(total billings)		(to maximum authorized rate)		

Or, in simpler terms:

Revenue = Effort (Rate) x Wealth (EAV)

Responses to Demands for Property Tax Relief

As described earlier in this chapter, economic changes affecting industrial, retail, and office properties have contributed to reduced valuations of these properties in recent years. The COVID-19 pandemic of 2020 and the resulting recession exacerbated these trends and severely impacted hotel, entertainment, and restaurant businesses, foretelling reductions in subsequent years. The impact on a district might include a shifting of the tax burden onto residential properties, delayed collections, more aggressive appeals, and demands by businesses and residents for general property tax relief. Forecasts of property tax revenues should be regularly updated during the budgeting process and preparation for the annual tax levy discussions in the fall. Citizen activism to reduce budgets and levies at the cost of drawing down reserves or making cuts in programs and support services may have to be addressed. Discussion of levy questions might well begin at the time of the tentative budget adoption in the spring or early summer to allow time for consideration of citizen views and the effect of options on the district's programs.

Table 4
School District Tax Rate Limitations*

Purpose	District Type	Percent Without Referendum	Percent With Referendum
Educational	Elementary	0.92	3.50
	Secondary	0.92	3.50
	Unit	1.84	4.00
Operations & Maintenance	Elementary	0.25	0.55
	Secondary	0.25	0.55
	Unit	0.375	0.50
Capital Improvements	All	N/A	0.75
Transportation	Elementary	0.12**	As Needed
	Secondary	0.12	As Needed
	Unit	0.20	As Needed
Summer School	All	N/A	0.15
Bond & Interest Payments	All	N/A	As Needed
Rent	All	N/A	As Needed
Municipal Retirement/Social Security	All	As Needed	N/A
Tort Immunity	All	As Needed	N/A
Health Insurance	All	N/A	As Needed
Working Cash	All	0.05	N/A
Fire Prevention, Safety, Energy Conservation, and School Security	All	0.05	0.10
Special Education	Elementary	0.02	0.40
	Secondary	0.02	0.40
	Unit	0.04	0.80
Area Vocational Education	Secondary	N/A	0.05
	Unit	N/A	0.05
Tort Judgment Bonds	All	As Needed	N/A
Leasing/Computer Technology	All	0.05	0.10
Temporary Relocation	All Eligible	0.05	N/A

*Tax rates may be affected by the Property Tax Extension Limitation Law. Chicago District 299 not included.
** Certain elementary districts of 2,600 or more students may levy .20. See 105 ILCS 5/17-2 for conditions.
Source: Illinois Department of Revenue, www2.illinois.gov/rev/localgovernments/property/Documents/newtaxrates.pdf

Public Act 101-0181, enacted in August 2019, created a Property Tax Relief Task Force to recommend by December 31, 2019, administrative, electoral, and legislative changes to create short- and long-term property tax relief for homeowners. Notable for the over 80 legislators who served on the task force, and following numerous meetings to review reports and testimony, its report recommended expansion of the sales tax to include services, addressed procedural and timetable matters, and recommended consolidation of government units and changes in TIF timeframes and definitions. No overhauls of the property tax system were recommended.

The Evidence-Based Funding formula, enacted in 2017 to overhaul the distribution of state school aid to improve equity and adequacy, allocates $50 million of an annual $350 million appropriation for property tax relief grants. These are grants to districts with high tax rates relative to other districts, enabling them to reduce an equivalent amount of local tax revenue. They are described further in *Chapter 6*.

Planning and Adopting the Levy

The steps for adopting and filing the tax levy must be followed exactly, because attorneys hired by property owners look for technical errors and may file tax objections over minor formalities. Such actions can be expensive to defend and settle.

1. The district must determine the total revenue required to operate the program for the coming school year. Therefore, the first step in levy planning is to develop a projected expenditure budget for each fund. Then estimate revenue from all sources other than tax revenue. The difference is the need for property taxes and is the justification for the levy. In reality, the district will probably need all of the tax revenue that it can legally secure.

2. If the need requires and tax rate limitations permit, the board may wish to levy above its operating needs to increase a fund balance. Conversely, a levy below needs, or the maximum available amount will work to decrease a fund balance. Such action might occur a) if the district had built up a surplus in one or more funds and needed the money in other funds; b) if the board concluded that the total operating fund reserves were at a sufficient level; or c) if the board wished to reduce the operating fund levy to partially offset an increase in that levy year's debt service levy. Decisions to levy below the maximum amounts have both short- and long-term consequences, and should be made only after review of the following year's projected budget and revenue and expenditure projections for the coming years. Those projections should include the additional costs due to enrollment increases and future program changes. *Chapter 22* and *Chapter 24* speak to fund balance policies and standards for an adequate balance. *Chapter 10* and *Chapter 20* address projections of revenue and expenditures.

3. Next, determine if the district's maximum operating fund rates will produce the desired revenue. In non-tax-capped districts, the maximum rates for the Education, Operations and Maintenance, and some "minor funds" (the operating funds) cannot exceed the rates that the voters have authorized for each fund. Nor can the maximum rate in any fund exceed the rate established by law. These rates appear in Table 4. When the operating fund tax rates (OTR) are fixed, and the levy is sufficient to "capture" the maximum rates in each fund, the total OTR times the total equalized assessed valuation (EAV) equals the money to be received. As EAV varies up or down, so does the money to the district from property taxes. See the calculation example on page 26 for a non-tax-capped district. See *Chapter 4* for rate limitation calculations in tax-capped districts, where voter-established fund rate limits do not apply, but the growth in total operating revenue is constrained by other factors.

4. If, in a non-tax-capped district, the most recent tax rate for a fund is at its maximum authorized rate, an increase in that fund's levy for the coming tax year will produce no additional revenue, unless the tax base also increases. If the EAV for the tax year being levied is known, and revenue is to be maximized, multiply the EAV by the maximum rate for the fund and levy that amount. It is wise to add a cushion in case the EAV is adjusted upward for new or updated EAV information. You don't want to get caught with your levy down if you need to maximize property tax revenue. See *Chapter 4* for levy calculation strategies in tax-capped districts. In a tax-capped district, the provisions of the Property Tax Extension Limitation Law (PTELL) control the total extension and determine the "limiting tax rate" for all operating funds. Any increase in property tax revenues is limited to the CPI adjustment, plus an adjustment for new property. The total limiting rate is a function of the previous year's extension times the CPI adjustment, divided by the current year's EAV, less the EAV of new property. The total operating tax revenue is the product of the current year's EAV and the limiting rate. The board must levy a sufficient amount to capture the available revenue and distribute that levy among the funds according to need so that each fund stays within its legal rate limit. Individual operating fund rates are subject only to the state limit for each fund, not to any previous voter-established limits. The tax rate and extension calculations for tax-capped districts are illustrated in *Chapter 4*. In 2022, Public Act 102-895 created Section 18-190.7 to the Property Tax Code that provides taxing districts subject to PTELL with the ability to levy below the maximum permitted levy in a given year and carry into a subsequent year the levy authority for a future year. The practical application of Section 18-190.7 is illustrated in *Chapter 4*.

5. If the new EAV is not known, the board may wish to hedge against yet-unknown increases or decreases in the tax base. These can occur as a result of new construction not yet assessed or

Tort Liability Fund Levy Requires Care

The Local Government and Governmental Employees Tort Immunity Act, 745 ILCS 10/9-101 et seq. (the "Act"), authorizes a local public entity, including a school district, to levy taxes to pay the costs of protecting itself or its employees against liability, property damage, or losses, including all costs and reserves of being a member of an insurance pool, to pay the principal and interest on bonds, and to pay the cost of risk management programs. Funds so raised may also be utilized to pay the cost of insurance, including all operating and administrative costs, and expenses directly associated with the maintenance of insurance, claims services, and risk management directly attributable to loss prevention and loss reduction, educational, inspectional, and supervisory services directly relating to loss prevention and loss reduction and legal services directly attributable to the insurance program.

The district may utilize its tort levy to pay all legal and consulting fees associated with investigating and defending itself against any claim or event, with a potential for or recognized exposure to liability. Similarly, the district may rely on its tort levy to pay for independent legal services, which are not otherwise covered by its general comprehensive liability insurer, and which are necessary to defend the district or its employees against any liability or loss.

The tort levy may also be used to pay the district's costs in purchasing comprehensive general liability insurance coverage for the district and its employees, including that portion of any premium paid for auto/bus insurance which relates to general comprehensive as opposed to collision coverage. Additionally, the tort levy may be used to pay the costs of surveying the district's facility for the presence of asbestos, however, it may not be used for defraying the actual costs of abatement.

One issue that has received attention from the courts in recent years is whether a school district may rely on its tort levy to pay a proportionate amount of the salaries of selected school administrative, maintenance, custodial, and support personnel whose duties and responsibilities include protecting the district, its staff, and students from liability.

Based upon recent case law, in order to justify the payment of employee salaries out of the tort fund, the public body must first establish a formal process of risk management. The public body must design the risk management process to identify, specifically address, and then reduce or eliminate exposures under the Tort Immunity Act before it may pay its employees' salaries with tort funds. According to a recent court ruling, a formal risk management program must contain the following four elements: 1) identifying and analyzing loss exposures, 2) selecting a technique or combination thereof to be used to handle each exposure, 3) implementing the chosen techniques, and 4) monitoring the decisions made and implementing appropriate changes.

Once the school district has established the appropriate risk management program, it may pay an employee's salary with tort funds if the employee's responsibilities include each of the four foregoing criteria and the employee actually performs the assigned risk management responsibilities.

---

correction of assessment errors. In preparing for a levy discussion, run various scenarios combining increases or decreases in EAV and in new property. The result may suggest a "balloon" levy. There is no legal limit to the amount that can be levied; however, the board must comply with the Truth in Taxation Act if it intends to levy more than 105% of the prior year's extension.

6. In levying for a fund with no tax rate maximum (e.g., pension or tort liability) an increase in the levy will produce additional tax revenue up to the amount of the levy. See "Tort Liability Fund Levy Requires Care" *above* for a discussion of the allowable uses of the tort liability/judgment fund. While there is no rate limit for this fund, substantiation of expenditures is required to justify the tort levy.

7. No annual levy action is needed for bond principal and interest payments. The county clerk will extend the necessary taxes each year, based on resolutions filed at the time the bonds were issued. However, it is wise to check the clerk's intended levy amount, which is filled in by the clerk at the bottom of the levy form when it is filed, against

ILLINOIS STATE BOARD OF EDUCATION
School Business Services Division
217/785-8779

Original: ☐
Amended: ☐

CERTIFICATE OF TAX LEVY

A copy of this Certificate of Tax Levy shall be filed with the County Clerk of each county in which the school district is located on or before the last Tuesday of December.

District Name	District Number	County

Amount of Levy

Educational	$ _____	Fire Prevention & Safety *	$ _____
Operations & Maintenance	$ _____	Tort Immunity	$ _____
Transportation	$ _____	Special Education	$ _____
Working Cash	$ _____	Leasing	$ _____
Municipal Retirement	$ _____	Other	$ _____
Social Security	$ _____	Other	$ _____
		Total Levy	$ ___0___

See explanation on reverse side.
Note: Any district proposing to adopt a levy must comply with the provisions set forth in the Truth in Taxation Law.

* Includes Fire Prevention, Safety, Energy Conservation, Disabled Accessibility, School Security, and Specified Repair Purposes.

We hereby certify that we require:

the sum of ____0____ dollars to be levied as a special tax for educational purposes; and
the sum of ____0____ dollars to be levied as a special tax for operations and maintenance purposes; and
the sum of ____0____ dollars to be levied as a special tax for transportation purposes; and
the sum of ____0____ dollars to be levied as a special tax for a working cash fund; and
the sum of ____0____ dollars to be levied as a special tax for municipal retirement purposes; and
the sum of ____0____ dollars to be levied as a special tax for social security purposes; and
the sum of ____0____ dollars to be levied as a special tax for fire prevention, safety, energy conservation, disabled accessibility, school security and specified repair purposes; and
the sum of ____0____ dollars to be levied as a special tax for tort immunity purposes; and
the sum of ____0____ dollars to be levied as a special tax for special education purposes; and
the sum of ____0____ dollars to be levied as a special tax for leasing of educational facilities or computer technology or both, and temporary relocation expense purposes; and
the sum of ____0____ dollars to be levied as a special tax for _____ ; and
the sum of ____0____ dollars to be levied as a special tax for _____
on the taxable property of our school district for the year _____ .

Signed this _____ day of _____ 20 _____ .

_____
(President)

_____
(Clerk or Secretary of the School Board of Said School District)

When any school is authorized to issue bonds, the school board shall file a certified copy of the resolution in the office of the county clerk of each county in which the district is situated to provide for the issuance of the bonds and to levy a tax to pay for them. The county clerk shall extend the tax for bonds and interest as set forth in the certified copy of the resolution, each year during the life of the bond issue. Therefore to avoid a possible duplication of tax levies, the school board should not include a levy for bonds and interest in the district's annual tax levy.

Number of bond issues of said school district that have not been paid in full _____ .

(Detach and Return to School District)

This is to certify that the Certificate of Tax Levy for School District No. _____, _____ County, Illinois, on the equalized assessed value of all taxable property of said school district for the year _____, was filed in the office of the County Clerk of this County on
In addition to an extension of taxes authorized by levies made by the Board of Education (Directors), an additional extension(s) will be made, as authorized by resolution(s) on file in this office, to provide funds to retire bonds and pay interest thereon.
The total levy, as provided in the original resolution(s), for said purposes for the year _____, is $ _____ .

_____
(Signature of County Clerk)

_____ _____
(Date) (County)

Source: Illinois State Board of Education. Certificate of Tax Levy (50-02). Retrieved from www.isbe.net/Pages/Certificate-of-Tax-Levy.aspx

district records to be sure they agree. Also, check the fund balance annually to be sure that previous errors or underpayments of taxes have not caused a deficit to accumulate. If it has, tax revenue will run out before the repayment obligations do. The cure is a resolution to request an additional levy to make up the deficit. A school attorney or bond counsel can draft such a resolution if it is needed. Taxes collected for principal and interest payments on bonds are deposited in accounts in the debt service fund group, from which these payments are made. Consult the Illinois Program Accounting Manual for applicable accounting regulations for the debt service fund.

8. The levy for the working cash fund need only consider the need for establishing, increasing, or decreasing the balance in this fund. No expenditures can be made directly from this fund. (See *Chapter 11* for information on laws governing transfers from this fund and allowable expenditures from the transferred funds.) The total balance in this fund, in a non-tax-capped district, is limited to 85% of the taxes last extended for the education fund. Caution is advised in all actions involving the working cash fund. The School Code specifies strong penalties for board members and school officials who willfully violate code provisions governing that fund. Fund levies and uses of the moneys are common subjects of taxpayer concerns and legal tax objections. It is advisable to review working cash levies and prospective transfers to other funds with legal counsel before they are finalized.

9. Levies for the capital projects fund, if established by referendum, are established at the level required for budgeted expenditures, subject to the approved rate limit. The levy for the leasing of educational facilities may also be used for computer technology or for both purposes.

10. The final step in the levy planning process is to add up the intended levies for all the funds. Then look at the result to answer several questions, which have political as well as financial ramifications.
    - What total tax rate will the levy produce?
    - What will be the school tax bill for an average homeowner, and how will it compare to the past year?
    - If a bond levy is required, how does it impact the total tax rate and bill?
    - Do the answers make any difference in the board's intended action?

    These questions should be answered before the levy is finalized. It is wise to avoid spikes in the tax bill; gradual increases from year to year usually go down better with taxpayers. While future trends in tax rates and bills depend on many factors, including property valuations, the district's financial consultant can assist in identifying the factors that may influence them. Knowing these factors is important before levy actions are taken and as any new borrowing is contemplated.

11. The school board must adopt an estimated tax levy not less than 20 days prior to the date it adopts its final levy. If the levy exceeds the previous tax year's operating fund extension by more than 5%, publication of the Truth in Taxation notice is required, and a hearing must be held before the levy is adopted. The hearing must be held on a separate date from the hearing on the budget. It is important to consult the school attorney to obtain the current notice and other compliance requirements of the Act.

12. The levy form, available from www.isbe.net, and illustrated on *page 24*, must be filed by the last Tuesday in December with the county clerk, who date stamps it and returns a copy to the district. Examine the levy form carefully before it is presented to board officials for signature, and again before it is filed with the county to be sure the amounts for each fund agree with the board's final actions. Many district officials file the levy in person to avoid the possibility of delivery delays during the busy holiday season.

4 / Determining Property Tax Revenue

This chapter on property taxes describes the procedures that determine a school district's actual revenue yield from its levy. These steps are performed by county and state agencies, and possibly the courts, and take place in the early months of the calendar year. They include the adjustment of counties' assessments to the legally mandated levels and calculation of each agency's tax rates based on its levy, tax base, and authorized rates. The cycle concludes in mid-year with the calculation, mailing, and collection of tax bills, and distribution of the proceeds to each agency. Chapter 4 also describes procedures and calculations that apply to districts subject to the Property Tax Extension Limitation Law (PTELL). It also identifies strategies that boards of education may employ, in certain circumstances, to maximize operating tax revenues while addressing taxpayer concerns over rising bills.

After the Board of Education files its levy in December, and the state certifies the equalized assessed valuation for the county, the remaining steps in the property tax cycle are the responsibility of county officials. The county clerk will extend the levy against the tax base (EAV) of the district, and compute its tax rates for each fund and the total rate. The county treasurer prepares and mails the bills to each property owner, receives and records the payments, and distributes the revenue to the taxing agencies.

The Extension Process

The county clerk is responsible for seeing that levies are adjusted, if necessary, so that they do not produce tax rates greater than those authorized by the district's voters or by law. The rate calculations differ for non-tax-capped and tax-capped districts. In non-tax-capped districts, the maximum rate for the Education, Operation and Maintenance, and some other operating funds cannot exceed the rates the voters have authorized for each fund, or the rate allowed by law (See *Table 4* in *Chapter 3*.) A levy communication is sent to the district by the clerk's office in the weeks prior to the calculation of the extension. This communication serves as confirmation of the levies, the maximum rates on file in the clerk's office, and the intended extensions for each fund. It is the last chance to correct errors and to designate the funds, if any, for which extensions are to be increased or reduced within the applicable rate limits. See the sample extension calculations for non-tax-capped districts and for tax-capped districts on the *next page*.

It is important for superintendents and school business officials to understand the process by which the county clerk calculates rates and extends tax levies for the various funds. Examine the past year's report that the clerk issued to the district at the time the final tax rate was computed, and follow the mechanics of the calculation. The report format differs for each county; Cook County reports reflect its unique prior-year EAV extension method. Meet with tax extension officials as necessary to gain a full understanding of the factors that affect the district's property tax revenues. Knowledge of the system will enable the official to develop levy recommendations to the board of education that, several months later, will produce the intended revenues.

Revenue Limits, Borrowing Options, and the Extension Process in Tax-Capped Districts

The Property Tax Extension Limitation Law (PTELL), ILCS 200/18-185 et seq., popularly known as the "tax cap," became effective with the 1991 tax year for school districts and other "non-home rule" government agencies in DuPage, Kane, Lake, McHenry, and Will counties. It was expanded to Cook County in 1994, and voters in 33 other counties have subsequently adopted the measure by referendum. (See *Table 5* on *page 28*.) These 39 counties include about 55% of Illinois' school districts and about 80% of its schoolchildren.

Computation of Allowable Tax Extensions in a Non-Tax-Capped District

The table here illustrates the process by which a tax levy for a non-tax-capped district is extended to produce the total billings to property owners. This is a simplified example; certain commonly used funds are not included, and amounts added to the levy by the county clerk to allow for "loss and costs of collection" are not shown. Rates are expressed as percentages.

The district's **authorized maximum tax rate** for each fund is established by referendum or by the state limit (see *Table 4* on *page 21*). However, there is no set limit for the IMRF/Social Security and Bond and Interest funds; extensions for these funds reflect the district's need as established by the levy.

Assume that the school district's equalized assessed valuation is $210 million and it has "balloon levied" to capture the maximum available revenue for the funds that have rate limits. The extension for each fund cannot be more than the amount levied for that fund.

The **computed tax rate** is found by dividing the levy for each fund by the EAV of $210 million. Where the computed rate for a fund controlled by a maximum is greater than the authorized rate, the authorized rate is multiplied by the EAV to compute the extension. **In the table here, the bold-faced rates are the ones used to compute the extension.**

Note that revenue in the three operating funds will be controlled by the authorized tax rate maximum. For budgeting purposes, the extension should be reduced according to historical loss of collections, an allowance for pending appeals, if any, and other factors that may be unique to the district.

An illustration of how the extension is calculated in a tax-capped district appears on *page 36*.

Fund	Tax Levy	Authorized Tax Rate	Computed Tax Rate (a)	Tax Extension
Education	$5,200,000	**2.350**	2.476	$4,935,000
Operations & Maintenance	800,000	**.350**	.381	735,000
Transportation	270,000	**.120**	.129	252,000
IMRF/Social Security	200,000	N/A	**.095**	200,000
Total Extension				**$6,122,000**
Total Tax Rate (Sum of bold-faced rates)			**2.915**	

(a) Rates may be calculated beyond three decimal places to allow the extension to be as close to the levy requested as possible.

No county has approved the cap since 2002; 10 counties have rejected the measure and it has not been brought to a vote in the other 53 counties. A referendum to impose the cap may be placed on the ballot by the county board at any regularly scheduled election except a consolidated primary election.

The stated purpose of the tax cap is to control recurring increases in property taxes. It does not directly limit the annual growth of school expenditures, although such limits do exist in several states. However, it effectively controls the growth of expenditures by limiting annual increases in schools' primary source of revenue, regardless of enrollment growth, program requirements, building repair needs, or other forces that create a need for new revenue. The result was devastating to the property tax revenues of schools in tax-capped districts in the years following its imposition. Severe budget cuts occurred as schools adjusted to the realities of lower growth in tax revenues.

The tax cap controls the property tax revenues of schools, parks, and other "non-home rule" agencies. Contrary to the expectations of many who voted for the tax cap, increases in individual property tax bills are not limited. Debt service levies rise and fall each year according to previously established schedules of principal and interest payments. Also, the growth in tax bills reflects the actions of both non-capped home rule government units and capped non-home rule agencies.

Under Illinois law, a "home rule" local government agency has authority to establish tax rates and to enact certain laws without regard to limits enacted by the Illinois legislature. Many cities and larger municipalities enjoy such home rule powers by virtue of the size of their populations or as a result of a referendum. Illinois school districts do not enjoy home rule powers, nor can home rule be conferred upon them by a referendum.

Table 5
Year of Enactment of Property Tax Extension Limitation Law
(And Levy Year for Determining Debt Service Extension Base)

1991	1994	1996	1997	1998	1999	2000	2002
DuPage Kane Lake McHenry Will (Base year for the DSEB is 1994.)	Cook	Boone Champaign Christian Franklin Jackson Kankakee Lee Logan Macoupin Menard Monroe Morgan Randolph Sangamon Schuyler Union Williamson Winnebago	JoDaviess Kendall McDonough Stephenson	Jefferson Marion Tazewell Washington	DeKalb Livingston	Greene Massac Shelby	Coles Cumberland

Source: Illinois Department of Revenue, Property Tax Extension Limitation Law Technical Manual

How the Cap Affects a District's Operating Tax Revenues

The cap limits the increase in total extensions (except for taxes levied for certain bond and interest payments) to the lesser of 5% or the 12-month rate of inflation as measured by the All Urban Consumer Price Index (CPI) published by the U.S. Department of Labor. For the first time since the tax cap limits were enacted, CPI for December 2020-December 2021 reached 7% resulting in a maximum CPI of 5% in the tax cap formula. The CPI averaged only a 2.1% annual increase from the 2017 to 2022 tax years. See *Table 6* on *page 29* for a list of CPI percentages used each year since 2001. The tax cap affects individual district property tax revenues in different ways, depending on the direction and relative changes in its property values and the rate of inflation.

The tax cap slows the growth of property taxes when property values and assessments are increasing faster than inflation. It increases the growth of property taxes when property values and assessments are increasing slower than inflation. In a capped district, as equalized assessed valuation varies, the total tax rate for the operating funds adjusts. Therefore, tax rates tend to decrease in those years where inflationary growth in property values has been greater than the CPI inflation rate, unless a substantial amount of "new growth" in a district's tax base has occurred. Refer to the tax rate and extension calculation (*Table 7*) on *page 30* and the worksheet (*Table 8*) on *page 31*.

Conversely, tax rates increase when property values decrease, new construction slows, and the CPI remains at low levels. These higher rates work to maintain districts' property tax revenues, even as their EAVs drop — up to the point that individual fund rates reach their maximum legal limits (lower referendum-approved fund rates no longer apply). But taxpayers note the increasing tax rates and assume, incorrectly, that school tax revenues are increasing at a higher rate than they are. This situation occurred during the Great Recession, confusing taxpayers and presenting a communications challenge to county tax officials and school districts. Tax revenue increases in capped districts can occur in the following ways:

- Provided that it levies a sufficient amount to "capture" the increase, a district receives an additional allowance in proportion to "new property" added to the tax base because of construction, annexations of territory to the district, and expired tax increment financing districts. It is essential to monitor TIFs so that the EAV from expiring or changed TIFs is considered in establishing the levy for that tax year.

Table 6
History of CPIs Used in PTELL Calculations

Levy Year	CPI %	Year Taxes Paid
2001	3.4	2002
2002	1.6	2003
2003	2.4	2004
2004	1.9	2005
2005	3.3	2006
2006	3.4	2007
2007	2.5	2008
2008	4.1	2009
2009	0.1	2010
2010	2.7	2011
2011	1.5	2012
2012	3.0	2013
2013	1.7	2014
2014	1.5	2015
2015	.8	2016
2016	.7	2017
2017	2.1	2018
2018	2.1	2019
2019	1.9	2020
2020	2.3	2021
2021	1.4	2022
2022	5.0	2023

Source: Illinois Department of Revenue

*The CPI used for the PTELL limiting rate calculation for a levy year is the percentage increase between the December to December CPIs for the two preceding calendar years or 5%, whichever is lower. It is worth noting that the CPI % for Levy Year 2022 was 7% prior to the reduction.

- "New property" is defined as changes that increase the assessed value of the property. Examples are home additions, new residential and commercial construction, including teardowns and rebuilds, development of previously tax-exempt property, such as former government property, and improved homes whose four-year improvement exemptions have expired. (See the PTELL Technical Manual described at the end of this chapter for other inclusions in the new property calculation.)
- The extension may be increased above the PTELL formula-determined amount if voters at a referendum have approved an increase in either the CPI-driven extension limitation or in the tax cap "limiting rate." For a discussion of the limiting rate, see *Computing and Managing Tax Rates and Extensions Under the Tax Cap on page 33*. When a district under PTELL requires a referendum, the wording of the question and ballot information requirements are strictly specified in law. For a discussion of specific provisions for — and limitations on — referendum options in tax-capped districts, see *Chapter 13*.
- If a district has a decreased aggregate extension base in the previous year, compared to the year before that, the limitation is based on the highest extension in any of the three preceding years. Note that this provision can be used only the first year after the aggregate extension is reduced, and applies to any reductions in extensions, including abatements. Otherwise, reducing any operating fund levies below those of the previous years will establish a lower base for future years' revenue calculations — a continuing gift to the taxpayers that keeps on taking from the school district. See the *text box* on *page 32* on strategies to reduce the levy for a description of debt service levy options that may allow boards to meet taxpayer demands for lower school tax increases while permitting operating fund tax increases.

Borrowing Options under the Tax Cap

PTELL has curtailed or limited the issuance of certain forms of debt that, prior to the cap's enactment, could be issued either without a referendum, or were subject only to a petition period or "backdoor referendum." These "limited bonds" include Fire Prevention and Safety Bonds, Working Cash Bonds, and Funding Bonds. A district may still be able to issue them, if certain conditions exist.

A district that levied to pay the principal and interest on non-referendum "limited" bonds in the levy year during which the tax cap was approved in that county (see *Table 5*) may issue new limited bonds. The limit on the annual levy for limited bonds is referred to as the Debt Service Extension Base (DSEB). The DSEB is the bond and interest levy for non-referendum bonds in the year the cap was approved (1994 is the base year for the five collar counties), increased (effective in 2009) by the CPI used for the limiting rate calculation. Working cash, fire prevention and safety, and funding bonds are the most common forms of non-referendum debt that are limited by the tax cap law.

Public Act 96-0501 allows a CPI factor to be applied to the DSEB. The increase for levy year 2022 is 5%. This provision gives districts additional flexibility to issue bonds in the future.

Table 7

Formula for Computing Allowable Tax Extensions Under the Tax Cap (outside Cook County)

The following definitions apply to terms in this formula:

Limiting tax rate: the calculated total allowable tax rate for all operating funds, excluding bond and interest. The aggregate rate for all operating funds cannot exceed this rate. The rate for bond and interest payments is in addition to the limiting rate.

Aggregate extension base: The prior year tax extension for all funds, except bond and interest.

New property: New improvements or additions to existing improvements that increased the assessed value of that real property during the tax year.

Step 1: Compute the limiting tax rate for the total of all operating funds.

    A. Multiply the **previous** year's aggregate extension base by the inflation factor applicable to the **current** levy year. The example uses 2% for simplicity.

    B. Subtract the value of new construction from the **current** year's EAV. Note that by subtracting the value of new construction from the denominator of the fraction, you thereby increase the limiting rate, as intended by the tax cap law to give districts access to tax base growth from new property valuation.

    C. Divide the result of step A by the result of step B. The result is the limiting tax rate.

Example: The district's total extension, not including bond and interest for the **last tax year** was $5,000,000. The district's total EAV for the current tax year is $210,000,000, of which $10,000,000 is due to "new construction" as defined in the tax cap law.

$$\text{Limiting rate} = \frac{\$5,000,000 \times 1.02}{\$210,000,000 \text{ minus } \$10,000,000} = \frac{\$5,100,000}{\$200,000,000} = \mathbf{2.550\%}$$

Step 2: Multiply the limiting rate by the EAV for the current year to determine the total extension for the operating funds.

    Limiting rate x EAV = Revenue
    Example: 2.550% = .0255 x $210,000,000 = $5,355,000 total limited extension

Step 3: Distribute the total extension to the various operating funds and complete the levy process. Consider the need for each fund for tax revenue, but do not exceed the statutory maximum tax rate for each fund.

Simplified example (Certain commonly used funds are not included. Rates are expressed as percentages):

Fund	Extension	Computed rate (a)
Education	$4,255,000	2.026
Operations & Maintenance	700,000	.333
Transportation	200,000	.095
IMRF/Social Security	200,000	.095
Total	**$5,355,000**	2.549
Limiting rate		**2.550**

(a) Computed by dividing the extension for each fund by the **current** year EAV of $210,000,000. The district's maximum rate for each fund is established by the state limit. There is no set rate limit for the IMRF/Social Security fund; it reflects the district's need.

Source: Elizabeth Hennessey, managing director of public finance at Raymond James Associates, Chicago.

Districts without a DSEB, and subject to the tax cap, must submit such borrowing to a referendum, thereby compromising for some districts a powerful financing tool for raising cash and funding safety-related building improvements that is available to others. Alternatively, a referendum may be held to establish a DSEB or to increase an existing DSEB. (See *Chapter 11* for more information on referendum options.)

A district subject to PTELL may still issue some forms of debt that are not "limited bonds." They include general obligation bonds approved by the voters, bonds to refund voter-approved general obligation bonds, debt certificates, and the back-up levies for "alternate bonds." (See *Chapter 11.*)

One additional provision to keep in mind is that a district subject to PTELL may not levy for a fund it has never used, or for a fund subject to backdoor referendum for which it has not levied in the last three years, without voter approval.

The Tax Cap and the School Program

The tax cap formula does not take into account changes in a school district's budgetary needs resulting from enrollment changes or new programs. It has had especially severe effects on the schools in older communities that are undergoing "generation turnover" in their populations where existing housing is being sold by childless residents to families with school-age children.

Enrollments and expenditures increase, but property tax revenues rise only at the rates controlled by PTELL, rather than the higher rates at which property has historically appreciated, and at which school expenditures must grow to meet the needs of an increasing population. Unless new growth occurs, which

---

Table 8

Worksheet for Estimating Limiting Tax Rate and Total Allowable Extension

Step	Information/Formula Component	Source of Information	Formula for Calculation	Result (insert figure)
A	Prior year aggregate extension	County Clerk's report of prior year extension	N/A	$_____
B	Prior year CPI applicable to the levy year being calculated.	Illinois Department of Revenue or U.S. Department of Labor	Limited to 5% increase (1.05 for calculation in step C)	_____ %
C	Numerator of limiting rate (to step G)	Calculation	(A*(1+B))	$_____
D	Estimated current year Equalized Assessed Valuation	Local or County Assessor or Clerk*	Estimate from trends and available information**	$_____
E	Estimated new growth	Assessor	N/A	$_____
F	Denominator of limiting rate	Calculation	(D-E)	$_____
G	Limiting tax rate	Calculation to 3 decimals	(C/F)	____._____
H	Estimated maximum current year aggregate extension	Calculation	(G/100)* current year EAV	$_____

* The source and amount of EAV information available prior to the extension of taxes vary by county. Township assessors should be contacted first, except in Cook County, where the information is made available at the county level.

** Until exact information is available, the current year EAV may be estimated using historical trends and available information on property valuation trends and new construction. A database on property valuations is an invaluable tool for projecting property tax revenues.

> ## Strategies to Reduce the Levy
> ## Without Affecting Long-Term Operating Revenues
>
> Taxpayer pressure is challenging many boards of education to establish annual tax increases below the maximum amount established by PTELL, by a "zero increase levy" to freeze the property tax extension at the current amount, or perhaps even to reduce it. In certain circumstances, a district may be able to increase its operating tax levy, but reduce the debt service portion of the levy to offset that increase.
>
> Some of the available strategies include use of money from operating fund balances for abatement of the Debt Service levy in combination with accumulated debt levies from sources such as "loss and cost" extensions. Other measures include refunding, prepayment or defeasance of debt, stretching out debt service payments, or a combination of these steps. Each option carries short- and long-term consequences. The district's financial consultant should be called in well in advance of the levy adoption season to explore available options, benefits, and costs.
>
> See *text boxes* on *page 61* in *Chapter 9* and *page 72* in *Chapter 11* for further information on this strategy.

requires that there be vacant land, home expansions, or redevelopment of large parcels of property, the school district's property tax revenues are not able to keep up with needed expenditures. Class size increases and a scarcity of money results, unless a referendum is successful.

In recent years, lower CPI adjustments, which averaged only 2.1% for levy years 2017 to 2022, have fallen short of the inflation of school costs, despite cost containment through restructuring salary and benefit plans and curtailing expenditures for other instructional and non-instructional expenditures. In some cases, class sizes were increased to reduce the need for teachers and classroom space. Some districts have outsourced cleaning and maintenance services, reduced administrative staff, deferred building maintenance, cut purchases of supplies and equipment, enacted early retirement incentives, and taken other cost-reduction measures. In 2022-2023 school year, with actual CPI above 7% and a national school staffing shortage, school labor costs are bound to outpace revenues limited to the tax cap maximum CPI increase of 5%.

Historically, the prospect of a tax-cap referendum generated a flurry of non-referendum borrowing. Districts floated working cash, fire prevention and safety, and other limited bonds to create a Debt Service Extension Base, and thereby lock in their entitlements to sell limited bonds in future years. Although there have been no successful tax-cap referenda since 2002, the idea of containing property taxes remains politically attractive.

If a county referendum on the tax cap is pending in the future, or if legislation to further limit or freeze taxes is successful, administrators and board members in currently non-capped districts need to be aware of the potential effects on tax revenues and of the steps that can be taken prior to enactment to mitigate the effects. In addition to issuing new limited bonds to utilize their full DSEB entitlement, boards of education should establish their annual levies at the maximum amount permissible under the district's tax rate limits, and levy for all operating funds. Monitor TIF distributions and calculate levies to capture the resulting new property the tax year of the distribution — or else lose the benefit forever. If the tax cap or a freeze were to come in the future, the base for the calculation of subsequent years' revenues would thereby be at the highest possible level. School officials should also inform the public of the anticipated effect on school revenues and programs. Public finance consultants can help prepare financial projections and identify borrowing options.

If a tax cap or other revenue limitation measures are proposed or enacted, the administration will need to employ all of its leadership and political skills to educate the board of education, staff, and community about the new revenue realities and what it will mean for the program, buildings, jobs, and morale of the school district. Few if any districts were unscathed financially by the imposition of the cap and most "bit the bullet" and acted quickly to bring their expenditures in line with projected revenues. While increases in state aid helped many of the state's poorest districts at the time, they did not remain sufficient to offset the loss of revenue caused by the property tax revenue limitations.

Computing and Managing Tax Rates and Extensions under the Tax Cap

A tax-capped district is limited in the maximum growth of its total operating fund property tax revenue (excluding debt service tax receipts). The conceptual formula for understanding the effect of the limit is:

Tax revenue (TR) = prior year TR x Consumer Price Increase + TR from new property growth

The operational formula that describes the revenue calculation in property tax terminology begins with the calculation of the following year's limiting tax rate.

$$\text{Limiting tax rate} = \frac{AEB \times (1 + CPI)}{CEAV - NP - AX - TIF + DIS}$$

Where:
AEB = aggregate extension base (prior year total taxes billed for funds subject to PTELL)
CPI = cost of living increase (CPI or 5% whichever is less; or other amount approved by the voters for the levy year)
CEAV = current year EAV of district, used in setting preliminary rates
NP = new property
AX = current EAV of any annexations
TIF = recovered tax increment value after the TIF expires
DIS = current EAV of any disconnections

The limiting rate formula allows a district to receive additional taxes in proportion to the value of property annexed, new property construction, and the expiring TIF. If property is disconnected from the district, the extension is reduced proportionately.

A detailed explanation of the calculations is provided on *pages 30* and *31*. The example in *Table 7* on *page 30* illustrates the steps by which the county clerk computes a district's tax rate and revenues in tax-capped districts. To follow the step-by-step instructions, start with the extension for the previous tax year. The worksheet (*Table 8*) on *page 31* will assist in estimating the maximum aggregate extension allowable for the operating funds under PTELL.

The tax cap requires districts to look at all of their operating funds and manage their levies accordingly. Effective with the 2006 levy year, Public Act 94-976 made significant changes that affect the maximum rates for the operating funds and provided districts with greater flexibility in allocating tax receipts to the various funds. A district may now exceed a voter-approved fund rate as long as it does not exceed that fund's maximum rate prescribed by law (if a prescribed maximum rate exists for that fund; see *Table 4* in *Chapter 3* on *page 21* for a table of maximum fund rates). The total rate for the operating funds may not exceed the limiting rate as computed under the PTELL formula. Most districts found that their total limiting rates decreased from year to year when property valuations increased at a faster rate than the COL factor in the rate calculation. As explained above, tax rates increased when valuations were decreasing with property values during the recession.

Levies are discussed in the Fall and must be adopted and filed with the county clerk by the last Tuesday in December. It is necessary for the district to estimate the available taxes before it adopts the levy. The estimate informs the amount of the levy and the estimated tax revenue for the preliminary budget used for planning the following year's budget.

In estimating a levy to assure that the district will receive the maximum available property taxes during the following year, with a cushion to cover unknown factors, first increase the prior-year total extension for the operating funds by the limitation inflation increase (COL). Then add a percentage increase that reflects the best estimate of the new property. It can be estimated based on recent trends and information from local building departments and assessors on new construction. Be sure to check for new recovered value from expiring TIFs.

Because the final EAV for the levy year may not be known until the district must levy, use the estimated EAV information, plus a cushion for unknown data. Then run the limiting rate formula (see *Table 8* on *page 31*), using the estimated EAV, the estimated new property, and the known CPI adjustment. Establish the levies for the operating funds (1) in relation to the needs of each fund, (2) to determine that the projected rate for each fund will not exceed the statutory limit for that fund, if any, and (3) to determine if the total rate for the funds subject to PTELL requires the district to publish a Truth in Taxation notice and hold the necessary public hearing. Be ready to explain the rationale for levying a cushion above the preliminary estimates of the actual amounts to be billed and received. The examples in *Table 7* on *page 30* and the worksheet (*page 31*) will be helpful.

When the actual extension and rates are computed, the county clerk will advise the district if the sum of all rates exceeds the limiting rate, or if any fund exceeds the maximum statutory rate. The district must then make adjustments among the funds to bring each fund and/or the total extension within limits. Such communications occur in the spring prior to the clerk's extension of taxes and setting of tax rates. Under PTELL, each Cook County school district has its levy adjusted to the maximum amount based on statutory rate ceilings and the previous year's total EAV plus the value of any new construction or the current year EAV, whichever is less.

If a district has had a successful referendum to increase the limiting rate, it may put that increase into effect for the levy year prior to the date of the referendum (the levy adopted the previous December), provided that the referendum is canvassed more than 30 days before the final rates are calculated and certified. The clerk of each affected county must be notified within two days after the canvass that the increased limiting rate is to apply to the prior year's levy. Adoption of a new levy is not required if the previously adopted levy is large enough to use the new limiting rate. Remember that the extension for any fund cannot exceed the amount of the levy.

If the district holds a successful referendum to increase the educational and/or operations and maintenance fund rates, it must approve a supplemental budget and file an additional levy for that year. The amended certificate of levy must be filed with the county clerk in time to be incorporated into the tax bills without materially impeding the extension and collection of taxes.

With election canvassing now the responsibility of county election officials rather than the school board, school officials should communicate with the appropriate county officials to assure that canvassing activities and communications with the county clerk are completed on the prescribed timeline.

Importance of Monitoring Tax Cap Calculations

The Illinois Department of Revenue establishes and oversees the procedures for calculating property tax extensions under the tax cap. However, individual county clerks may have their own interpretations of several fine points in the law, which can result in increases or decreases in tax revenues of substantial amounts. Since the extension of one year becomes the starting point for the following year's calculation, an interpretation adverse to the school district repeats itself and accumulates its effects in future years.

Therefore, school administrators should consider consulting the school district auditor, financial advisor, and/or attorney at the time the county clerk communicates on the proposed calculation and distribution of the district's extension. This usually occurs in the early spring. One of the best ways to come to an understanding of the arithmetic of the tax cap is to collect and study the prior year's working papers relating to the extension of the tax levy by the county clerk, along with the corresponding property tax bills sent to residents. Explaining the effect of tax revenues to the public is especially complex. A good starting point is to collect school board reports and budget documents from other districts that have built such explanations into their communications.

Billing, Collection, and Distribution

Billing begins in the spring when the extension is completed. Deadlines for the two installments may vary from year to year depending on the speed, or lack of it, with which the assessment/equalization process takes place. It is advisable to research recent practice in a given county to accurately project revenue flow. Legally specified payment dates for the two installments outside Cook County are June 1 and September 1.

The first installment bill in Cook County, computed at 55% of the previous year's bill, is due March 1. All changes due to revisions in EAV and tax levies are calculated into the second installment. Combined with the confusion over the multiplier, tax cap, exemptions, and triennial assessments, this practice contributes to the annual summer/fall tax shock that reverberates around public offices throughout Cook County. Second-installment billing in Cook County formerly ran well into the fall due to the large amount of property data required for computing the equalization multiplier. The second installment in recent years has been more timely, and second installment bills have been due by early August. However, for levy year 2021 the second installment was four months late due to software changeover at the Cook County Assessor's Office and delays at the Board of Review. This means some Cook County school districts and municipalities were required to use fund balance not only for salaries and operations but also for bond payments, typically due December 1.

It is prudent to budget tax revenues assuming a less than 100% collection of the extension. Collections may be reduced or delayed by late payments, appeals, foreclosures, bankruptcies, or other adverse

Tax Caps and the Effects of Decreasing Property Values
(applicable to non-tax-capped and tax-capped districts)

Some areas of Illinois are experiencing a downturn in residential property sales and values, and in the valuation of some types of non-residential property. Property value trends during recessions are not uniform throughout the state. Therefore, school officials need to research local trends to determine their impact on revenues from property taxes and state aid. The effects of the pandemic will require additional research to determine these trends over coming years.

The effect and duration of a property value trend on school tax bases will depend on the length and scope of the decrease or increase as well as local market conditions. According to one assessor, a true sales trend needs to last for three years or more to cause significant changes in assessed values. This is because sales data for the previous three years are used to reassess property in general reassessment years and multi-year averages are also used for computing equalization factors. For example, assessments for tax year 2021 reflected market values for 2018-2020. Therefore, recent years of lower, stable, or higher property values will not be reflected in current year assessments. The immediate effect of upturns and downturns is thereby dampened and deferred.

Tax revenues are a function of the tax base, the levy, and applicable fund rate limits. (See *Figure 6* on *page 20*.) A decrease in the tax base may, but will not necessarily, lead to a decrease in tax revenue. In a non-tax-capped district, the future revenue impact of a decline in the tax base will depend on the amount of subsequent levies for each fund, and whether a given fund rate is at its maximum level. When an operating fund tax rate is fixed, property tax revenues adjust as the equalized assessed valuation varies. Therefore, if a fund is already at its maximum rate, a decrease in the tax base will result in a proportionate decrease in revenue to that fund. But if a fund is not at its maximum rate, a constant or increased levy will produce revenue up to the levy amount or until the rate limit is reached, whichever is lower.

Therefore, boards may wish to increase levies for funds that have not reached their maximum rates to mitigate losses in other funds. Each fund needs to be evaluated for its need for additional revenue, with special attention to expenses charged to the Tort Liability Fund. (See the section on the Tort Fund in the previous chapter.)

In a tax-capped district, the provisions of the Property Tax Extension Limitation Law (PTELL) control the total extension and "limiting tax rate" for all operating funds. Any increase in property tax revenues is limited to the CPI adjustment, plus an adjustment for new property.

The total limiting rate is a function of the previous year's extension times the CPI adjustment, divided by the cur-rent year's EAV, after subtracting the EAV of new property. The limiting tax rate thereby adjusts according to changes in the equalized assessed valuation. A decrease in the current year EAV will cause the limiting rate to increase. When the higher rate is applied to the lower EAV, the result will be a total amount of tax revenue equal to that of the previous year. (Rounding of the tax rate may result in a slight variation.) In addition, the district will gain tax revenue attributable to any new construction. The school board must, of course, levy a sufficient amount to capture the available revenue, and distribute that levy among the funds according to need so that each fund stays within its legal rate limit. Individual operating fund rates are subject only to the state limit for each fund, not to any previous voter-established limits.

Work through various scenarios of tax base changes and levies, using the applicable formulas, to determine how a declining tax base will affect a district's revenues.

Source: Wayne Township (DuPage County) Assessor website, posted in November 2007. Dates updated by author.

---

developments, especially where refunds are approved for large taxpayers to be deducted from the current year's distributions. The district's audits for recent years will provide guidance for adjusting the budget for probable uncollected taxes and designating an amount to be budgeted as "prior year" taxes.

The COVID-19 pandemic may delay the distribution of taxes to schools as some counties have provided taxpayers with penalty-free options to defer a portion their payments that would otherwise have come due around June 1 and September 1. The economic distress of commercial and industrial taxpayers has been reflected in appeals and bankruptcy proceedings which, until resolved, may suspend their tax payments. Monthly financial reports to boards of education should compare monthly receipts as

New Law Provides for a Voter Initiated Referendum to Reduce Education Fund Levies

The education funding formula allows voters in a district that has resources that exceed 110% of its Adequacy Target, a state calculation in the Evidence-Based Funding formula described in Chapter 6, to force a referendum to reduce by up to 10% the next Educational Fund levy below the previous year's levy. It applies to all districts. The reduction may not cause the district's adequacy target to fall below 110% for the levy for which the reduction is sought. Such a referendum must be held at a consolidated election at which board members are elected, and once held, it may not be submitted for the next two consolidated elections, regardless of the result. The consequences of a successful referendum would impact most severely schools that are primarily funded by local resources. In the event that a referendum petition is circulated, consult the Illinois Department of Revenue's PTELL Technical Manual and the school attorney to determine how tax extensions would be affected by a successful referendum.

Recent PTELL Legislation

In 2021, Public Act 102-0519 created Section 18-233 of the Property Tax Code, which implements an automatic levy increase to be applied by the county clerk each year in the amount of the aggregate property tax refunds paid by a taxing district in the prior year for certain types of refunds. The refund recapture authority applies to three categories of property tax refunds: the issuance of a certificate of error, a court order issued in a valuation tax objection complaint, and a State Property Tax Appeal Board (PTAB) decision. For each taxing district that is subject to the provisions of PTELL, Section 18-233 directs the county clerk to automatically apply an additional amount to the annual levy made by such taxing district equal to the taxing district's refunds paid out during the prior 12-month period. By November 15 of each year, the county treasurer must certify the aggregate amount of refunds paid in these three categories during the preceding 12-month period.

Sample Extension Calculation for a Tax-Capped District

LakeCounty Tax Year: 2019   PTAX-253   E31112

NORTH SHORE SCHOOL DISTRICT #112

Residential EAV:	2,153,411,911	Residential EXT:	65,446,753.26
Farm A EAV:	970,375	Farm A EXT:	29,491.75
Farm B EAV:	1,995	Farm B EXT:	60.63
Commercial EAV:	265,462,963	Commercial EXT:	8,067,982.23
Industrial EAV:	486,076	Industrial EXT:	14,772.88
Railroads EAV:	3,508,602	Railroads EXT:	106,633.85
Total EAV:	2,423,841,922	Total EXT:	73,665,694.60
New Property:	9,594,422	Annexations:	0
Recovered TIF:	0	Disconnections:	0
PTELL Limiting Rate:	3.039212		

Fund	Levy	AR	MAR	Extension
EDUCATIONAL	57,620,000.00	2.349806		56,955,582.92
IMRF	100,000.00	0.004078		98,844.28
OPERATION & MAINT.	13,000,000.00	0.530154	0.550000	12,850,094.91
SOCIAL SECURITY	100,000.00	0.004078		98,844.28
SPECIAL EDUCATION	700,000.00	0.028547	0.400000	691,934.16
TRANSPORTATION	3,000,000.00	0.122344		2,965,425.17
WORKING CASH	5,000.00	0.000205	0.050000	4,968.88
Total:	74,525,000.00	3.039212		73,665,694.60

The county clerk will then automatically add such amount to the next taxes to be extended for such taxing district.

In May 2022, Public Act 102-0895 created Section 18-190.7 of the Property Tax Code. Pursuant to Section 18-190.7, school districts that have a designation of "recognition" or "review" according to the State Board of Education's School District Financial Profile System and for which taxes were not extended at the maximum amount permitted under PTELL in a given levy year may be to recapture all or a portion of such unrealized levy amount in a subsequent levy year. Section 18-190.7 directs county clerks, in calculating the limiting rate for a given taxing district, to use the greater of the district's last preceding aggregate extension or the district's last preceding aggregate extension if the district had utilized the maximum limiting rate permitted without referendum for each of the three immediately preceding levy years. The aggregate extension of a district that includes any recapture for a particular levy year cannot exceed the district's aggregate extension for the immediately preceding levy year by more than 5%. If a district cannot recapture the entire unrealized levy amount in a single levy year, the district may increase its aggregate extension in each succeeding levy year until the entire levy amount is recaptured. To be eligible for recapture in a subsequent levy year, the district must certify to the county clerk that it did not levy the maximum amount permitted for a particular levy year within 60 days after the district files its levy resolution with the county clerk.

The Future of the Property Tax

The property tax has a long legacy. It is an important source of government revenue in English-speaking countries throughout the world, despite the development of a more easily valued method of gauging wealth — that is, income. Although politically unpopular, it has proven to be resistant to change.

Pressures to shift the burden from residential property have and may continue to result in tinkering, such as exemption increases, circuit breakers, and other devices favorable to homeowners. Businesses and homeowners pursue assessment appeals in increasing numbers. Pressures from organizations representing taxpayers, business, agriculture, and mining may result in further restrictions on tax growth. The Illinois General Assembly has considered proposals to transfer some teacher pension obligations to school districts, without provision for additional taxing authority for those payments.

Although initiatives to restrict property tax revenues are now common events in the legislatures of Illinois and other states, the tax is unlikely to disappear as an important source of school revenues. It has several desirable traits from a public policy point of view. Among them are visibility and understandability regarding costs and benefits, a large measure of local control of the tax level and purpose, relative stability of revenue yield, and a high collection rate. Therefore, it falls on educational leaders to continue to strive to understand the system and to apply its ever-changing, intricate mechanisms for the benefit of the schoolchildren in their charge.

Additional Resources

There are many details that affect calculations and tax rates and revenues under PTELL. They are found in the Property Tax Extension Limitation Law Technical Manual published by the Illinois Department of Revenue. The manual also illustrates how rising and declining EAVs interact with PTELL to lower and raise tax rates. The manual is available on the Illinois Department of Revenue website.

5 / Personal Property Replacement Tax Revenue

Illinois property taxes were once assessed in two classes: real estate and personal property. Both classes were assessed and distributed by the counties and were included in local government units' tax bases. The personal property tax on individuals was abolished in 1978. The 1970 Illinois Constitution abolished the personal property tax on businesses effective in 1979.

The Personal Property Replacement Tax, or PPRT, is collected from Illinois businesses and distributed to government units by the Illinois Department of Revenue. PPRT is intended to replace revenue lost by local governments when their ability to impose taxes on business entities was eliminated. As such, it is categorized for revenue accounting as a local source of revenue and as a "payment in lieu" of taxes. PPRT is collected and distributed by the Department of Revenue as part of the State Corporate Income Tax.

Distribution of the Replacement Tax

The Department of Revenue computes each taxing agency's share of the total PPRT payments collected for the previous year. The total collections are divided into two portions. Cook County receives 51.65%; the other 101 counties share the remaining 48.35%. The distribution to taxing agencies is determined by multiplying the total of the applicable pool by the agency's allocation factor. The allocation factor is determined by the amount of the agency's personal property tax collections for the 1977 tax year (tax year 1976 in Cook County). Allocation factors for each agency and estimates of the amount to be received by government units are found on the Department of Revenue website, tax.illinois.gov/.

Budgeting Replacement Tax Revenues

Because the allocation factors remain constant, increases and decreases in PPRT revenues depend on statewide personal property replacement tax collections. These collections in turn depend on the health of the Illinois business economy. The FY 2022 replacement tax allocations were estimated at $2,107 million, an increase of 14.3% over the FY 2021 allocation which totaled $1,843 million.

Budgeting for FY 2023 and beyond will reflect the health of Illinois' business economy.

Estimates of coming-year PPRT payments to school districts and other agencies are available from the Department of Revenue website cited above. The payments are made in eight unequal installments during the fiscal year and draw from the replacement tax collections over the previous two calendar years.

The fund assignment for replacement tax revenue is at the annual discretion of the district, except for an amount that must be designated for the IMRF/Social Security Fund. Otherwise, the money can be assigned to any operating fund for which property taxes are levied.

Districts can borrow against anticipated replacement revenue for the current and two succeeding years by issuing Personal Property Replacement Tax replacement notes in an amount not exceeding 75% of an amount certified by the Director of the Illinois Department of Revenue. Another option is to pledge PPRT revenues for repayment of alternate bonds. Alternate bonds are described in *Chapter 11*. A financial consultant can advise on the amount of projected revenue that can be approved for such borrowing.

PPRT revenues work to the benefit of school districts that are issuing certain types of bonds and debt obligation, because the calculation of the maximum amount of debt that can be issued takes replacement revenue into account.

The historical association of the replacement tax with a district's local property wealth manifests itself as a dollar-for-dollar reduction in the calculation of a district's available resources in the Evidence-Based Funding formula which is discussed in *Chapter 6*.

Essentials of Illinois School Finance 39

6 / Evidence-Based State Funding

Several years of studies and debate culminated in the summer of 2017 with enactment of SB 1947, the Evidence-Based Funding (EBF) for Student Success Act (PA 100-0465). This chapter relates EBF to previous state funding programs, describes its vocabulary, summarizes the research supporting the EBF model, demonstrates how a district's EBF aid is calculated, and discusses the impact of EBF on current and future state budgets.

The publications of the Center for Tax and Budget Accountability, information on the website of the Illinois State Board of Education and the Principles of School Finance workshop materials of the Illinois Association of School Business Officials provided much of the information in this chapter, and special thanks go to the authors of these materials.

The Goals of Evidence-Based Funding

The Illinois Evidence-Based Funding (EBF) model addresses long-standing concerns of parents, educators, and the public. Its goal is to improve statewide achievement overall by closing the funding and achievement gaps between districts with property wealth and districts without. The model strives to improve equity by increasing state funding for school districts with less resources to fund their schools adequately, based on research regarding what resources are needed to educate students with different needs. The EBF model intends to raise funding to meet the costs of an adequate education for all children in preparation for achievement and success after high school. The model also affords property tax relief to some districts with high needs and lower resources. Additionally, it improves oversight, accountability, and transparency of school districts' planning and budgeting processes. When fully funded and operational, it will advance Illinois from the bottom of state school funding quality rankings to the upper ranks of states with well-funded schools and an advanced school funding system.

EBF Blends the Former Foundation State Aid and Some Major Categorical Grants

The EBF replaced the old formula that was based on a one-size-fits-all "Foundation Level" of per-pupil funding that was both inadequate in amount and inequitable in distribution. Before the 2017-18 fiscal year, the state aid formula was referred to as General State Aid (GSA). It was "unrestricted" revenue usable for any purpose for which it was legal for school districts to expend funds. Most districts designated their GSA for the education fund, but it could be allocated in whole or part for building operations, transportation, and other operating purposes. That previous formula was in place since 1997, while the concept of state "foundation support" goes back to the 1920s.

The GSA foundation level, $6,119 in FY 2017, was an outcome of the annual budget appropriation process. It was the same amount for all the state's districts, regardless of their students' needs or program costs. It did not relate to the actual costs of operating a school program adequate to enable all students to meet the state's educational goals. The foundation amount was unchanged from Fiscal Years 2010 through 2017, except for five years of proration when the appropriation was insufficient to fund formula claims. When fully funded, the poorest 10% of Illinois' districts received $4,000 to $5,500 per pupil of GSA. During that time, the median foundation grant was between $2,500 and $3,000 with the state's property-wealthiest school districts receiving less than $1,000 per student of GSA.

The foundation formula's goal was served by distributing state aid in inverse proportion to a district's local tax resources. Districts were required to fill the gap between necessary expenditures and GSA allocation with other state grants, federal funds, and local property taxes. Therefore, the spending power of a school district was highly correlated to its property tax base. That fact violated the principal requirement of an equitable funding system, known as "fiscal neutrality." In a fiscally-neutral funding system, the quality of a child's education is independent of the fiscal resources of his community.

While a second goal of the foundation formula was to help districts fund an *adequate* educational program, the FY 2017 foundation level was about $3,000 below the research-based level recommended by the General Assembly's Educational Funding Advisory Board.

Funds previously in the state budget for General State Aid, the supplemental low-income grant, English Language Learning, and for special education personnel, student programs, and summer school were integrated into the Evidence-Based Funding (EBF) budget line beginning in 2017-2018. Together, they constituted each district's Base Funding Minimum (BFM) state aid. In subsequent years, each district's BFM has increased by the amount of its Tier Funding, which is distributed in inverse proportion to the district's capacity to fund an adequate program from its local resources.

Reaching EBF's Goals Poses a Long-Term Funding Challenge

ISBE's FY 2024 EBF contribution was $8.143 billion, an increase of $350 million over the prior year's contribution. While this increase moves many districts closer to equity, the law establishing EBF called for annual increases of $300 million which did not occur during the COVID pandemic. The frozen EBF appropriation of 2021 set back hopes for achieving full funding of EBF by June 2027, 10 years after its implementation.

A May 2023 report by the Center for Tax and Budget Accountability found that, at the beginning of FY 2023, the formula was underfunded by $3.38 billion. Appropriating in future years only the $300 million annual minimum increase called for in the EBF law would extend the date at which full funding of EBF is achieved to 2035. Adjusting for inflation, the full funding target date advances to FY 2038.

Gaining the rewards anticipated in the Evidence-Based Funding model and funding their costs pose an immense challenge to state and local leaders to secure the necessary money over the coming years. Money in the state budget needs to be found to restore reductions in essential state services, fund pension obligations, reduce outstanding debt, and establish a "rainy day fund" to meet needs yet unknown. Local school leaders must gain and retain community support for the property taxes and other measures to fund local expenditures concurrently with the state initiatives to increase taxes that are likely to persist.

A critical time for EBF comes with the development of the FY 2025 budget in the spring of 2024. Sufficient reliable revenues to meet the growing needs for EBF funding will be required if funding reform is to retain its momentum and enable all school districts to operate quality programs and achieve both local and state goals for their students. In order to meet the statutory deadline of fully funding EBF by June of 2027, Illinois would need to increase K-12 funding threefold, by $1.149 billion each year.

Overview of the Evidence-Based Funding (EBF) Formula

Evidence-Based Funding draws on a large body of work by Allan Odden of the Wisconsin Center for Education Research at the University of Wisconsin, Lawrence Picus of the University of Southern California, and other researchers. The research identified the level of resources needed to meet the performance goals established by a prototypical school district. The prototypical resources are then adjusted to reflect a district's unique student characteristics and costs to determine the adequacy target for that district. The adequacy target may also be adjusted to reflect regional cost differences.

The district's adequacy target is allocated equitably between the district and the state by a formula, which expresses its local capacity to fund its needs as a percentage of its adequacy target. A district's local capacity is a function of its property tax wealth, receipts of state personal property tax replacement revenue, and its Base Funding Minimum state aid for the current year. The percentage of a district's adequacy target that can be funded by its local capacity determines its share of Tier Funding, which is the equalizing component of the EBF formula. The graphic, "How Close is the School District to Adequacy?" *Figure 7* on *page 41* illustrates the EBF equation.

Statewide equity is achieved when the state contribution due to each district is fully funded at a future date (discussed in the previous section). Meanwhile, a four-tier phase-in methodology ensures that districts with the highest gaps between their funding capacity and adequacy target (Tiers I and II) receive 99% of the appropriation for Tier Funding. The Base Funding Minimum (BFM), described in the previous section, establishes a base or "hold harmless" amount of state funding during the transition years to full funding of

Figure 7
How Close is the School District to Adequacy?

Final Resources: Base Funding Minimum + PPRT + Final Local Capacity Target

Adequacy Target: Core Investments + Additional Investments + Per Student Investments for Central Office Operations & Maintenance + Per Student Investments (All other)

= FINAL PERCENT OF ADEQUACY

Core Investments and Additional Investments: Subject to Regionalization Factor

---

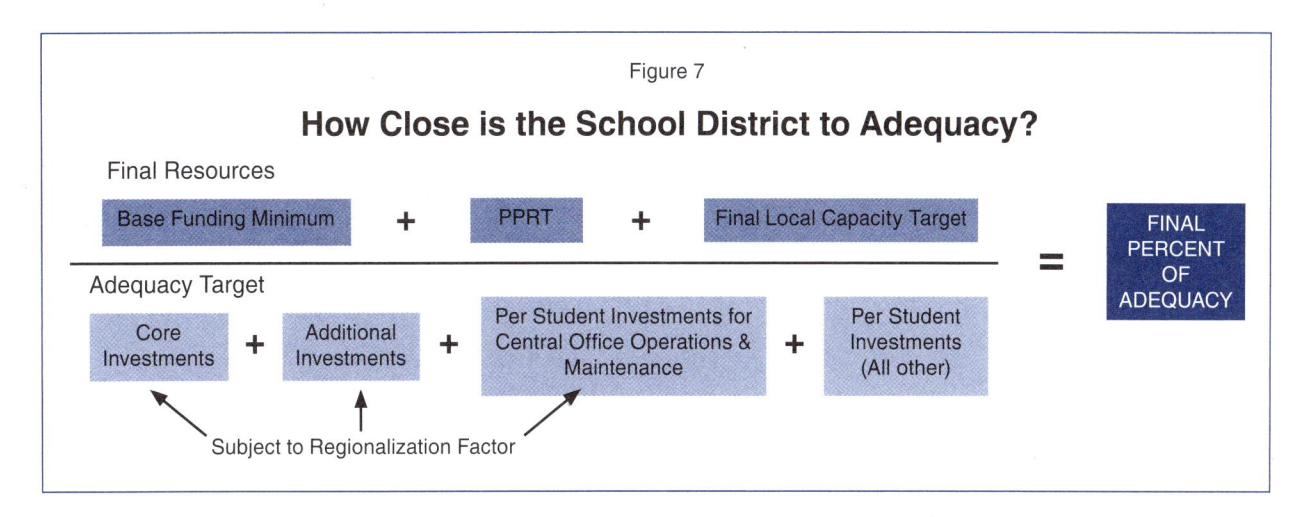

EBF, so that no district suffers a revenue loss compared to the previous year.

The EBF Funding Elements

The table of Funding Elements in Table 9 summarizes the evidence underlying the EBF model. Together, the elements describe the resources found in a school district budget, with the exception of those whose level varies by non-controllable factors such as geography. Transportation is one such variable resource.

The evidence is of two types and is the result of many studies of practices and costs in Illinois and other states. In the introduction to the March 2007 report of the Wisconsin School Finance Adequacy Initiative, which contained a cost table similar to the Illinois elements, the authors stated that "The evidence relies much more strongly on evidence of the resources needed to meet pre-determined performance goals than on the professional judgment of educators."

Some of the evidence for the core program elements comes from studies of the performance of students of similar characteristics enrolled in programs that vary in class size, student and teacher support, and other variables. Other data, including expenditures for materials, administration, and non-instructional services, come from research on Illinois averages. Several Illinois cost studies were prepared by outside researchers for the Educational Funding Advisory Board and a subsequent Educational Funding Advisory Council which were formed to advise the General Assembly on establishing foundation levels under the previous formula and on constructing the new EBF formula. Elements tied to school size, including administration, represent best practices research findings on efficient elementary, middle, and high schools.

The list of elements in *Table 9* on *page 42* serves both state and local purposes. They are not mandates.

The Illinois State Board of Education (ISBE) uses the elements, along with student and cost data, in calculating each district's Adequacy Target. The elements provide guidance to the local district in making research-supported decisions based on its needs, and a framework for reporting its planning to ISBE. They also provide best practice benchmarks to districts reviewing their budgets to identify where resources might be increased, decreased, or transferred to better serve the program as a whole.

The Weight of the Evidence

Michelle Mangan of Concordia University Chicago identified "gold standard research-based practices" that, if implemented in accordance with research-based assumptions, are associated with gains in student achievement. The gains are stated in terms of *effect size*, defined as "the amount of standard deviation in higher performance the program produces for students who participate in the program versus students who do not. An effect size of 1.0 would indicate that the average student's performance would move from the 50th to the 83rd percentile. The research field generally recognizes effect sizes greater than 0.25 as significant and greater than 0.50 as substantial."

The practices with the greatest benefits are shown in *Table 10* on *page 43*.

Overview of the Calculation of a District's EBF

The EBF process involves three stages of calculations to determine the state and district's funding shares. Refer to the *Glossary* on *page 45*, *Figure 7 above,* and *Table 9's (page 42)* EBF elements as you follow these steps. The calculations are performed by ISBE based on enrollment, student, staff, cost, and revenue data submitted by the district

Table 9

The Elements of the Evidence-Based Model

Core Staff	Class Size
Core Teachers K-3 Low Income	15
Core Teachers K-3	20
Core Teachers 4-12 Low Income	20
Core Teachers 4-12	25
Specialist Teachers	20% of Core Teachers (elementary and middle school)
	33.33% of Core Teachers (high school)

	FTE* Staff per Number of Students
Instructional Facilitators	200 K-12
Core Intervention Teachers	450 K-8 / 600 9-12
Core Guidance	450 K-5 / 250 6-12
Nurse	750 K-12
Supervisory Aides	225 K-8 / 200 9-12
Librarian	450 K-8 / 600 9-12
Library/Media Aide/Technician	300 K-12
Principal	450 K-8 / 600 9-12
Asst. Principal	450 K-8 / 600 9-12
School Site Admin. Assistants/Clerks	225 K-8 / 200 9-12
Substitutes	Average daily salary x 5.7% of 176 days x FTE

Per Student Investments	$ per Student (subject to annual recalibration)
Gifted and Talented Students	$90
Professional Development	$125
Instructional Materials	$325
Assessment	$34
Computer Technology	$285.50
Student Activities	$125 K-5 / $249 6-8 / $859 9-12

Central Services	
Maintenance and Operations	$1,361
Central Office	$937
Employee Benefits	30% of salary
	$472.18 (central office)
	$479.70 (Maintenance & Operations)
	Pension costs (Chicago Public Schools only)

Additional Investments	FTE* Staff per Number of Students	
	Low Income (DHS**)	English Language Learner
Intervention	125	125
Pupil Support	125	125
Extended Day	120	120
Summer School	120	120
English Learners	—	100
	K-8 Students	
Special Ed Teachers	141	
Psychologist	1000	
Special Ed Aides	141	

* FTE = Full Time Equivalent
** DHS = Illinois Department of Human Services count of children receiving certain state benefits.
Source: Illinois State Board of Education, August 2023

Table 10

Effect Sizes of Key Evidence-Based Model Elements

An effect size of 1.0 would indicate that the average student's performance would move from the 50th to the 83rd percentile. The research field generally recognizes effect sizes greater than 0.25 as significant and greater than 0.50 as substantial.

Recommended Program	Effect Size
Full Day Kindergarten	0.77
Class size of 15 in Grades K-3	
Overall	0.25
Low income and minority students	0.50
Multi-age Classrooms	
Multi-grade Classrooms	-0.1 to 0.0
Multi-age Classrooms	0.0 to 0.50
Professional Development with Classroom Instructional Coaches	1.25 to 2.70
Tutoring 1-1	0.4 to 2.5
English Language Learners	0.45
Structured, Academic-Focused Summer School	0.45
Embedded Technology	0.30 to 0.38
Gifted and Talented	0.5 to 1.0
Accelerated instruction or grade skipping	0.5 to 1.0
Enrichment Programs	0.4 to 0.7

Source: The effect sizes in the table were reproduced in the article by Drs. Jacoby and Mangan cited above, and credited by them to the report, *An Evidence-Based Approach to School Finance Adequacy in Washington*, by Allan Odden, Lawrence Picus, Michele Mangan and others, prepared in 2016 for Washington Learns, North Hollywood, CA.
---

and other agencies. Based on the data, ISBE reports to the district the amount of its EBF funding for the current year. Spreadsheets showing the data are available in the Evidence-Based Funding section of the Illinois ISBE website.

Stage 1: Determine the District's Adequacy Target (Needs)
- ISBE determines the cost of educating the district's students, according to the 27 defined cost factors in the table of EBF elements. The sum of all education cost factors is the district's initial Adequacy Target (AT).
- The AT reflects the needs of the district's actual student population, considering total enrollment, and district reports to ISBE on counts of low-income and English Language Learners and staff serving special needs students identified on that ISBE census.
- The costs of elements in Core Investment and Additional Investment are then adjusted by a regional cost factor. These factors are based on average salaries, using either the ISBE Employment Information System or the Employment Cost Index (clerical and instructional assistants), and have been narrowed from their actual range to a low of .90 and to a high of 1.06.
- The result is the district's Final Adequacy Target.

Stage 2: Measure the District's Adequacy Level (Local Resources)
- The district's resources consist of the sum of its Local Capacity Target (LCT), plus its Personal Property Replacement Taxes (PPRT), plus its Base Funding Minimum (BFM).
- The LCT identifies how much of its Adequacy Target (AT) the district should cover from its local resources.
- LCT is based generally on a ratio of a district's real taxable property compared to the value of the property of all districts in the state. Example: AT=$20 million/EAV=$100 million=20%.
- Put all districts' ratios into a 1-100 normal distribution.

- Assume the 20% calculates into an LCT of 25% on the all-district distribution.
- Thus, the district's ideal contribution from its local resources is 25% of its AT of $20 million=$5 million. Variations may apply; see the ISBE spreadsheet for explanations.
- The LCT provides a measure of fairness in an inequitable property tax system. Low property tax wealth districts with high tax rates are not expected to contribute as much towards covering their ATs as are higher wealth districts.
- Add the LCT, PPRT, and the BFM to determine Local Resources.
- The FY 2021 LCT calculation uses PPRT received in calendar year 2019 and the BFM component of EBF funding for FY 2021.

Stage 3: Determine the District's Percent of Adequacy and Tier Funding Level

- Dividing the District's Resources (Stage 2) by its Needs (Adequacy Target-Stage 1) produces a ratio that determines how far away it is from adequate funding. That "Target Ratio" will determine which, of four tiers, will determine the district's EBF distribution for the next year.
  Example:
  Resources...................... $9,000 per student
  Adequacy Target (Needs)...$12,000 per student
  Percent of Adequacy................................75%
  Tier Funding....….................…............ Level 2

New EBF Money is Distributed According to Tier Funding Level

- A district's total EBF funding includes its BFM and Tier Funding from the new money appropriated in the ISBE budget for the current year. There are four tiers. Figures are from FY 2024.
- Tier 1 districts are the least well-funded, having the biggest gap (averaging 72.4%) between their resources and their adequacy targets. These districts received 81.4% of the annual appropriation of new EBF dollars.
- Tier 2 districts had average resources of 82.5% of their Adequacy Targets. This tier received 17.6% of the new state funding. As a result, 99% of new funding for education went to those districts least adequately funded — a powerful step towards equity.
- Tier 3 districts had resources that averaged 94.8% of their Adequacy Targets. They received just 0.9% of the new money.
- Tier 4 districts had resources which averaged 136.6% of their Adequacy Targets. They shared 0.1% of the new EBF funds.

The FY 2021 ISBE budget froze EBF funding at the FY 2020 level. Consequently, no money was designated for Tier Funding to districts in 2020-2021. In each of the past three years, tier funding of $300 million was allocated. If a future year budget were to fail to cover the BFM portion of the grants, the BFM of the most adequately funded districts will be the first EBF dollars cut. If that does not cover the full amount of the under-appropriation, further reduction will be made on a per-pupil basis. The EBF legislation contains "doomsday" provisions in the event of even more severe budget reductions. The most drastic of these could reduce aid to the level of the inception of the EBF formula in 2017-2018.

The Annual EBF Plan

School districts, laboratory schools, Regional Offices of Education, and Intermediate Service Centers are required to submit an EBF Spending Plan by October 31. The plan instructions and a submission template are found on the EBF section of the ISBE website. Districts are to describe the student outcomes expected as a result of their EBF investments and other focused efforts, and their plans for their EBF Tier Funding. Other sections cover plans for special education students, children from low-income families, and English Language Learners from all federal, state, and local funds.

Since EBF is unrestricted funding, it can be used for staff and material needs for core programing, including reduction in class size, additional materials, and technology. Districts may also add support staff including counselors, deans, assistant principals, social workers, psychologists, intervention teachers, and other specialists to work with students. Enhanced professional development programs, which show a substantial effect size, may also be implemented. Additionally, EBF may be used for capital projects to replace aging infrastructure.

The EBF plan is not audited, nor is it expected to tie out or link to a district's Annual Financial Report. However, ISBE has integrated the plan into the public budget process and annual budget template.

Other Provisions of the EBF Legislation

The funding reform law contained provisions that impact specific districts and circumstances. Affected entities may obtain information on these provisions

Glossary of State Aid and EBF Terminology

This glossary is intended as a roadmap to assist the reader in navigating the specialized vocabulary used in the discussion of the reforms that culminated in Illinois' EBF system, and the calculations and communications under EBF.

Adequacy — A dollar level of support that, if distributed to districts on an equitable basis, and spent to its greatest effect, will fund a program sufficient to enable most students to achieve at or above the state's specified competency levels. Adequacy also implies that additional support will be provided to educate students with learning and/or language impediments and to compensate for the effects of low family income.

The District Adequacy Target (DAT) — Calculated by ISBE each year and communicated to the district, it is based on the per-pupil costs of research-supported elements that are listed on the chart in this chapter.

The Base Funding Minimum (BFM) — Assures that no district will receive less state funding than it received the prior year. For FY 2018 it consolidated five grants received in FY 2017: Gross General State Aid, English Learner Education, Special Education Personnel, Special Education Funding for Children, and Special Education Summer School. Chicago Public Schools also receive the calculated FY 2017 Block Grant Overage. The BFM is calculated each fiscal year to include the additional EBF Tier Money for the previous year.

Block Grant — Since 1995, the Chicago Public Schools (CPS) alone received grants that encompassed mandated categorical reimbursed to other districts by special formulas and certain other categorical programs. Its calculation was based on state and CPS populations in 1995, and did not adjust for population and demographic changes. Most of the block grant goes away under EBF, except for programs not incorporated into EBF such as early childhood and transportation. The prior Block Grant became part of CPS's BFM and moved it closer to, but still well below, its adequacy target.

Categorical Aid — A system of grants to support a portion of the costs of certain mandated programs (MCATS), including special education and transportation and other programs such as bilingual and early childhood education. Prior to EBF, for instruction-related grants, each district received amounts related to the number of students served and the related costs. Beginning in FY 2018, some MCAT grants were integrated into districts' BFMs. Exceptions include transportation, early childhood education, programs funded by federal dollars, private special education tuition, "orphanage" special education grants, and programs that serve populations that cluster in certain districts, including grants on behalf of students in state facilities.

Equity — A fair and just means of distributing resources. There are three dimensions:
- Taxpayer equity exists when taxpayers with equal ability bear the same tax burden. Tax rates should be equal across the state and districts should receive equal resources from local and state funds for equal local effort.
- Student equity is achieved in two ways. Horizontal equity requires that equals are treated equally, with no variation in resources. Vertical equity recognizes that special needs and poverty require additional resources. Vertical equity has underlain Illinois' school aid programs since 1970.
- Equal opportunity requires that students have access to equal resources despite differences in district type and wealth. It is a key issue in deciding equity-based legal challenges to school funding systems that are based on the education clauses of various states' constitutions.

General State Aid (GSA) — Prior to FY 2018, a per-pupil state grant paid to all school districts in inverse proportion to the district's ability to fund its program from property taxes and under several "breakout" provisions from the GSA appropriation.

Local Capacity Target — The sum of a district's local resources, or the amount of its Adequacy Target that it should contribute from its local resources. Under EBF, the LCT is the district's Base Funding Minimum (BFM) plus its receipts of Personal Property Replacement Taxes (PPRT). LCT = BFM + PPRT.

Private School Tax Credits — Authorized under the School Reform Act as the "Invest in Kids" tax credit. Under the Act, donations made by individuals, corporations, or partnerships for funding scholarships to private schools are

continued

eligible for a 75 percent credit against their state income taxes, up to a $75 million annual statewide maximum. With no identified revenue appropriation, these credits will draw from the same General Fund that supports public schools and many state services.

Property Tax Reduction Referendum — Required to be held at the next non-partisan (November) election if 10 percent of the district's registered voters petition for it. It applies to districts whose resources exceed 110 percent of the Adequacy Target. If successful, the extension for the levy year when the vote took place is reduced by the specified percentage, up to 10 percent.

Property Tax Relief Fund — A pool, the size of which is determined by an annual legislative appropriation, from which districts with high tax rates and low property tax values may apply annually for a limited amount of relief funds.

Proration — The practice of reducing state aid claims when appropriated funds in the state budget are insufficient to pay districts' claims in full. Prorations have been applied during several periods of state budget distress.

Regionalization Factor — A regionalization factor or Comparable Wage Index (CWI) is applied to the Initial Adequacy Target to produce the Final Adequacy Target. The CWI compares the salaries of non-education employees with a bachelor's degree across all counties, compares those differences and computes an index for each region. The actual ranges are narrowed so that the regional ranges used in the CWI are from .9 to 1.06.

Salary Factor — ISBE will calculate and communicate annually the district's cost of the 27 essential elements, using data from its Employment Information System for all positions except clerical and instructional assistance. It will use weighted average salaries based on the district's enrollment. Baseline salary information for clerical and instructional assistants will be multiplied by the Employment Cost Index.

State Budget — The annual appropriation for discretionary expenditures enacted by the General Assembly and approved by the governor for the fiscal year beginning July 1. Many expenditures, including those for state pension contributions, are required by law and the required amounts do not fall within the discretionary budget.

Tier Funding — A district falls into one of four tiers, based on the percentages of its Adequacy Targets that is covered by the sum of its Base Funding Minimum, and its Local Capacity Target divided by its Adequacy Target. The resulting "Percentage of Adequacy" determines the district's tier for that year. Tiers I and II include the districts with the lowest percentage (64-90 percent) of adequacy and in FY 2018 will receive $175 million of the $350 million of the available tier funding allocation. Tier III districts, with ratios between 90 and 100 percent, collectively receive $2.15 million of the new funds. Districts with ratios over 100 percent receive $350,000 of the allocation.

An October 2017 report by the Center for Tax and Budget Accountability commented, "How powerful this distribution mechanism is from an equity standpoint, allocating 99 percent of the new funding for education to those districts that are least adequately funded."

Wealth Neutrality — A situation where the total resources available to a school district in a state do not correlate positively with that district's ability to raise its share of its costs from property taxes, and therefore the quality of the district's education is independent of the community's wealth. A low or negative correlation indicates the state's school funding system provides an equitable amount of state funds to enable all districts to spend at the specified adequate amount.

from the ISBE website and their attorneys, auditors, and financial advisors. Among the provisions are:

- A narrowing of the range of charter school funding from 75 to 100% of the school's "per capital student tuition," to a range of 97 to 103%. The majority of charter schools are in Chicago, and the change has ramifications for Chicago Public Schools.
- Elimination of most of the Chicago Block Grant, except for early childhood education and transportation. The remainder of the grant becomes part of the BFM, moving it closer to its adequacy target and reducing its EBF tier funding. Changes in the Pension Code provide a measure of equity for Chicago taxpayers in comparison with taxpayers in downstate districts.
- A provision for voter-initiated referenda to reduce property taxes. Voters in a district whose resources exceed 110% of its state-calculated adequacy target may petition for a referendum to require the district to reduce its property tax levy by up to 10%. Only one failed referendum was held in 2020.

- A program allowing individuals and businesses to donate funds to private schools for scholarships (but not for specific students). Donors receive credit against their Illinois income taxes up to a $1 million annual limit per donor. Credits are subject to a $75 million aggregate statewide maximum.
- A streamlined process for waiver relief for School Code mandates, giving ISBE authority to approve most waiver requests, reducing the physical education mandate, and allowing districts to contract with commercial driving schools.
- Creation of a task force to review state policy on Tax Increment Financing districts.
- Property tax relief for districts with high tax rates and low property wealth that may apply for a limited amount of relief annually. For example, a unit district can lower its tax rate by about 1 percentage point; a district with a 7% operating tax rate could lower it to 6%. Upon ISBE approval of its application, districts file tax abatements with the county clerk. In FY 2020, 130 districts received a total of $49,703,174 in grants.
- The threshold for eligibility and the amount available for relief will depend on ISBE regulations and the annual budget for the property tax relief fund. A state appropriation is required to fund the grants each year. To the extent it is funded, it reduces new state money for distribution through the EBF formula. With state education funding uncertain beyond FY 2024, the future of the property tax relief grant may also be uncertain. Instructions and a list of recipient districts are found on the EBF section of the ISBE website.

Accountability and Transparency

EBF carries with it new requirements for accounting and transparency. School officials will need to keep current on forthcoming changes in ISBE regulations governing budgeting, accounting, and reporting, and modify their charts of accounts and coding procedures accordingly. Revenue categories reflect the integration of some previous categorical grants into EBF funding. While these categorical grants have been integrated into EBF, student and cost data on pupil services is still required for other state and federal reporting purposes.

ISBE has published rules for three formerly separate categorical grants that were integrated into EBF.

- English Language Learners – District funding attributable to these students must be spent on EL services and documented on an end-of-year report to show how EL funds were spent for the year.
- Special Education – ISBE calculates the total special education funding generated for each organizational and specially funded unit, including any special education funds generated under the BFM and Tier Funding. These funds must be used for special education facilities and services as defined in Section 14-1.08 of the School Code.
- Low Income – Each unit of a participating district is required to describe in its Annual Plan how it will use the BFM and Tier Funding it receives, with specific identification of how it intends to use low-income resources. No expenditure reports for low-income funds are required.

The elements of the EBF formula include data of interest to the public and media. Information about the district's resources related to its adequacy target and other EBF information is included in its Illinois Report Card distributed to school families and posted for public information. Boards of education in districts that receive substantial amounts of new state funding are faced with allocating these funds among competing, worthy alternatives. Some boards may choose to reduce property taxes or set aside some of the funds to build up reserves or allocate them to capital needs. EBF revenue is unrestricted revenue in the sense that the previous General State Aid revenue could be allocated among the operating funds, programs, and expenditure categories. The process of engagement and communication used by the board with its stakeholders to make such allocation decisions is as important as the results of that decision.

Time will tell how accounting and communication changes will play out. Meanwhile, superintendents, business officials, principals, and board members will need to reflect on the communications they may be required to conduct in the future and develop some formats and language with which to make them.

7 / State Categorical Funding

Categorical Funding in the ISBE Budget

A substantial amount of the state's education budget reimburses districts for a portion of the costs of educational programs and support services to targeted populations. Such grants are referred to as "categorical grants" and, for budgeting and reporting, as "restricted revenues." Categorical grants in the ISBE budget that support mandated programs (MCATs) include special education, orphanage, and private school tuition; regular, vocational, and special education transportation; and lunch and breakfast programs. They are entitlements, as opposed to competitive grants, in that districts need only offer the service and file with ISBE the necessary data and claims to qualify for the funds. Most categorical grants reimburse only a portion of the costs of the programs and services they support. Reimbursement occurs in the year following expenditure of funds. Categorical grant amounts in the ISBE budget vary over time, depending on numbers of children in need of services and annual legislative appropriations.

The rules and regulations for the various categorical grant programs are found on the ISBE website. Careful compliance with these rules and associated reporting requirements and claim deadlines is necessary to gain the full value of the grants and to avoid claim reductions due to audit exceptions. ISBE has online reporting of student, personnel, program cost, and other data pertinent to categorical grant administration. New requirements and procedures appear frequently, and business officials and the administrators responsible for special education and other grant-supported programs should regularly check their knowledge of these procedures and their data banks well ahead of the reporting and claim deadlines.

MCAT claims have sometimes not been paid on time or have been prorated during periods of state budgetary distress. However, districts expected to receive all four of their quarterly payments for 2022-2023 claims on time.

Table 11

FY 2024 Budget Allocations for Mandatory Categorical Grants (MCATs)

Special Education - Orphanage Tuition ...	$118,919,500
Special Education - Private Tuition	202,732,400
Special Education - Transportation	437,366,100
Free Lunch/Breakfast	9,000,000
Orphanage Tuition (Non-Special Ed)	8,000,000
Transportation - Regular/Vocational	340,000,000

Source: ISBE FY 2024 Budget, May 26, 2023

Major Illinois Categorical Funding Programs

Tables 11 and *12* identify the major categorical grants by group and their FY 2023 budget appropriations. The ISBE budget, found on the ISBE website, shows appropriations for each state grant program, federal grants administered by ISBE (described in *Chapter 8*), and for ISBE operations and services. These budgets may change during the fiscal year; checking the latest numbers is advisable, especially during periods of fiscal uncertainty.

Many of the MCAT claims have not been paid in full during periods of state budgetary distress. Even prior to the onset of the pandemic in March 2020, ISBE announced that some FY 2020 special education and transportation claims would be prorated at 80 to 90% of the approved claim amounts. In addition to proration, claims scheduled to be paid in installments are not paid on time when the state has a bill backlog. Some districts budget only the anticipated prorated amounts with an informational note as to the amount of the expected reductions.

Provisions of Mandated Categorical Grants

Special Education: Reimbursement for tuition paid for students in non-public special education programs is based on state-approved rates for each institution, including summer school where required, less twice the district's per capita cost. Non-public school tuition is governed under Section 14-7.02 of the School Code and associated ISBE regulations.

Costs of "orphanage" special education services provided to foster children and wards of the state, including residents of children's homes and certain state institutions, are reimbursed fully under provisions of 14-7.03 of the School Code, once known as the "Orphanage Act." It is important that local administrators identify these students and maintain cost records on their special education services so that these costs are recovered. Orphanage payments have generally not been prorated in recent years, as the outlays for these services are substantial parts of the budgets of school districts where large state and private institutions are located.

Transportation costs for students for whom special transportation is specified in their Individual Educational Programs are reimbursed at 80% of eligible costs. Rules for allocating transportation expenditures to special education and claim procedures are found on the ISBE website in the transportation funding and disbursement section.

Early Childhood Education: According to the Illinois State Board of Education, access to preschool provides an essential foundation for the trajectory of a child's well-being and academic outcomes. As such, the state budget for FY2024 includes an increase of $75 million dollars to expand access to preschool opportunities across the state with a focus on areas identified as "preschool deserts" where low-income children lack sufficient access to publicly funded preschool. These funds are part of the four-year Smart Start Illinois plan to be implemented in 2024.

Transportation: Reimbursement for student transportation over 1.5 miles or from areas designated as hazardous or with a pattern of criminal gang activity is paid on a sliding scale related to the district's tax base. A higher percentage of costs is reimbursed to higher poverty districts; a flat grant of $16 per reimbursement-eligible pupil transported is paid to the wealthiest districts. ISBE budget reductions in recent years have required proration of transportation claims, thereby requiring higher local contributions from taxes and fees. Rules for transportation reimbursement, including procedures for designating areas as hazardous, are available from ISBE's website, along with links to resources on operating transportation programs.

The State School Lunch and Breakfast Program: These funds supplement the amounts from federal funds for children who meet the guidelines for free and reduced-price meals. Every public school must have a free lunch program to provide free

Table 12

FY 2024 Budget Appropriations for Selected Grants and ISBE Programs

Grant/Program	2024 Budget
Early Childhood	$673,138,100
Mental Health Services	7,500,000
ROE/Safe Schools	20,000,000
Truant/Alternative/Optional Programs	11,500,000
Career/Technical Education	47,726,400
Agricultural Education	7,050,000
GATA/Budgeting for Results	300,000
Autism	100,000
Blind and Dyslexic	846,000
Tax Equivalent Grants	275,000
Technology Support	2,443,800
Computer Science Education	3,000,000
Dolly Parton Imagination Library	1,600,000
Youth Build Illinois	5,500,000
After School Matters	5,000,000
After School Programs	25,000,000
Adv. Placement Courses, Test Fee	2,500,000
Assessments	40,000,000
National Board Teacher Certification	4,500,000
Teacher Vacancy Grant Pilot Program	45,000,000
District Consolidation Costs	80,000
Driver Education Fund*	10,000,000
Technology Loan Fund*	7,500,000
School STEAM Grant Program Fund	2,500,000
Charter School Loan Fund*	200,000
District Emergency Financial Assist Fund*	1,000,000
Temporary Relocation Expenses*	1,000,000
ROE Salaries and Services*	31,170,000
ISBE Agency Operations	42,548,900
ISBE Special Purpose Trust Fund	8,484,800
After-School Rescue Fund	200,000

* Grants from funds other than the General Revenue Fund

Source: ISBE FY 2024 Budget, May 26, 2023

lunches (and breakfasts if a school offers breakfast) to students eligible to receive free meals as defined in the Illinois School Code and related Administrative Rules. Alternatively, high-poverty schools may utilize the Community Eligibility Provision (CEP), which allows schools meeting certain eligibility criteria to forgo the household income eligibility requirement. Federal meal reimbursements are discussed in *Chapter 18*.

Other Categorical Grants and Budget Appropriations

Other major categorical grants in ISBE's FY 2024 budget are listed in *Table 12*. Also, from time to time, special grant programs administered by state agencies other than ISBE are announced. To identify such funding opportunities, regular reading of ISBE communications and those of other grant-making agencies is encouraged. These grants have specific and often short application timelines, so diligence in seeking them out is advised.

Where to Find More Information on ISBE Grant Programs

The ISBE publication "Fiscal Year 2023 Recommended Investment in Public Education" details the purpose, history, appropriation, participant statistics, and reimbursement/distribution method for all ISBE grant programs and many federal programs as well. This 200-page publication is a starting point for educators shopping for grant support or browsing to appreciate the wide umbrella of assistance available to schools. Familiarizing oneself with the description of a grant in this publication will assist in the preparation of the formal grant applications, which will be found on the appropriate section of the ISBE website. Some programs authorized in law for which there is no current appropriation are included. The publication may be found by entering "FY 2023 Budget Book" in the search field on the ISBE website (www.isbe.net). The Budget Books are normally available in February prior to the beginning of each fiscal year, e.g. February 2023 for FY 2024.

8 / Federal and Other Grant Revenue

This chapter describes the federal education budget process and the major federal grants to Illinois schools. It also discusses techniques and resources to assist the administrator in matching available federal and other outside funding sources with the programs and priorities of the school district.

Background

The history of federal government support of public education begins in the early years of the Republic, with land allocations for public schools in the Northwest Territories and for public universities. The early 20th century saw the emergence of federal support for vocational and agricultural education. Later came the establishment of the Federal School Lunch Program following World War II, and grants for science education and teacher training during the "space race" in the 1950s and 1960s.

The late 1960s and the 1970s saw a burst of "social legislation" with profound consequences for school programs, budgets, and operations. Some of this legislation, such as student records law, was confined to regulating specific aspects of school operations. Other initiatives included both regulatory and funding aspects. Notable among the funded programs have been those for students with disabilities, early childhood education, low-income children, immigrants, and English language learner students. Meanwhile, many funded programs, including vocational education and school meal programs, continued or expanded in scope and federal funding.

The Elementary and Secondary Education Act (ESEA), passed in 1965, became the umbrella legislation for many long-standing federal aid programs, often referred to by their "Title" numbers. Title I of ESEA was intended to help districts cover the costs of educating disadvantaged children. Subsequent reauthorizations of the law have increased the federal role in education. Each version of ESEA got a new name. In January 2002, it became the No Child Left Behind Act (NCLB).

NCLB significantly increased the federal role in holding schools responsible for the academic progress of all students. And it focused on ensuring that states and schools boost the performance of certain groups of students, such as English language learners, students in special education, economically disadvantaged and children of color, whose achievement, on average, trails their peers. States did not have to comply with the new requirements, but if they didn't, they risked losing federal Title I money.

After the passage of NCLB in 2002, appropriations for Department of Education programs grew from Fiscal Years 2002 through 2006. Elementary and Secondary Education Act, Title I grants, and Individuals with Disabilities Education Act (IDEA) state grants were allocated significant funding increases. Appropriations leveled during the recession of 2007-2008. In Fiscal Year 2009, significant funding increases for new and existing education programs were included in economic stimulus legislation, the American Recovery and Reinvestment Act of 2009.

Every Student Succeeds Act (ESSA)

The December 2015 Every Student Succeeds Act (ESSA) followed NCLB and is the latest iteration of ESEA. ESSA outlines how states can use federal money to support schools' plans to achieve equal opportunity for all students. ESSA also establishes an accountability framework for all districts, which is now extending to the school building level. This section illustrates how three programs within ESSA provide funding for Illinois schools.

States submitted an ESSA plan to the U.S. Department of Education. The Illinois ESSA plan was approved on August 30, 2017. ESSA eliminated NCLB's Adequate Yearly Progress requirements that imposed sanctions on districts failing to meet specified achievement goals. It also eliminated the Highly Qualified Teacher designations that defined preparation standards and limited local districts' staffing options. Other changes affected school improvement categories. An amended Illinois plan was approved by the Department of Education in September 2019. Both the original 2017 plan and the amended plan are found at www.isbe.net. Search for ESSA and you will find the plans and the extensive process by which they were developed.

The Illinois State Board of Education administers ESSA Title IA, Title IIA, and Title IV programs.

Title IA is the largest federal grant program administered by ISBE. Funds are based on the numbers or percentages of children from low-income families. Poverty counts and low-income rates are generated by the U.S. Census Bureau and do not equate to the numbers of students eligible for free and reduced meals. In some schools that meet criteria defined in terms of the percentage of children from low-income families (40% of enrollment), the funds are targeted to provide academic enrichment services for schoolwide programs that serve all children. Other schools focus the grants on specific groups of eligible students who are failing or most at risk of failing to meet state academic standards. Districts also must use Title I funds to provide services to eligible children enrolled in private schools.

Title IIA seeks to improve the achievement of all students by supporting the preparation, training, and recruiting of high-quality teachers, principals, and other school leaders. Title II funds are generated based on districts' numbers of 5-17 year-olds (20%) and number of low-income 5-17 year-olds (80%). Districts may use funds for intensive, focused professional development and on evidence-based class-size reductions. A portion of the state allocation may be used for State Board of Education activities including certification reform, teacher and leader academies, and providing equitable access to teachers.

The mission of ESSA Title IV is to improve academic achievement by providing access to technology to support digital literacy; foreign language instruction; art and music education; science, technology, engineering and mathematics (STEM) courses; Advanced Placement and International Baccalaureate programs; and other subjects. Other eligible uses include Safe and Supportive School programs, and those designed to improve students' physical and mental health. The extensive list of eligible programs appears on the ISBE website under Title IV. The funds distribution formula is based on districts' relative share of Title I funds. Districts may form consortia and combine their funds.

ISBE's FY 2021 Title IV grant awards, which may be spent over a 27-month period, are $51,305,680 for Community Learning Centers and $50,043,672 for Title IV-A (Student Support and Academic Enrichment).

Coronavirus Relief Funding

Schools were major beneficiaries of Section 18003 of Division B of the Coronavirus Aid, Relief and Economic Security (CARES) Act enacted on March 27, 2020, and of Section 313 of the Coronavirus Supplemental Appropriations (CRRSA) Act enacted on December 27, 2020. Selected provisions of the two Acts are shown in the excerpted table on the *next page*. LEA refers to Local Educational Agency; SEA refers to State Educational Agency.

In addition to CARES and CRRSA, school systems, their employees, students, and families benefitted from other COVID relief programs. Among them are Families First Coronavirus Relief (FFCRA) including provisions and flexibility for school nutrition programs and mandated sick paid/family leave; the Paycheck Protection Program and Health Care Enhancement Act; and Economic Stabilization Fund provisions for paid leave during coronavirus-caused disruptions, extension of unemployment benefits, and various tax and payroll credits for businesses and educators.

The Federal Education Budget

The federal fiscal year runs from October 1 through the following September 30. As a result, federally funded programs in schools with July 1-June 30 year overlap two federal fiscal years, requiring grant administrators' attention to the designated federal year for which funds are received and expenditures made.

Federal grants are "forward-funded." Reading the progressive drafts of the Department of Education budget prior to the beginning of the federal fiscal year in October will give an indication of the amount of funds that will be available for the current and following school years. The progress of the federal budget and enacted appropriations, when available, can be found on the U.S. Department of Education website, www.ed.gov/budget. The figures may change several times between the President's initial budget proposal and finalization of the budget appropriations, which may be delayed past the October 1 beginning of the federal fiscal year.

A description of the federal education budget process, including descriptions of the goals and budget for each grant program, and the budget calendar are at www.ed.gov/budget. The budget appropriations for the current year and proposed appropriations for the following year can be also found there. A list of all federal education grants and links to eligibility requirements and application procedures can also be found at www2.ed.gov/fund/grants-apply.html. The President's FY 2023 Budget Request called for $88.3 billion in discretionary budget authority, a $15.3 billion or 20.9% increase from the FY 2021 appropriation.

Advocating for the Federal Budget

Accessing federal decision-makers is a skillset with which many administrators and board members are not familiar. It is important to develop an information network through professional organizations, monitor publications and legislative websites, and develop personal contacts with representatives and especially their staff members who work on education legislation and appropriations. Many of these staffers are early in their careers, and their knowledge of education has been shaped by their own recent experiences. Educating them in the issues as seen in the "big picture" is essential. State and national organizations of school board members and administrators offer information, websites, publications, and workshops on federal educational developments and lobbying, and some organize events in Washington that include informational presentations and meetings with agency officials, members of Congress, and their staffs.

Table 13

Federal Education Spending, FY 2023 Budget Appropriations for Selected Programs

	($ billions)
Department of Education Total Appropriation for Elementary and Secondary Programs	88.3
Title 1 Grants (Mandatory)	16.0
Title 1 Grants (Discretionary)	20.5
School-Based Health Professionals	1.0
Impact Aid	1.541
IDEA Grants	16.259
Career and Technical Education Grants	1.570
English Language Acquisition	1.075

Source: U.S. Department of Education FY 2023 Budget Summary

Information on Grant Funding

Information on federal and other grants, as well as federal budget developments, is regularly published in *Education Week*, www.edweek.org. Keeping current on non-governmental sources of grants is necessary, since

	ESSER Fund (CARES Act)	ESSER II Fund (CRRSA Act)	ARP ESSER (ARP Act)
Availability	March 13, 2020 – September 30, 2022	March 13, 2020 – September 30, 2023	March 13, 2020 – September 30, 2024
Uses	Specified in Act for preventing, preparing for, and responding to COVID-19	Same as CARES Act including addressing learning loss, preparing schools for reopening, and testing, repairing, and upgrading projects to improve air quality in school buildings.	Not less than 20% must address learning loss through the implementation of evidence-based interventions, such as summer learning or summer enrichment, extended day, comprehensive afterschool programs, or extended school year programs, and ensure that such interventions respond to students' academic, social, and emotional needs and address the disproportionate impact of COVID-19 on underrepresented student subgroups. The remaining funds uses same as ESSER and ESSER II, including hiring new staff and avoiding layoffs.
Equitable Services	LEA must provide to non-public schools, students, and teachers as provided under Title I of ESEA.	Act includes a separate program for non-public schools, which may apply to SEA. LEAs not required to provide services.	After seeking public comment on it, the district must make its plan for a safe return to in-person instruction and continuity of services available on its website.

Table 14

Selected State-Administered Federal Grants

Career and Technical Education	$70,000,000
Child Nutrition	1,250,000,000
Individuals with Disabilities Act	996,376,400
Title I	1,200,000,000
Title II	160,000,000
Title III English Language Proficiency	56,000,000
Title IV	250,000,000
Title V-Rural and Low-Income Schools	2,200,000
Title X	9,000,000

Source: ISBE FY 2024 Operations Budget, May 26, 2023

grant-making agencies and their programs undergo frequent change.

The U.S. Department of Education website lists available discretionary grants and the timelines and procedures for applying for them at www.ed.gov/programs/gtep. Consult the websites of other agencies for information on programs under their jurisdictions, e.g., www.usda.gov for information on federal lunch and breakfast programs, and www.hhs.gov for information on early childhood and childcare grants.

Information on foundation grant programs can be accessed from the various foundations currently funding public education initiatives. While some foundations consider applications from throughout the United States, others have regional emphases. A good source of philanthropic information is the *Chronicle of Philanthropy*, www.philanthropy.com.

The book, *Winning Grants Step by Step* (5th Edition, 2019) by Tori O'Neal-McElrath, offers a guide to securing funding from private foundations or the government. Filled with examples, this guide directs the novice grant-seeker and offers a refresher course for experienced grant writers. It is available from the IASB online bookstore at www.iasb.com.

Matching Needs to Outside Funding Sources

Long-standing local, state, and federal revenue sources are stressed as a result of the 2020 COVID-19 pandemic. Recovery to past levels, let alone increases to meet future needs, may not be rapid. Therefore, school leaders are looking to grant-making agencies, including foundations and businesses, and are applying for state and federal competitive grant programs. This section outlines a process for determining whether a grant would be of benefit to the district and for developing the grant proposal.

Several questions must be asked when researching outside funding for an educational program or support service. The questions may be educational, political, legal, managerial, financial, or any or all of these. Some can be answered by a careful reading of the information contained in the Request for Proposal (RFP) or other government bulletins that describe the grant program. Others require consultation with the leadership, faculty, and governing board of the school district.

Involvement of the school district's business administrator at the early stages of consideration and in preparing an outside funding proposal is desirable. Such consultation will assure that, if the proposal is successful, the money will be spent and accounted for according to the terms of the grant and other applicable laws.

The first step for an administrator who is considering applying for a grant is to define and answer key questions. These questions are applicable whether the funding is to come from federal, state, or private sources, such as a foundation. Listed below are representative questions; the remaining ones will be situational in nature, but equally important in deciding upon, preparing, and administering the funded program. Take time to develop and answer the questions appropriate to the situation.

- Do we want to do this? Is the purpose of this funded program one that meets the educational needs of the district or social needs of the student body? Does it complement or conflict with our present program? Will it require that student time be devoted to the funded activities? Are the school day and/or year to be lengthened and will the grant pay the extra costs? If no more student time is to be added, what programs or services are to be discontinued? In short, how do the funded activities impact the "big picture" in the school district?
- Who else in the school system may have a stake in the decision? A funded program for a small

Education Grants 101

Many school districts find it more and more difficult to function effectively on the support received from state and federal funds. Most school administrators and teachers are aware that grants are available from both federal agencies and private organizations. However, they usually do not know the sources of grant funds, and they do not have the time to research what grants are available and how to obtain grant funds.

Grant seeking and grant writing are time-consuming endeavors that require concentrated effort, commitment, and persistence on the part of the grant seeker and grant writer. Some districts have realized that these efforts amount to full-time activities that require the support of a grant development office.

Through such an office, a district can better coordinate the technical skills of grant writing with the expertise of program specialists to develop more effective grant proposals. Office personnel also become knowledgeable on the types of grants available, the standard application procedures, and the differing requirements of each grant.

Grants offices typically collect a variety of information and set up their own reference library, which includes books, directories, newsletters, and names of organizations and contacts who can provide current information on federal, corporate, and foundation grants. Listed below are the four basic steps in the process of seeking grant funds.

1. Conduct Needs Assessment

Before undertaking any grant seeking, a district or campus must first identify its needs by conducting a thorough needs assessment. Successful grants are always designed to meet compelling and clearly defined needs, not just to secure funding. If the needs statement does not contain substantial, justifiable needs, the proposal will be turned down.

Furthermore, the very process of defining needs helps a prospective grantee match its needs with the requirements of specific grant sources. This translates, in turn, into more efficient use of time and a greater likelihood of successful funding.

2. Investigate Grant Opportunities

The best way to start investigating grant opportunities is to visit one of the regional foundation libraries, which are located at most major universities. These libraries provide current and comprehensive information, free of charge, on funding sources and grantsmanship. With advance notice, library personnel can also compile materials in your particular area of interest.

Make an appointment with a librarian to review the available materials and then decide if you need to purchase additional publications to inform and assist in the grant-seeking process. At the same time, obtain the names and addresses of corporate grantors and private foundations that fund organizations similar to yours; later, you can request in writing to be placed on their mailing lists.

If you are interested in federal funding, make a habit of reviewing the Federal Register for Requests for Comments, which are required of all federal programs. The comment period not only provides an opportunity to comment on the program but also outlines the preliminary program priorities of the potential funding source. With this information you can begin working on your proposal right away instead of waiting for a formal Request for Proposal (RFP) to be issued.

This extra time is especially valuable since the period between the announcement and the deadline is usually too brief to accommodate the typical in-district approval process, particularly if it involves the local board of education.

3. Learn to Write a Grant

After becoming acquainted with the different aspects of grants, attend training classes on grant writing. Grant writing is an art that needs to be developed through continuous practice. Volunteering to be a reader of grants can increase your writing skills. This activity will familiarize you with the terms and styles used in grant writing and with how to address federal agencies, corporations, and private foundations when you request funding.

4. Prepare and Submit the Grant Application

Most grants are designed for institutions rather than individuals, which means teachers face special challenges when seeking grant funds to implement innovative ideas in the classroom. In those districts with established grants departments, teachers should confer with the campus principal to determine the availability of individual grants. Depending on district procedure, either the superintendent, the principal, or the teacher would contact their school district grants department and request that all available information be forwarded to the teacher.

In those districts without such services, the teacher should still consult with the appropriate administrative personnel, but ultimately he or she will need to become a campus-level specialist on grants. Individual teachers would use the process suggested above for acquiring information on grants and grant writing. Additionally, however, they would likely have to present their findings to central office administration in order to secure district-wide support for the grants process.

Once the grant process is underway, the applicant must be careful to meet all the requirements outlined in the RFP or other grant guidelines. Since these requirements are described in narrative form only, it might be helpful to devise a checklist to ensure that all necessary information is included.

Copyright © 2023 Illinois State Board of Education, reprinted by permission. All rights reserved.

amount of computer equipment in a single school will have fewer ramifications (if it doesn't cause system problems) than a program to change the service delivery model for gifted children in all of the schools. Although the single school grant might contribute to inequity of computer resources among the schools, it is not as pervasive or probably as controversial as a district-wide initiative in a "hot button" topic such as gifted education.

- Which local decision-makers must sign off on the proposal? The grant-seeking administrator requires a sensitive antenna to determine who must be informed and consulted before a grant application is prepared. Topics with district-wide implications may require involvement of the superintendent and discussion and approval by the board of education. It is not always possible for the beginning administrator, especially, to see the wider ramifications of what seems like a small, contained program-improvement proposal. Therefore, informing upper levels of administration of intended grant-seeking activity is good practice.

- Can we buy what we need with the grant funds? If we need services for students, does the grant permit them, or is it limited to training and start-up expenses? Are matching local expenses required, and if so, can the budget support them? Are such items as equipment, travel, and consultants necessary and, if so, are they permitted or limited? Who will run the program, and are there sufficient funds to support the cost of its administration and other overhead, unless the school district is to support these expenses?

- How long will the grant last, and might it oblige us to expand or continue a program or service after the outside funding has ended? If so, can we afford it? While a pledge of continuation may not be contained in the grant terms, a grant-seeking school district must consider the political ramifications of discontinuing or limiting a successful program when the grant funds run out.

- Is this an "entitlement" or a "competitive" grant? Entitlement grant funds are commonly distributed on a formula related to the number of eligible pupils. Lunch and breakfast and Title I basic grant programs are examples of entitlements. While application paperwork and accounting reports must be filled out, the supporting narrative of objectives, activity descriptions, and budget detail is usually substantially less cumbersome than for competitive grants. Examine the program information on agency websites and application materials to determine up front the nature of the grant program in this respect.

- What are our chances of getting this money? If the grant is competitive, what percentage of applications has been funded in recent grant cycles? Is there a pattern of types and locations of funded projects, and do the school district's proposal and demographics match those of successful districts? Does someone in the district know the people who will read and score the proposals, and their interests and predilections? It is good strategy for the grant writer to volunteer to serve as a reader for the grant-awarding agencies to learn first-hand how the game is played. One will not, of course, be allowed to read applications for grant programs for which one's district is applying.

- Is the district able and willing to abide by the terms of the funded program? Federal RFPs and the associated regulations have the force of law, and misspending of government funds can lead to financial sanctions against the district and professional embarrassment, or worse, for the offending grant administrators. Termination of a grant and repayment of misspent money are among the penalties for violating grant terms. Items purchased with grant funds may be considered federal property, and federal laws may influence even the process of purchasing them. Federal as well as state grants are routinely audited, and compliance or non-compliance with their terms is noted on the district's accounting reports, which are sent to boards of education and government agencies and are open to public inspection.

9 / Local Funding Sources

This chapter identifies the major categories of local revenues and discusses the uses and, where applicable, some of the legal parameters in their administration.

Background

Local funding sources contribute over half of Illinois public school revenues. However, in districts with relatively rich tax bases, which receive minimal state funding, the percentage of local funding can run 80% or more. While most local revenue consists of property taxes, schools statewide rely on many other forms of locally raised money to fund their educational programs and support services.

Some local funding sources are unrestricted in that they can be applied to any operating fund at the discretion of the local board of education. Most of the interest earned on bank balances and investments is unrestricted. Other sources are restricted and must be applied to the fund and purpose for which the revenue is collected. Examples are fees collected for driver education, school meals, and transportation.

Managing Local Revenue Sources

Tuition is collected by districts for non-resident students. The district is required by law to charge tuition to non-resident students, excepting special education students or others in a joint program with other districts. Limited exceptions apply to students from an adjacent school district in cases where a student's health and safety are served, and for dependents of military personnel in temporary housing. Consult the district's attorney when such exceptions are considered. The tuition rate is established by ISBE based on the receiving district's actual expenditures for the previous year, a statistic known as the per capita tuition cost. The rate is found on the school district's annual financial report (AFR). Do not confuse the tuition calculation with that of the per-pupil operating cost, also found in the AFR.

Whether to accept non-resident tuition students or to waive tuition for future residents are policy decisions of the local board of education. Restrictions can be placed on non-resident enrollments. However, to avoid allegations of discrimination, some attorneys advise that any restrictions be based on "applicant-neutral" factors such as class size, and not on the individual characteristics of non-resident applicants.

Policing non-resident enrollments can be time-consuming and must follow procedures specified in law to assure due process for students and their families as well as the district's protection from the costs of ineligible students. Researching current residency law and incorporation of key provisions in the district's policies, procedures, and employee handbooks will assure that administrators, teachers, and support personnel will be familiar with residency law and policies, alert to the signs of possible residency errors or fraud, and minimize errors and possible legal actions resulting from challenges to a student's residency.

Summer school tuition rates are established locally based on the actual costs of salaries, supplies, building use, and other costs associated with the program. A separate fee may be charged for transportation. No fee may be charged for special education students whose summer services are included in their individual educational plans. State reimbursement for a portion of the costs is available for eligible students in special education summer school programs of at least 60 clock hours, provided the student is eligible under Private Facility (14-7.02) or Children Requiring Special Education Services (14-7.02b). No tuition may be charged to families for these services.

Districts or cooperatives that operate special education programs in which students from several districts are enrolled receive tuition paid by the student's home district, based upon the cost of providing the class and related services to the non-residents.

The tuition calculation follows procedures specified by ISBE. The tuition cost sheet (Form 50.66A) and related forms can be found at www.isbe.net.

Inter-district agreements establishing agencies for vocational education and other programs provide formulae within state regulations for students' home districts to reimburse the cooperative or operating district for the cost of the program. Districts that operate adult education programs collect tuition related to the costs of adult classes.

School districts outside Chicago may rent or sell textbooks to students unless the voters of the district have authorized free textbooks in a referendum. Therefore, a profusion of registration, book, and material fees exists and is applied to the costs of textbooks and consumable instructional materials. In recent years, fees were waived due to the COVID-19 pandemic. In fiscal year 2022-2023, many districts returned to charging student fees. Such fees are widely resented, often difficult to collect, and awkward to explain to parents, especially to former residents of states where textbooks are provided free of charge. With the costs of printed materials and technology rising faster than school revenues from taxes and state aid, fees in most districts have shown a steady trend of increase. State law requires that a district waive most student fees for low-income families.

With technology such as tablet and laptop computers taking the place of some printed materials, districts are taking varied approaches to funding the necessary equipment and content. Some schools furnish the equipment, and charge students an insurance fee as a condition of take-home privileges. Others sell the equipment to students, allowing payment over several years. Some share the lower costs of content compared to expensive textbooks by reducing the fees previously charged for textbook rental. A policy for financing new technology and associated content is an essential step in planning for a major technology implementation.

Districts that provide transportation that is not subsidized at the state level commonly charge fees related to the cost of providing this service. The amount of transportation fees is determined by the board of education. Few districts have the tax base to provide free or low-cost optional transportation. Moreover, the tax cap law has required districts to lower transportation tax rates to permit higher rates in educational funds. With the costs of vehicles, drivers, and operations rising at a greater rate than the cost of living, transportation fees have responded accordingly, with fees now as high as several hundred dollars per pupil.

While the state does subsidize student transportation for students more than 1.5 miles from school or in areas identified as serious safety hazards, reimbursements do not cover 100% of the expenditures for this service.

Reasonable fees may be charged for participation in extracurricular activities, sports programs, music groups, and other services and activities that are tangential to the educational program. They must be waived for students identified as low income. These fees have become increasingly common as budgetary pressures have increased. Activity participation fees are regarded as a necessary alternative to discontinuing popular programs. It is wise to consult the school attorney before initiating a fee for classes and activities that fall within the legal parameters of the school day or which are for activities related to the instructional program.

Admissions to sports and other school events are school revenues and are established by local policy, as are the regulations regarding "booster clubs" and fund-raising events in support of specific activities.

A district must provide, at its expense, catastrophic accident insurance for high school students participating in IHSA sanctioned events. This coverage is in addition to any other health insurance. To the extent possible, it is to be paid from funds derived from athletic activities; any remainder must be paid from the Education Fund.

The total amount from driver education fees and state reimbursement must not exceed the total cost of the program, and must be deposited into the district's driver education fund as a separate line item budget entry. Moneys in that fund must be used solely for the funding of a high school driver education program approved by ISBE and using state board-certified instructors. While the maximum fee for driver's education is $50, many districts have increased this fee to as much as $250 by school board resolution following a public hearing. Districts that choose to increase the fee above the $250 amount may only do so after receiving an approved waiver from ISBE. Again, the fee must be waived for low-income families.

Fees for breakfast and lunch programs are established to cover the operating costs of the program, which may also include related costs for cleaning and maintaining food preparation equipment and spaces. Districts that participate in federal and state reimbursement programs establish meal fees to cover costs not covered by government reimbursements. The highest rate of reimbursement is paid for meals served to low-income students, who are eligible for a free lunch or breakfast. Current reimbursement rates can be found at www.isbe.net/nutrition. While boards of education may opt to subsidize meal programs, the costs must come out of the Educational Fund. Therefore, most districts will keep a close eye on food service programs to assure that they are self-sufficient from fees and reimbursements. In recent years, many districts transitioned to the Community Eligibility Provision which provides free meals to all students in low-income districts. Additionally, as part of the pandemic relief legislation, free meals were provided to all students regardless of family income during 2021 and 2022 fiscal years. The School Nutrition Association, www.schoolnutrition.org, has valuable resources for management and cost control of breakfast and lunch programs. Providers of contract food services are familiar with the regulations, funding sources, and cost containment measures for school meal programs, which can also be found on the ISBE website, www.isbe.net.

The Illinois School Code requires that the annual budget separately identify revenue that comes from taxes and revenue that comes from other local sources, including vending machines. The budget must also disclose all board-sanctioned contractual agreements and the resulting estimated revenues. Additionally, the board must approve contracts and agreements that are intended to produce additional revenue in excess of $1,000.

State law (PA 94-0981) requires districts to operate a breakfast program in each building in which 40% or more of the students are eligible for free or reduced lunches — unless the district petitions the regional superintendent to opt out if the program would not cover its costs from federal, state, and local sources. PA 95-0155 requires districts with over 50% free/reduced eligible students to offer breakfast and lunch programs for the duration of summer school, provided that expense reimbursements meet costs.

Waiver of Meal and Required School Fees

Under Illinois law, school districts are required to waive charges for textbooks and other fees for children whose families are identified as low income, including children eligible for the federal free lunch and breakfast program, and for any other extenuating circumstances for which the school board will waive fees as communicated in its adopted policy (e.g., reduced-price lunch or medical emergencies). [105 ILCS 5/10-20.13 and 34-21.6]

Currently, a school district is obligated to waive at least the cost of textbooks and instructional materials for any student whose family income is within the federally established guidelines for free meals, regardless of the student's participation in the federal meals program (i.e., National School Lunch, School Breakfast, Special Milk, or After-School Snacks). In addition, the district cannot verify the eligibility to receive a school fee waiver of a student who is receiving free meals outside of the verification requirements established for the federal meals program.

Some districts with 40% or higher low-income enrollment, by school, school group, or in the aggregate, qualify for a Community Eligibility Process (CEP) for free meals, doing away with the necessity for securing individual family applications. Districts must meet the costs of the meals from federal reimbursements, making up any shortfalls from other revenues.

Because CEP schools do not collect annual individual family income data, they are unable to determine individual student eligibility for waiver of other school fees by using such data. The district may choose to discontinue student fees for educational services, especially if the low collection rate diminished the proceeds from these fees, when the administrative cost of billing and collecting them was considered. Or, the district may use an alternative household income form and application process. Information on the alternative process is available from the ISBE Rules and Waivers Division.

As a result of the COVID-19 pandemic, schools closed their doors in March 2020 and resumed instructions in 2020-2021 under various instructional models and schedules. Meals were provided during the shutdown period, including the summer break, to eligible children and adults under special regulations and reimbursement programs. During 2020-21 and 2021-2022, districts developed procedures to furnish meals to students receiving remote, hybrid, and in-school instruction under a variety of schedules. Some eligible families of students who were not furnished meals received equivalent monetary payments instead. Current regulations and reimbursement claim information can be obtained from isbe.net/nutrition.

Source: Information taken from the Nutrition Programs section at www.isbe.net

Initiatives to eliminate or restrict sales of certain beverages and food items may require school officials to modify revenue expectations from meal programs and vending machines and to adjust menus and meal prices accordingly.

Short-term rental of school facilities and sometimes long-term leases of surplus space provide additional revenue to many schools. Governed by local board policies and state law, rental income is unrestricted but is commonly applied to the district's operations and maintenance fund for building upkeep. Rental rates and eligibility policy are often a hot topic at school board meetings; courts have limited local boards' ability to approve and disapprove organizations wishing to rent facilities.

Some school districts have established tax-exempt foundations for receiving gifts from residents, businesses, and other sources. A separate board from that of the district governs foundations, and specific federal and state legal requirements apply to their governance and accounting. Consultants specializing in establishing school foundations can assist in their formation. It is also useful to talk to districts that have established successful foundations.

Other strategies to enlist support from community members and businesses include partnerships with organizations for services (e.g. upkeep of athletic fields by park districts); corporate partnerships, which may, for example, involve advertising space on scoreboards; booster clubs for athletic and non-athletic organizations; and expanded fundraising.

Investing School Funds

Investing school funds until they are required to be expended produces interest revenue, most of which is unrestricted and can be transferred to the fund most in need. The term of investments may range from one day to a year or more. Astute cash managers regularly sweep school funds into interest-bearing accounts. The district treasurer must manage cash flow based on the anticipated flow of revenues and expenditures. The treasurer uses cash flow data to develop an investment strategy that assures that funds are available when needed, while maximizing safety and interest yield. (See the Cash Flow Worksheet in *Chapter 10*.)

Illinois law governs investment of school funds. Legal investments include

- United States obligations guaranteed by the full faith and credit of the government;
- Obligations of U.S. government agencies, as defined in the state law;
- Accounts, certificates of deposit, and other direct obligations of banks;
- Certain short-term obligations of large corporations;
- Eligible municipal securities; and
- Eligible money market mutual funds. One such fund is the Illinois School District Liquid Asset Fund (ISDLAF), an investment pool co-sponsored by the Illinois Associations of School Boards, School Administrators, and School Business Officials.

Board of education policies also govern investments, and those policies may further restrict the investment of school funds, confining them to obligations of the U.S. government, bank instruments, and possibly money market funds. Effective January 1, 2020 investment policies of public agencies must include a statement that material, relevant, and decision-useful sustainability factors are regularly considered by the agency within the bounds of financial prudence.

Regular review of investment policies and practices is essential, because opportunities for investments are numerous, and the options may include instruments that do not meet legal requirements for investment of school funds. School attorneys and auditors can provide model investment policies and other guidance in this area. The IASB Policy Reference Education Subscription Service (PRESS) includes a sample investment policy that describes legal school investments. A board can use its policy to select legal investments that fit its philosophy and financial circumstances, or adopt the PRESS policy in its entirety. Either way, discussion of the administration's/treasurer's reports on current investments, their yield, and market conditions should be a regular agenda item throughout the year.

Investments should be undertaken with great caution and with knowledge of money markets and the characteristics and risks of each investment instrument. Safety, liquidity, yield, and diversification must be considered in that order, and the investment portfolio should be diversified as appropriate to the nature, purpose, and amount of funds. Public officials who do not comply with the terms of the Public Funds Investment Act may be personally liable for losses related to such investments. An investment consultant, independent of any bank or investment pool, is a valuable resource to assist districts in developing investment strategies with attention to safety and yield. Treasurer' should know with whom you are investing and check out unfamiliar

Taking New Initiatives with County Sales Tax

Local money generated through the property tax is not able to meet the increasing demand for either facility improvements or new buildings in many school districts. To help remedy the problem the County Schools Facility Occupation Tax law took effect in 2007.

This law provides an opportunity for school districts to generate money through sales taxes rather than property taxes. This tax money is available to all school districts having territory within the county where the tax is implemented, providing revenue that is dispersed based on the number of enrolled students residing in the county.

The sales tax increase is limited to a maximum of 1% and can be raised in increments of 0.25%. General merchandise (excluding vehicles, watercraft, aircraft, trailers, mobile homes, and medical supplies) is taxable; the county sales tax is not collected on food and drugs. Agricultural sales such as farm equipment, feed, seed, fertilizer, chemicals, and livestock reproduction are not subject to the tax.

Under the Act, money generated through the county sales tax can only be used for "school facility purposes," defined as "acquisition, development, construction, reconstruction, rehabilitation, improvement, financing, architectural planning, and installation of capital facilities consisting of buildings, structures, and durable equipment." It can also be used for the "acquisition and improvement of real property; interest in real property required, or expected to be required, in connection with the capital facilities." Usage also extends to updating systems for fire prevention, safety, security, energy conservation, and disabled access, school safety, and mental health.

The tax is collected by the Department of Revenue and placed into the School Facility Occupation Tax Fund. Each month, the Department of Revenue dictates the specified amount to the state comptroller. This amount is then distributed to the regional superintendent of schools in the county where the tax was collected. The amount distributed to each local school is based on the number of each district's resident pupils that reside within the county collecting the tax, divided by the total number of resident students within the county.

Both the school district and the community can reap benefits by implementing a countywide sales tax. While the district benefits from access to additional funds, the community benefits as money generated through the county sales tax can potentially replace some of the dependence on local real estate taxes.

The county sales tax also allows all school districts to benefit directly from tax generated based on their student enrollment, not just on the local business base. This revenue source for school facilities is also significant because the tax is not based on property wealth and state foundation level funding sources, but whether the student attends a school where the county sales tax has been adopted. Because each district's percentage of the tax is adjusted annually, if enrollment increases, the school district will be eligible for more money from the pool generated.

While the county sales tax has its positives, it also has a few negatives. The first is that this is a tax and will result in a slight cost increase in merchandise for consumers. Another negative is that it is regarded as a "regressive tax," one that affects lower-income population more than upper-income brackets.

The County Schools Facility Occupation Tax Law provides significant revenue potential for school districts and is beneficial because it spreads the income generated to all the school districts in the county, even when the majority of the sales revenue may only be accrued in one part of the county.

By encouraging voters to support a local sales tax increase, the school district could gain significant revenue without making the voters in their district incur a property tax increase. Like any referendum, voters require information. In Champaign County, the regional superintendent acted as point person to get information out. Presentations were made to realtors, service clubs, the Farm Bureau, the newspaper editorial board, legislators, and university leadership. Key information was that lower property taxes due to abatements would more than offset the additional sales tax on routine purchases.

Changes in 2011 — Public Act 97-0542 (2011) — amended the School Facility Occupation Tax Law. It changed the referendum provisions of the law by removing the county board from the election process. For sales tax referenda held after August 23, 2011, the regional superintendent of schools for the county must, upon receipt of resolutions adopted by school boards representing more than 50% of the student enrollment within the county, certify the sales tax question to the proper election authority for submission to county voters.

continued

> The Act also removed the authority of the county board to impose the sales tax or to prevent a referendum. Once approved at a referendum, the sales tax will be imposed by law at the rate set forth in the ballot question. However, the county board may certify a ballot question for the reduction or elimination of the sales tax. If such a referendum is successful, the sales tax will be reduced or ended by law, provided that such action does not adversely affect a school district's ability to pay debt service on bonds that are secured by the proceeds of the sales tax or necessitate the extension of additional property taxes to pay debt service on a school district's bonds. Using sales tax revenue to retire alternate revenue bonds is discussed in *Chapter 11*/Borrowing Options. Finally, the Act clarified that sales tax moneys and the proceeds of bonds or other obligations secured by sales tax revenue may be used to construct or purchase a new building for classroom instruction without direct referendum approval.
>
> The 2011 changes required more active roles from school districts and regional superintendents in the referendum process. Previously, the county board of its own volition could certify the sales tax question for voter approval. Now, the sole burden rests on school districts to gather support for sales tax referenda.
>
> School districts located in counties where the school facility sales tax is in effect should be aware that the tax can be reduced or eliminated by the county board only with referendum approval, although the county board can initiate such a proposition. Prior to any referendum to reduce or discontinue a sales tax, school officials should determine whether such action would adversely affect the district's ability to pay debt service on bonds secured by the tax or require the extension of additional property taxes to pay debt service on district bonds. If it will, the school board will need to determine whether to challenge the referendum question.
>
> When a referendum is successful, it takes about a year for districts to receive any funds as the state revenue department only changes the tax rates for counties twice a year, on January 1 and July 1. It then takes about four months after the county tax goes into effect for funds to be distributed from the state through the regional office of education to local schools.
>
> As of July 2023, these 57 counties have passed the sales tax proposition: Bond, Boone, Brown, Calhoun, Cass, Champaign, Christian, Coles, Cumberland, Douglas, Edgar, Edwards, Fayette, Franklin, Fulton, Greene, Hamilton, Hardin, Henry, Jackson, Jasper, Jersey, Jo Daviess, Knox, Lawrence, Lee, Livingston, Logan, Macon, Macoupin, Marion, Mason, Menard, Mercer, McDonough, Monroe, Montgomery, Morgan, Peoria, Perry, Pike, Platt, Randolph, Richland, Rock Island, Saline, Sangamon, Schuyler, Scott, Shelby, Union, Wabash, Warren, White, Whiteside, Williamson, and Woodford.
>
> Sources: Illinois Department of Revenue The information on the County Schools Facility Occupation Tax is adapted from an article in the July-August 2008 issue of the *Illinois School Board Journal*. The information on the 2011 amendment is adapted from a newsletter of the law firm Hodges, Loizzi, Eisenhammer, Rodick and Kohn, LLP.

vehicles thoroughly, especially in times when economic circumstances cause interest rates to fall.

While accurate forecasting of interest rates is difficult at best, certain risks can be avoided by attention to the safety of principal. Bank deposits or certificates of deposit that exceed the federal insurance limit should be backed by collateral, such as U.S. government securities dedicated only to the individual school district's deposit, held by a third party, and at least equal to the current market value of the investment. In today's tumultuous investment climate, it is prudent to periodically review collateral arrangements with an attorney who is knowledgeable about the investment world.

When interest rates increase, the market value of investments decreases. Districts or investment pools that hold commercial paper are also subject to losses resulting from misfortunes of the issuing corporation. Commercial paper, and such instruments as repurchase agreements and collateralized debt obligations, require sophistication beyond that found in most school district business offices. Investment losses suffered by schools during the economic downturns emphasize the dangers inherent in high-risk investments where school officials may have not understood or been told about those risks.

Extraordinarily complicated federal regulations control the yield to the school district from investing the proceeds of tax-exempt borrowing and school construction grants. A law firm or financial advisor knowledgeable about such regulations is an essential guide to the legal investment of these funds, lest the Internal Revenue Service become the unintended beneficiary of a share of the investment income.

The size of a district's fund balance is a function of its budget revenues and expenditures over a period of several years. The topic of fund balance size is often hotly debated by boards of education, especially when tax levies are being considered. School auditors can assist in relating a district's fund balance to those of similar districts and to its cash flow needs. Many boards of education have implemented fund balance policies in recent years.

How much of a fund balance is enough? The size of the opening fund balance for the year is a heavily weighted component of the state's measure of school district fiscal health. Depending upon circumstances of tax collection schedules, enrollment changes, and other variables unique to each district, a case can be made for a fund balance equivalent to four to six months, or 35-50% of the year's budgeted expenditures. Illinois statutes provide few limits on fund balances, with the exception of the Working Cash Fund. The Illinois Supreme Court ruled in a 1969 case that a fund balance in excess of two or three times the annual expenditure in a fund is illegal. Litigation on this issue occurs from time to time involving challenges to individual districts' reserves. The school attorney can advise whether the district's fund balances might raise issues of "excessive accumulation" and the possibility of legal action, including a tax objection.

The relationship between fund balances and fiscal health, plus fund balance size and policy considerations, are discussed in *Chapter 22,* while the role of school board policy in managing fund balances is set forth in *Chapter 24.*

Additional Resources

The ISBE School District Budget Form and the Illinois Administrative Code Part 100: Requirements for Accounting, Budgeting, Financial Reporting, and Auditing provide a useful catalog and index to available local revenue sources. Specific state statutes and administrative regulations may also apply to the administration of certain revenue sources. ISBE regulations and the school attorney should be consulted for guidance when questions or challenges occur.

School Business Affairs, a monthly publication of the Association of School Business Officials International, offers articles on management of support programs, including transportation and food services, investment practices, and other financial management topics.

The district's financial consultant(s) who advise on investments and debt issuance have current information on interest rate trends and forecasts and are familiar in detail with prudent options within the broad categories of legal investments, including United States obligations and money market funds.

Investment and fee practices and laws are discussed in the *Illinois School Law Survey* by Brian A. Braun, published by and available from the Illinois Association of School Boards

10 / Projecting Revenue

This chapter discusses strategies for projecting the flow of revenue for the coming fiscal year and for the years beyond. Short- and long-term revenue estimates should be prepared in the late spring or early summer and discussed with the board along with the tentative budget. Projections can be adjusted during the year as additional information becomes available on property assessments, legislative action, board of education decisions, grant awards, and other revenue-determining factors.

The COVID-19 pandemic introduced uncertainty into finances and programs of all school districts and affected the amounts of state and federal money received from emergency funding. It is necessary to identify and separate one-time revenues and expenditures and develop long-term projections with consideration for pre-pandemic financial data as well as post-pandemic revenue and expenditure estimates.

Long-term projections involve development of several scenarios. It is helpful to use the district's financial consultant to assist in developing the projections and in presenting them to the board.

Property Taxes

Projecting property tax revenue begins with the current year's budget. In tax-capped districts, revenues for the following year can be estimated by multiplying current tax year receipts by the Consumer Price Index adjustment used for computing the extension limitation. If information from the assessor indicates new property growth, tax revenue from that property can be added to the cost-of-living-based projection.

If a district is not subject to the tax cap, property tax revenue for the coming years will be the product of individual fund tax rates and each year's property tax base. Therefore, it is important in the fall to determine the district's new equalized assessed valuation if it is available, or to estimate it if it is not. The assessor's office and local building officials can assist in projecting changes in the tax base.

Each fund's tax revenues must be analyzed separately. In a non-tax-capped district, if the fund's tax rates are not at authorized maximums, an opportunity may exist to increase the levy for that fund if required to meet expenditures. The following year's revenue budget will reflect the increase, but only if the board of education levies the additional taxes in December.

Several other developments can influence property tax revenues, and the official preparing the projections must determine if these factors are to be considered. A significant consideration when preparing tax projections is the impact of Tax Increment Financing (TIF) districts. If a TIF district is created, there will be no tax growth for the TIF area for the duration of the TIF, typically 23 years. If that same TIF is extended for additional years, that will impact projections as well. Conversely, if a TIF expires, there will likely be a substantial increase in property tax revenue for the TIF area.

Long-term projections of tax revenue are commonly done by taking a three- to five-year trend and projecting the rate of change into the future. It is especially important in long-term tax revenue projections to adopt a conservative stance, especially with respect to the prospects for changes in assessment levels, new construction in the district, and the cost-of-living factor applied in the tax cap calculation. The real estate market is volatile and susceptible to interest rates and other factors. Even though the best information and opinion on real estate growth may have been consulted, it is risky to bet the future of the school program on overly optimistic estimates of property tax growth.

> **Changes in Assessments and Revenues Lag Changes in Property Values**
>
> Assessors employ multi-year averaging in arriving at the valuation of properties for each tax year. The common "look-back" period is three years. Therefore, the effects of increases or decreases in property values reflect in tax bases for a number of years after they occur, thus dampening the property tax revenue effect of such changes. For example, the January 2023 valuations (the record date for the 2023 tax year assessments) will reflect market values for 2020, 2021, and 2022.
>
> Taxpayers who experience a drop in their property values during a recession may see only a gradual decrease in their assessments, as their falling property values are dampened by the three-year look-back period. The impact on tax rates and bills and school revenues depends on whether a district is subject to the tax cap. The effects of a future recovery of property values will similarly be dampened. Chapter 4 describes how the impact works. Taxpayer confusion and concern are likely to result, and school leaders need to be able to explain to the public how the factors that affect tax bills operate during periods of large changes. Assessors may be able to assist in developing this message.

In projecting property tax revenue, the district's tax base must be considered by its major components individually. Commercial, industrial, residential, farmland, mineral, and other classifications may trend up or down at varying rates. Use a weighted average to determine an overall rate of change.

Some Boards of Education are choosing to contain the growth of property tax bills by freezing the levy at the previous year's extension. The effects of such a decision on subsequent years' tax revenues must be considered in projections. The long-term effects will depend on whether the board extends the freeze beyond the first year or chooses to capture only the cost of living and new property increments. Since the actions of school boards may vary from year to year, it is helpful to project long-term tax revenues under various assumptions, so the consequences of containing the levy to control tax bill increases are clear.

State Revenues

Information in this section alludes to the provisions of the Illinois School Funding Reform Act and the Evidence-Based State Aid system. They are described in *Chapter 6*.

Personal property replacement tax revenue is a function of state tax rates and collections, which rely on the health of the Illinois business economy. This revenue can be forecast based on information available from the website of the Illinois Department of Revenue, as well as from the school district's recent experience. *Chapter 5* details Personal Property Replacement Tax Revenue.

Predictions of Evidence-Based school funding for fiscal years 2024 and beyond must consider the financial position of the state, which remains burdened by underfunded pensions, and a high level of "structural" obligations for pensions and other costs that reduce the discretionary amounts available to the General Fund budgets.

Categorical state aid projections for those grants not integrated into the EBF formula begin with preparing and analyzing present-year claims to compute the maximum entitlement under the law for reimbursement in the coming year. Among the grants that remain separate from EBF are regular, special education, and vocational transportation; special education private school; and special education and general orphanage tuition. Other major continuing categorical grants include early childhood education, bilingual education, and Illinois free lunch/breakfast grants.

Projecting long-term categorical aid involves trending, adjustments for probable and known changes in state appropriation levels, and allowances for increases and decreases in program staffing levels and students. Analyzing each grant separately will lead to the most accurate projections. Many of the categorical grant entitlements have been pro-rated in recent years. Projections for FY 2024 and beyond will depend on the health of state revenue collections. It is worth noting that growth in the number of students served in many of these programs is outpacing the growth of the associated categorical funding source.

Current information on legislative developments in Springfield can be obtained from the websites of the various professional and school management associations. Especially useful are IASB's Legislative Reports, which can be accessed www.iasb.com, as well as those of the various administrator associations.

Other Revenues

Personal property replacement tax revenue is a function of state tax rates and collections, which rely on the health of the Illinois business economy. This revenue can be forecast based on information available from the website of the Illinois Department of Revenue, as well as from the school district's recent experience.

Federal programs depend on congressional appropriations, which are determined for fiscal years beginning October 1. The quality of information available for school budgets depends, therefore, on the timing of final action on the federal budget. Estimated budgets appear on the Department of Education website in the fall and continue up to final appropriation action in the spring or summer. Federal grants are "forward funded" and, therefore, can be budgeted for the current year with a high degree of accuracy.

Since the federal and school district fiscal years do not coincide, it is common for school budgets to include funding from two federal fiscal years. Grant administrators at the State Board of Education monitor the federal budget process and provide estimates for school budgeting purposes. They should be consulted for questions on specific programs.

Long-term projections of federal and other grant revenues must consider the nature of the grant program. Conservative revenue projections for entitlement programs can be constructed from current funding

Sample Cash Flow Worksheet – Education Fund

The flow of revenue shown in this example is for a school district where property taxes are paid to the county on June 1 and September 1 and distributed to taxing bodies shortly thereafter. Note, therefore, that this school district has received virtually all of its tax revenue in the first half of the fiscal year, and the second half of the fiscal year will show little if any property tax revenue. However, expenditures will continue at about the rate shown for September through December, months when school is in session. Typically, payroll expenditures will be higher in June due to the availability of teachers' summer paychecks. Also note that separate cash flow worksheets for each fund should be consolidated into a single projection as an aid in making investment decisions. See explanatory notes on *page 67*.

	JULY	AUGUST	SEPTEMBER	OCTOBER	NOVEMBER	DECEMBER	PERIOD
Beginning balance	$ 750,000	$3,385,000	$3,313,000	$2,823,000	$4,791,000	$4,254,000	$750,000
REVENUE							
Taxes	$2,750,000	$ 250,000	$ 250,000	$2,700,000	$50,000		$6,000,000
Corp. Tax Replacement	50,000	50,000		50,000		50,000	200,000
Fees	75,000	25,000	15,000	5,000			120,000
Cafeteria receipts		8,000	20,000	20,000	20,000	20,000	88,000
Tuition			40,000				40,000
EBF state aid	100,000	100,000	100,000	100,000	100,000	100,000	600,000
Special education aid			200,000			200,000	400,000
Other state grants						50,000	50,000
Interest							
Federal ESSA Title I			25,000	25,000	25,000	25,000	100,000
Federal lunch subsidy				8,000	8,000	8,000	24,000
Other federal aid						5,000	5,000
Transfers in							
Total revenue	$ 2,975,000	$ 433,000	$ 650,000	$2,908,000	$ 203,000	$ 458,000	$7,627,000
EXPENDITURES							
Salaries	$ 100,000	$ 100,000	$ 500,000	$ 500,000	$ 500,000	$ 500,000	$2,200,000
Benefits	125,000	125,000	125,000	125,000	125,000	125,000	750,000
Services	25,000	25,000	40,000	40,000	40,000	40,000	210,000
Supplies	50,000	200,000	100,000	40,000	40,000	25,000	455,000
Capital outlay	15,000	30,000	150,000	10,000	10,000	10,000	225,000
Tuition			200,000	200,000			400,000
Other	25,000	25,000	25,000	25,000	25,000	25,000	150,000
Transfers out							
Total expenditures	$ 340,000	$ 505,000	$1,140,000	$ 940,000	$ 740,000	$ 725,000	$4,390,000
Monthly balance	$ 2,635,000	$ (72,000)	$ (490,000)	$1,968,000	$ (537,000)	$ (267,000)	
Ending balance	$ 3,385,000	$3,313,000	$2,823,000	$4,791,000	$4,254,000	$3,987,000	$3,987,000

Notes to Sample Cash Flow Worksheet – Education Fund

These notes provide a brief explanation of each Revenue and Expenditure item appearing in the Cash Flow Worksheet.

Beginning balance	Enter July 1 fund balance. Each month's opening balance should equal the closing balance of the preceding month.

REVENUE

Taxes	Enter property tax distributions. Many districts enter the June 1 installment payment as of July 1. Use historical information to project tax distributions for subsequent months.
PPRT	This revenue is received in eight unequal payments in July, August, October, December, January, March, April, and May. Use information on Department of Revenue website to estimate amounts.
Fees	Much of this revenue will be collected in the summer. Lesser amounts from activities, new enrollees will be received during the year.
Cafeteria sales	Spread the budgeted amount evenly throughout the school year, unless historical patterns suggest otherwise.
Tuition	Most tuition will be received as a result of interdistrict special education agreements and billing schedules.
EBF state aid	The law provides for semi-monthly GSA payments from August to June, equal to 1/22 of the total amount.
Special education aid	Quarterly payments are the norm; however, check with ISBE as to the schedule for each grant program; delayed payments may occur during times of state fiscal distress.
Other state grants	Check ISBE for the expected distribution date for each grant.
Interest	Estimate the interest due each month on bank balances, CDs, treasury instruments and other investments. Consider balance changes during the year and interest transfers. Distribute to funds per board action.
Federal ESSA Title I	Title I and many federal grants are forward-funded; check ISBE or DOE websites and historical information for distribution schedules.
Fed lunch subsidy	Meal subsidy payments are based on breakfast and lunch sales and claims which are filed monthly; use historical receipt schedules to project cash flow.
Other federal aid	ESSA Title I and many other federal grants are forward-funded, and the schedule of receipts may not coincide with the school year in which they are expended. Check the U.S. Department of Education or ISBE for information on distribution schedules for each grant and reflect those schedules in the cash flow worksheets.
Transfers in	Add amounts that will be loaned or transferred from other funds. Enter the reverse transaction for the month when a loan will be repaid.
Total revenue	Add the total receipt and loan/transfer amounts.

EXPENDITURES

Salaries	Project salary and pension payments for 12-month personnel throughout the year. Insurance payments for 10-month personnel may be spread over 12 months.
Benefits	Teacher and other 10-month salary payments will occur throughout the school year. Deferred summer payments, although budgeted in the fiscal year, will draw down cash during the following summer months.
Services	Absent large payments to architects or other major summer payments, service payments can be projected throughout the year.
Supplies	Supply payments will concentrate in the summer and early fall months, as new books and other supplies are checked in. Some supplies, such as food, will spread out through the year.
Capital outlay	One-time payments for equipment and summer construction will concentrate early in the year. Monthly payments for equipment will occur throughout the year.
Tuition	Tuition for interdistrict services will be due according to the billing practices of special education cooperatives and should be projected accordingly.
Other	Use this line for insurance payments, settlements, and other large expenditures usually paid in one sum.
Transfers out	Subtract the amounts that will be loaned or transferred to other funds. Enter the reverse transaction for the month when a loan will be repaid.
Total expenditures	Add the total expenditure and loan/transfer amounts.
Monthly balance	Subtract the total expenditures from the total revenues. Shows annual operating surplus/deficit.
Ending balance	Each month's ending balance becomes the opening balance of the following month. June 30 balance is the next year's opening balance.

NOTES:

Projecting revenues to be received one month later than usual and expenditures to be made one month earlier produces a conservative cash flow estimate that is less likely to lead to unpleasant surprises during the year.

Separate cash flow worksheets for each operating fund can be consolidated into a single projection for decisions on investments.

Cash flow for the Debt Service and Capital Projects Funds should be projected separately as their revenues and expenditures follow unique patterns.

levels and projected program enrollments. However, if a grant program expires at the end of a given year, that fact must be considered in the overall projection of outside revenues for the long-term period, lest the total be inflated by money that will not be forthcoming after the end of the grant period. In some cases, the cash flow from the grant will continue for a few months into the year following its conclusion, as final expenditure claims are filed and paid.

Projections of budget allocations for federal programs can be found at Department of Education website, www.ed.gov. The Illinois State Board of Education may also provide assistance with grant budgeting and for the federal grants that it administers.

Most local funding sources, such as book and bus fees, special education tuition, summer school tuition, and meal fees, depend on locally determined actions, program enrollments, and participation levels. Accurate following-year budgets for these items can first be prepared based on trending of recent years. Consider the effects of the current economy and family income trends on fee collections. While many Illinois districts waived fees during the pandemic, waivers reduce revenue. Fee revenue estimates are updated later in the year, following board of education action on fee levels and current enrollment and program participation projections for the coming year. Trending also develops long-term budgets for these sources.

Interest income is a function of the school district's average monthly cash balances and available rates on investments. Interest budgeting for the coming year begins with cash flow projections that consider both income and expenditures for the year. Projecting future interest rates is a futile exercise, especially in a period of economic volatility such as occurred in 2022 and 2023. Averaging rates for the past five years is a conservative approach in developing five-year projections of interest income.

A simplified cash flow projection is shown in the *Sample Cash Flow Worksheet* on *page 66*. It is prepared by charting historical and projected revenue and expenditures by category and fund. The consolidated projection should reveal any needs for borrowing and the possibilities for investing idle funds.

A surplus budget will tend to increase interest income; as an unbalanced budget will decrease it. Since it is difficult for even sophisticated economists to predict future interest rates, use of current rates applied to projected balances is a common short-term budgeting technique. Long-term interest projections are developed by the same method. Because an expenditure projection must also be prepared, interest income budgets are often adjusted in the final days before the budget is presented for discussion and adoption. Financial advisors can provide information on current and near-term projections of interest rates on common school investments.

The notes on *page 67* provide some explanation of the items in the *Sample Cash Flow Worksheet (page 66)*.

Projecting the future is an art as much as a science, and intuition plays an important role. A database on the variables that influence major sources of revenue is an invaluable tool for short- and long-term revenue budgeting. A detailed history of increases and decreases in each revenue source over past years greatly facilitates the use of trending in revenue budgeting. Creation of such a database and trend history, if it does not exist, can be a major contribution of a financial administrator to a school district's planning process. Past-year audit reports are good places to look for historical information on both revenues and expenditures by categories.

The financial administrator's network of colleagues can assist with the substance and format of financial projections, and it might prove helpful to review short- and long-term budget projections from nearby districts, especially those similar in enrollment and property tax trends. Not only can specific calculation assumptions be compared, but ideas can also be gained for formats for presenting information to the public and board of education.

Essentials of Illinois School Finance 69

11 / Borrowing Options

Special thanks to Kyle Harding, Partner of Chapman and Cutler, Chicago for his contributions to this chapter. Other contributors are listed in the bibliography in Appendix B.

Illinois schools enjoy many short and long-term credit options. Short-term borrowing may be used when additional funds are needed to cover a temporary cash shortage. Long-term borrowing may be employed for educational programs, new facilities, repairs to existing buildings and capital items including school buses.

This chapter introduces the most common borrowing options. While the authority for borrowing rests in Illinois law, federal laws and school board policies govern the sale, investment, and use of bond proceeds. Therefore, school districts seek advice of their attorneys and financial advisors as they plan a borrowing issue.

It is a long-standing principle of school finance that the public has a say before a district incurs long-term debt. When a district issues such debt, it is backed by the full faith and credit of the real property within the district. If necessary, the district can levy taxes up to the value of each property owner's real property to repay the debt. Therefore, most means of long-term borrowing require a referendum or public hearing to provide the public with a voice before their property is pledged for debt repayment.

Public borrowing falls under disclosure and tax compliance regulations enforced by the Securities and Exchange Commission and the Internal Revenue Service. These regulations govern the information that must be disclosed to potential buyers. Compliance is necessary to sell the debt as exempt from federal income taxes to the buyer.

Tax-exempt status enables the school district to pay a lower interest rate than if the interest were taxable to the buyer. However, in some instances, it may benefit the district to sell the bonds on a taxable basis, since some restrictions on the use of proceeds from tax-exempt borrowing may not apply when bonds are issued on a taxable basis.

The tax compliance requirements continue after the bond sale is completed. The law imposes post-issuance reporting obligations until after the debt has been repaid. Failure to comply may lead to penalties, including revocation of the tax-exempt status of the bonds.

Commonly Used Borrowing Options

The information on short- and long-term borrowing options in this chapter consists of summaries of the commonly used instruments. When planning for borrowing, consult a public finance advisor and attorney well ahead of the anticipated need for the funds.

Interfund Loans and Permanent Transfers

A district may be able to borrow from itself, avoiding the expenses of issuing and paying interest on debt. Surpluses in some funds can be transferred or temporarily loaned to other funds as specified by state law. *Table 15* on *page 70* indicates with an "A" which interfund transactions are allowed. Board of education approval is required for an interfund loan or transfer, and public notice and a public hearing are required for certain interfund transfers. Except for the Working Cash Fund, all loans must be repaid to the loaning fund within three years. Transfers are usually from the smaller to the larger funds, and therefore produce limited benefit.

Transfers among the Education, Operations and Maintenance, and the Transportation funds after June 30, 2020 are limited to meet one-time, non-recurring expenses. The Working Cash Fund may also be abated or reduced under certain conditions.

Taxpayers have brought actions against some districts for "unnecessary accumulation" of moneys in certain funds. Districts may wish to consult their legal counsel to determine if permanent interfund transfers would avoid challenges to tax rate objections in an operating fund.

Table 15

Loans and Transfers

Consultation with legal counsel is recommended in planning for loans and transfers to assure compliance with applicable laws and ISBE regulations and for updated resolutions and other documents.

Permissible Interfund Loans

LOANING FUND	RECEIVING FUND			
	Education	Operations. & Maintenance	Fire & Safety	Transportation
Education (a)	-	A	A	A
Operations & Maintenance (a)	A	-	A	A
Transportation (a)	A	A	A	-
Working Cash (b)	A	A	A	A

(a) Loans must be repaid within three years.

(b) In anticipation of next taxes or state funding for the receiving fund in the year the loan is made. The loan must be repaid upon receipt of anticipated taxes or state funding (whichever anticipated). A board resolution is required.

A = Allowed

Permissible Permanent Interfund Transfers
A board resolution is required for most transfers.

SOURCE FUND	RECEIVING FUND		
	Education	Operations. & Maintenance	Transportation
Education (c)	-	A	A
Operations & Maintenance (c)	A	-	A
Transportation (c), (e)	A	A	-
Working Cash (d)	A	A	A
Life & Safety (e)	-	A	-
Tort Immunity (c)	-	A	-

(c) Upon proper notice and hearing. Due to expiration of statutory language expanding interfund transfer authority, after June 30, 2024, the transfer must only be for the purposes of meeting one-time, non-recurring expenses, unless legislative action again suspends this limitation.

(d) To the fund most in need, upon abatement of the Working Cash Fund, after which the balance in the Working Cash Fund must be at least .05% of the district's EAV. If abolished, the balance must be transferred to the Education Fund. A Board resolution is required.

(e) Permanent interfund transfers require notice and hearing. Consultation with the district's legal counsel is also advised as to potential applicability of the Illinois Constitution's "transportation lockbox."

(f) Applies to excess life safety and restricted funds, but not to bond proceeds, with Operations and Maintenance tax abatement.

A = Allowed

Notes: Refer to the Illinois School Code and Local Government Debt Reform Act for specific provisions for all transfers, and confirm the requirements for notice, hearing, resolution, and other procedures for any transfer. The school board generally has authority to transfer interest from the fund in which it was earned (except for IMRF, tort immunity, life-safety, or certain capital improvement tax proceeds) to the fund(s) most in need, provided the interest is not otherwise earmarked for a designated purpose (e.g. certain grant/bond proceeds). Consultation with legal counsel is advised if such a transfer is planned. Additional transfers of specific funds are authorized by statute. Pursuant to ISBE regulations, unless otherwise provided by statute or specified by board resolution adopted prior to June 30 of a fiscal year, interest earnings shall be added to and become part of principal as of June 30 of the fiscal year. Thus, districts should consult with legal counsel to ensure appropriate earmarking of any interest intended to be transferred in a year subsequent to the year earned.

Information in the above tables is adapted from A School Board Member's Handbook, 2023 edition, published by Hodges, Loizzi, Eisenhammer, Rodick and Kohn; *Illinois School Law Survey*, 2020; and P.A. 101-0643 at www.ilga.gov.

Short-Term Borrowing for Operating Expenses

These instruments are designed to provide short-term cash to cover expenditures when cash balances are low and expected property taxes and other revenue have not been received. The need for them must be proven by financial projections as specified in federal law. They do not require public approval in a referendum, nor do they provide additional money to the district. Rather, they speed up receipt of money to which the district is already entitled. Frequent use of these forms of debt indicates current or impending financial difficulty. Conversely, failure to use them can create a liquidity crisis and distasteful consequences. Policies on fund balance and on cash flow borrowing are helpful in alerting the school board and administration to the need to borrow. Fund balance policies are discussed in *Chapter 21*.

The information on short- and long-term borrowing options in this chapter consists of summaries of the most commonly used instruments. Each option requires observance of certain procedures and timelines, and carries conditions. In planning for borrowing, consult a public finance advisor and attorney well ahead of the anticipated need for the funds.

- **Tax anticipation warrants** are issued against taxes levied but not yet collected and are repaid from the taxes levied for the particular fund against which they are issued, either upon their receipt or on a specified maturity date. Up to 85% of the anticipated taxes may be borrowed.
- **Establishing a line of credit** with a bank or other financial institution within the general limits applicable to tax anticipation warrants is an alternative way of assuring adequate cash on hand if revenues are delayed or unexpectedly reduced.
- **General obligation tax anticipation warrants** are repaid on a specified date through a special tax levy, which is subtracted from the tax rate for the applicable fund.
- **Tax anticipation notes** are similar to general obligation warrants but count against a district's debt limit. A longer repayment period may be possible.
- **State aid anticipation certificates** may be issued against Evidence-Based Funding state aid due for the year, up to 75% of the balance to be received, subject to offsets and limits related to the Working Cash Fund and tax anticipation borrowing. Principal and interest are repaid from state aid revenues.
- **Personal property replacement tax notes** are similar to state aid anticipation certificates and are payable from replacement taxes when received.
- **Revenue anticipation notes** are issued in anticipation of federal aid, revenue sharing, or certain fees, up to 85% of expected revenue, and are payable from these receipts.
- **Teachers' orders** are issued to pay wages of teachers when there is no money in the educational fund. A financial institution provides the funds at an established rate. Principal and interest are repaid when funds are available and can also be repaid by the issuance of funding bonds.

Long-Term Cash Flow Borrowing

These tools can provide substantial amounts of new cash to fund a variety of needs. Unlike the tools described earlier, they do provide additional funds to the school district and are secured by a direct annual tax levy. The regulations governing their issuance and uses of the funds are complex. Referendum requirements differ according to the type of borrowing instrument and whether the district is located in a county subject to the property tax cap. (See *page 75*, "Borrowing under the Tax Cap.") All non-referendum tax bonds require a public hearing prior to issuance, under the provisions of the Bond Issue Notification Act. Consultation with a public finance attorney is essential if such borrowing is contemplated.

Instruments identified as subject to a voter-initiated referendum requirement may be issued after publication of a notice, followed by a 30-day period during which registered voters may petition for a referendum on the bond sale. This process is sometimes referred to as a "backdoor referendum." Absent a petition calling for a referendum, the bond sale may proceed within a three-year period. If a petition is received, the sale must either be put to a referendum or abandoned. Typically, a backdoor referendum requires a petition signed by at least 10% of the registered voters of a school district to pass.

- **Working Cash Fund bonds** are issued to create or increase that fund, after which the money can be loaned to any fund for which taxes are levied to avoid the need to issue warrants or notes or transferred to any other fund determined to be most in need. The bonds may be issued up to an amount of 85% of the last Education Fund levy, plus 85% of the district's Personal Property Replacement Tax entitlement plus 85% of its Evidence-Based Funding state aid. These bonds are subject to a backdoor referendum process. Money may be transferred from the Working Cash Fund to any other fund, so long as a school district adopts a resolution abating its

Sales Tax Can Support Alternate Revenue Bonds for Facilities

In 2007 legislation was enacted to provide for a countywide sales tax to fund capital projects for Illinois school districts. The law is referred to as the County School Facility Occupation Tax or County School Facility Sales Tax ("CSFST") or commonly referred to as the sales tax.

The sales tax is a tax of up to 1% on goods sold in the county with excepting automobiles, farm equipment, boats, aircraft, and qualifying food and drugs, among other items. Current law provides for a countywide referendum that must be passed by a simple majority for the sales tax to go into effect.

All counties are eligible for this tax, excluding Cook. School districts with 51% of the student enrollment in a county can initiate a referendum question by submitting a resolution to the Regional Office of Education. The law also allows that a school facility occupation tax may be reduced or discontinued if the electors later vote to reduce or discontinue the tax.

Money received under the sales tax is distributed to school districts based on the number of students that reside in the county and the percentage of students that attend a school district. As an example, if 100 students live in the affected county and 25 of them attend each of four school districts in the county, then each school district will receive 25% of the total sales tax distribution. If 25 students of those 100 students attend a school district in a neighboring county, then the school district in the neighboring county will receive 25% of the total distribution.

Money is collected by the Illinois Department of Revenue and is distributed to the Regional Office of Education. The ROE distributes the sales tax revenue to individual school districts based on enrollment calculations.

The sales tax was created to fund facility needs, and may not be used for operating purposes. Sales tax revenue may be used to abate bond and interest levies involving capital expenditures or serve as a source of revenue for alternate revenue bonds. It may not be used for a working capital bond issue.

Districts that fund new school buildings through the issuance of alternate revenue bonds do not have to go to referendum so long as alternate revenue bonds are paid entirely by CSFST revenues. Alternate revenue bonds may be issued up to 40 years and are not included in the formula for calculating a district's debt limit.

The list of counties that have passed the sales tax proposition appears in *Chapter 9*.

Working Cash Fund and retains a balance in the fund of at least 0.05% of its EAV. If the Working Cash Fund is abolished completely, the balance must be transferred to the Education Fund. Working Cash Fund bonds may also be issued without a referendum for improvement, repair, alterations, and equipment of existing school buildings, but not to build entirely new structures.

- **Funding bonds** are a means of "rolling over" short-term debt, such as debt certificates and teachers' orders. They may also be used to fund teachers' salaries, retirement obligations, technology purchases, or other claims or invoices. They are subject to a backdoor referendum and do not fall within the debt limit restriction.
- **Tort judgment funding bonds** may be issued without referendum for payment of obligations from judgments or settlements.
- **Insurance reserve bonds** may be issued without referendum to create a reserve fund as part of a self-insurance program. State and federal law regulates the amount of such a reserve and its investment. They are excluded from the debt limitation.

Long-Term Borrowing for Buildings and Other Capital Expenditures

Like the debt issues described above, these options are authorized in state law and regulated by both state and federal rules:

- **Building bonds** are used to fund land, building, and equipment costs for new schools, as well as alterations, additions, and repairs. They require a referendum.
- **Life-Safety bonds** (fire prevention and safety, environmental protection, school security, and energy conservation bonds) may be used to fund projects approved by both the regional and state superintendents (including replacement buildings in some cases). They do not require a referendum if a district is not subject to the property tax cap. If a district is subject to the tax cap, it may be possible to issue life-safety bonds as "limited bonds." See "Borrowing under the Tax Cap" on *page 75*.
- **Debt certificates** may be issued to fund capital or real property payments due under lease and installment contracts. The outstanding principal amount of debt certificates, combined with

existing debt, must fall within the district's statutory debt limit. There is no separate tax levy for their repayment.
- **Guaranteed energy savings contracts** are secured by a contract that guarantees a 20-year payback of the cost of a project from its energy or operational cost savings; the contractor must reimburse any shortfalls to the district. They are funded by debt certificates; no referendum is required. Relying on the creditworthiness of the contractor may add layers of complexity to this funding option.
- **Alternate bonds**, which are subject to a backdoor referendum and public hearing, are repaid by pledging an operating revenue source equal to at least 1.25 times the amount of the borrowing. Typical pledged revenue sources include operations and maintenance fund taxes, county school facility sales taxes, EBF state aid, personal property replacement taxes, developer donations, and revenues from tax increment financing districts. A backup tax levy is provided for if the pledged revenues fall short of the amount required to repay the bonds. This backup levy makes them a less expensive form of financing than debt certificates. See the text box on page 72 for information about alternate revenue bonds.
- **Refunding bonds** are commonly used to restructure the district's debt, reduce interest costs, or avoid default. They do not require a referendum but must comply with federal regulations.

Planning for a Debt Issue

The available options and associated laws and procedures for issuing debt require that the board of education, financial administrator, and superintendent have a sound grasp of the district's need for short- and long-term financing for various needs. Since bond referenda can be held only on general primary and general election dates, planning for a referendum often begins two years or more before the target date for the vote. If prospects for passage are uncertain, additional time must be allowed to "resell" the public should the referendum fail.

The steps in planning and communicating the need for marketing a debt issue vary according to the specifics of each need and debt instrument selected. The steps listed on the next page are necessary for most of them. Administrators will do much of the background work; board of education understanding and approval are necessary as the debt issue moves from concept to market and public communication. The steps include

- Make enrollment and financial projections, and conduct other relevant planning, to determine borrowing needs, including a comprehensive facilities plan.
- Open and maintain communications channels among school board, staff, and community regarding school district borrowing needs.
- Research the repayment schedule of existing debt, if any, and project the tax impact of repaying both old and new debt. Be conservative in projecting the growth of the district's tax base in light of recent trends in residential property valuations and the uncertainty of values in the coming years. Should a lower equalized assessed valuation occur than the EAV on which the tax impact of the repayment schedule was predicated, the tax rate necessary to meet future obligations will be higher than expected. When that happens, boards may examine debt restructuring options, especially if new borrowing needs exist.
- If they do not already exist, adopt school board policies governing fund balances and borrowing and discuss the impact that borrowing will have on tax rates. This requires consideration of alternative repayment scenarios. If possible, structure repayment schedules for new issues to avoid large increases and decreases in annual debt service levies and tax rates when new issues and existing issues are combined.
- Appoint an attorney and select an independent financial advisor and an underwriter.
- Select borrowing option(s) and define limits and an approval process.
- Establish a timetable for issuing debt instruments, including a referendum if required.
- Organize and carry out a referendum campaign if required.
- Prepare documentation of compliance with state and federal laws.
- Determine the mode of sale — by a competitive bid, negotiated sale, direct placement with a bank or a unit of local government — following consultation with the financial advisor.
- Prepare and distribute an official statement to potential bidders in a competitive sale or bond investors in a negotiated sale to buyers.
- Hold a public hearing if required by the Bond Issue Notification Act.
- Submit application to a credit agency for a rating on the debt issue.
- Receive and present bids for board of education action.

- Prepare post-sale documents and close the sale to receive the money.
- Develop a plan to meet post-sale disclosure requirements.

While there is no legislation requiring a financial advisor for bonds, there is a fiduciary duty assigned to municipal advisors by the Securities and Exchange Committee (SEC) and the Municipal Securities Rulemaking Board (MSRB). In selecting a financial advisor or consultant, first determine the types of assistance that are required of the firm. All consultants will guide the sale process from marketing through closing. In addition, will the consultant be asked to assist in preparing financial projections and identify options for the board of education, or is the administration able to perform these steps? After identifying the required services, talk to the district's bond attorney and to several districts that have recently sold bonds, and prepare a short list of firms that are to be invited to prepare proposals for service. Requests for proposals should clearly specify the services required.

Fees for bond counsel, financial consultants, rating services, insurance, and various incidentals should be researched far enough in advance of the sale for them to be included in the district's budget. Payment for financial consultant services and bond counsel can be quoted in terms of a flat fee or, in the case of a negotiated or a competitive sale, included in the cost of the issue. The consultant will assist in evaluating these two marketing options, which is a decision of the board of education. Various costs of issuance, including printing and distribution of official statements, advertising, and fees for registration of the issue and paying agents will be additional. Some costs of issuance must be factored into the amount of the total debt for determining compliance with debt limitations.

The Rating Process

A district's bond rating reflects the rating agency's assessment of its ability to repay the debt. Each issue carries a separate rating. The agency typically reviews several years' audit reports, the current year's budget, trends in the property tax base, local population and employment statistics, and the outstanding debt of overlapping taxing agencies. Submission of the information is typically followed by a meeting during which questions are answered and opinions formed on the strength of the district's financial management as well as its fiscal outlook. An analyst queries the district on the purposes to which the borrowed funds will be put and on its plans for future borrowing. The outcome is one of several ratings on a scale measuring the relative risk to buyers of the debt issue. The higher the rating, the lower will be the interest rate paid on the bonds.

Prepare for this rating assessment as you would for a comprehensive examination. Do not assume that the rating analysts know all of the important facts about the district. However, it is possible that they do know many of them and are evaluating your knowledge and financial management skills. Explain increases or decreases in fund balances in recent years and plans to reduce or eliminate deficits. Call attention to any accounting change from cash to accrual or modified accrual, so any changes in fund balances as a result of accounting changes can be evaluated accordingly. Be ready to tell how you maintain good relations with the voting public.

Other factors being equal, a growing tax base; favorable community wealth indicators, especially median family income; larger fund balances within a district policy; a history of balanced or surplus budgets; absence of short-term borrowing;, and a remaining margin for long-term borrowing will be favorably looked upon. Be familiar with the positive economic factors in the community and its other government agencies. Evidence of long-term planning and capital planning, investment and debt management policies are other positives. Repayment of bonds can extend for 20 years or more. Therefore, the bond rating not only reflects and amplifies a school district's current fiscal position; it also speaks to its financial outlook for future years. Unfortunately, there are suggestions in the credit markets of an "Illinois penalty" that may diminish school districts' ratings and raise borrowing costs as a result of the budget and credit problems that have beset the state, the City of Chicago, and the Chicago Public Schools. The severity and duration of the pandemic-caused financial distress on the Illinois and national economies and the finances of public agencies may also impact school debt ratings.

Buyers of public debt have increased their scrutiny of issuers' financial strength and ratings as a result of the last recession and its impact on the credit markets generally. Some do their own credit assessments before bidding on the debt. Securing the most favorable possible rating for a debt issue requires considerable research and preparation. Fitch (www.fitchratings.com), Moody's (www.moodys.com) and Standard and Poor's (www.standardandpoors.com) issue quality ratings on school bonds. Such a rating is not legally required but may lower interest costs. In planning for a bond sale, talk to some administrators who have recently gone through a credit rating process and ask to examine their submissions and the rating agency's final report. Watch for presentations at conferences by representatives of the rating firms, and attend them if borrowing is contemplated.

Financial consultants will assist in preparing for the rating conference, but the rating agency analysts often talk to them separately and expect superintendents and business officials to display an in-depth knowledge of their community's economic characteristics and their district's financial condition and plans.

In June of 2021, Moody's, a widely used rating agency changed its rating methodology for school districts. The changes consider how they rate the district independent of bonds and how they rate each bond issued by the district. Additionally, Moody's will consider if the district is reporting its results on a Generally Accepted Accounting Principles' (GAAP) basis or a cash basis. If a district utilizes a cash basis of accounting, this will result in a lower rating for the district.

Bond Insurance

Some districts have opted to purchase municipal bond insurance as a means of securing a more favorable rating, essentially "renting" the favorable credit rating of the insurance company. The market uncertainties as a result of the pandemic are reflected in a robust market for bond insurance. If a district's finances point to the possibility of a poor rating, a financial advisor can price bond insurance and compare the cost against the resulting savings in interest. Selling non-rated debt, especially short-term cash flow obligations, is also an option. Again, seek advice on the cost savings and possible future implications of selling non-rated debt.

Borrowing under the Tax Cap

As discussed in *Chapter 4*, a district subject to the Property Tax Extension Limitation Law may be constrained in its ability to issue bonds without referendum. Affected are such borrowing options as life-safety bonds, working cash fund bonds, funding bonds, and insurance reserve bonds. Such bonds may be issued as "limited bonds," without a referendum, only if the district levied for non-referendum bonds in the tax year when the property tax cap was approved in the county in which the district is located. The levy year for the Debt Service Extension Base calculation for Cook and the five collar counties is 1994. The applicable levy years for the other counties subject to the tax cap are shown in *Table 5* in *Chapter 4*.

The amount of the levy to repay such bonds in that year, called the Debt Service Extension Base (DSEB), defines the maximum available levy for non-referendum bonds in future years, even if a period of time with no such levy has elapsed since the repayment of earlier bonds. For example, if a district in a county where the tax cap was imposed in 1996 levied and collected $750,000 for repayment of limited bonds that year, it may levy up to $750,000 each year for repayment of new limited bonds. Applicable backdoor referendum petition period and public hearing requirements still apply. A DSEB can be established or increased by referendum. Beginning in 2009, a district's DSEB is increased annually by the CPI figure used to compute the limiting rate under the tax cap law.

County clerks and public finance consultants can provide information on a district's historical levies and determine whether a DSEB exists and in what amount. Consultants can assist the district in structuring future bond sales to gain maximum funding power from the available DSEB, while taking into account the effect of such actions on property tax bills.

Uncertainty about future CPI levels must be taken into account in establishing annual levies when long-term bonds are to be issued. The annual CPI adjustment used for the property tax extension limitation averaged only 2.1% for levy years 2017-2022. A conservative projection of future DSEB levels in structuring debt service levies will reduce the possibility that a levy could exceed the authorized level in a year when the CPI is low. The financial consultant can project alternative debt schedules under various assumptions about DSEB growth.

12 / Revenue Management and Control

Schools have less control over revenues than expenditures. Therefore, it is important that the controls that are available be regularly exercised. The list of tips listed below is used by successful school leaders to assure the highest possible yield from local, state, and federal revenue sources. Part two of this book (*Chapters 14-22*), which discusses expenditure budgeting and management, includes management tips on the overall budgeting process and expenditure control.

Property Tax Revenue
- Know your tax base and its outlook by establishing and maintaining contact with township and county assessors, with persons in the community knowledgeable about local real estate values and trends, and with the officials responsible for tax extensions (billing) and collections.
- Maintain a database on large commercial and industrial property valuations and compare the valuation trends to changes in the condition of the property, occupancy, and other determinants of value. Consider appealing under-assessment and reductions of property valuations that lead to significant revenue losses.
- Monitor tax receipts monthly; watch for unusual discrepancies that suggest an error by the county treasurer in distributing taxes to public agencies. Errors do occur from time to time.
- In budgeting property tax revenue, allow for delayed receipt or refunds due to non-collection of taxes, bankruptcies, appeals, and other factors. Research historical rates of uncollected taxes and be alert to increases in the percentage of problem collections. Examine selling delinquent taxes and other old receivables to generate current revenue.
- Monitor and intervene in assessment appeals and tax objection complaints; tax refunds can be substantial in the case of large commercial and industrial property. Appeals filed in circuit court are not routinely reported to taxing agencies; if these are a problem, ask the school attorney to monitor court actions to discover them. Negotiate the schedule for repayment of refunds over a multi-year period if refunds are awarded. Allow for possible refunds in budgeting property tax revenue in the event that pending appeals and objections are decided in favor of the taxpayer.
- Work with local government officials to secure impact fees, upfront transition fees, and developer donations of land and/or money to offset the cost of building facilities to house students from new homes.
- Become involved in matters concerning tax increment financing (TIF), enterprise zones, municipal incentives, abatements, and other redevelopment incentives, and attempt to negotiate benefits for the school district, including periodic payments of revenues from the TIF district. Other negotiable provisions include the TIF's time period and geographic area, distribution of incremental revenue, infrastructure improvements that benefit the school district, a requirement that property owners waive their right to property tax appeals, and waiver of municipal utility charges for the school district. Educational benefits may include funding for the district's job training and vocational education programs.
- See *Chapter 3* for additional information about the school's rights in the formation and governance of a TIF, and for other strategies to control losses from appeals, incentive classifications, and tax abatements.

Levies
- Plan tax levies carefully so that levies for each fund provide for current budgetary needs, adequate

reserves, and are within applicable tax rate limits. In tax-capped counties, research trends in new property valuations as well as the cost-of-living statistic and simulate the extension calculation under different scenarios before finalizing levies. This will work to avoid under-levying and the consequent loss of tax revenue entitlement for the year and following years.
- Make use of special-purpose levies such as tort liability and life-safety funds to the extent and for purposes permitted by law to relieve pressures on the major operating funds. Keep current on legal interpretations of allowable uses of these funds, especially the tort liability levy for which ISBE has established budgeting and accounting procedures.
- Consider the tax bill effect while planning levies, bond issues, and referenda to increase the tax rate; this will maximize the chances for the success of actions which require voter approval. Avoid sharp increases or decreases in future levies.
- Levy sufficiently to capture increases in EAV from new construction and those that may arise from TIFs and expired incentives. Research and keep current these expiration dates to be sure that the levies for that tax year are sufficient to capture increased taxes.
- Be cautious with abatements; consider the possible effect on the extension base if located in a PTELL county.
- Monitor any proposed legislation to freeze property taxes to understand how the short- and long-term effects on revenue for the operating funds and debt service. Inform legislators of the financial and program impact of restricting growth in property tax revenue, especially at a time of restricted state funding. If a petitioned referendum is called to reduce property taxes as provided for by the 2018 School Funding Reform Act, develop a plan to communicate to voters the importance of the property tax in assuring adequate funding for the school program.

Enrollment and Attendance
- Maintain an accurate monthly record of both enrollments and attendance, along with an audit trail. Understand the process of calculating state aid under the Evidence-Based Funding formula, and the importance of enrollment reports in that calculation. In addition, other financial communications require both attendance reports. See that staff is trained on recording and documenting enrollments and on state rules for counting enrollment and attendance. This will work toward maximizing revenue and minimizing audit reductions. Correct the causes of any audit reductions in previous claims.
- Maintain surveillance on the residency of pupils and collect tuition for, or dis-enroll, non-resident students, being careful to observe due process procedures and rights to a board hearing that are specified in law.
- PA 99-0670 changed residency hearing procedures in cases of disputed residency and added rights to appeal to the Regional Office of Education. Review registration and residency policies and procedures, and train staff members, so that entry of new students proceeds according to law.
- Avoid scheduling events that reduce attendance, in the interest of student learning.

Fees
- Community service programs can contribute to the costs of district overhead. Establish fees for childcare, lunch, summer programs, and adult education to recover their costs, including building costs and administration.
- Make use of federal meal program cash and commodity subsidies; keep and maintain accurate records substantiating student eligibility for free and reduced breakfasts and lunches. Consider qualifying a school or the entire district for meal benefits if the poverty rate is sufficiently high.
- Keep current with regulations for providing meals to students and families during the pandemic-caused disruption in the school schedule and the incomes of the district's families, so that the food necessary to their health can be provided while minimizing the net costs to the district.
- Keep textbook, transportation, and other fees current with their related costs.
- Develop and keep up-to-date policies on the funding of technology used by students, including provisions for cost sharing and insurance.
- Streamline procedures for collecting fees by offering online payments and credit card options.
- Consider athletic and other activity participation fees, but have a policy and subsidy for those unable to pay such fees.

Grants and Other Revenue
- Understand the purposes and claim procedures for the various state and federal categorical grants.

- Maintain the necessary databases on special education and bilingual students and program costs so as to secure the maximum amount of available revenue from these grants.
- Avoid losses of funds by closely observing the rules for spending and accounting for grant funds. Be certain that principals and others who authorize grant expenditures understand the rules.
- Employ or train a staff member in the art of seeking and writing grants from state and federal agencies, foundations, and other sources, and to lobby for funds for the district's special program needs and initiatives.
- Lease or rent surplus land and facilities at rates that reflect costs and the market for such real estate. Consider the sale of obsolete buildings and unneeded school sites.
- Sell services to other agencies to fully utilize specialists and facilities.
- Sponsor special fundraising events, such as golf tournaments, that will attract the community's business and professional leadership, and thereby expose them to the school's needs.
- Establish a foundation to solicit and channel contributions to the schools. The National School Foundation Association provides resources on its website, www.schoolfoundations.org.
- Invite businesses to establish mutually beneficial partnerships with the district.
- Attract cell and wind energy towers, but be prepared for lengthy communications and negotiations with municipal officials and nearby property owners.
- Consider selling naming rights to field houses, athletic fields, and stadiums, and other non-school building facilities.
- Become familiar with the provisions of the County Schools Facility Occupation Tax. Explore with other districts the feasibility of holding a referendum to institute the tax in those counties where it is not in place. *Chapter 9* provides information on this tax.

Investments and Borrowing

- Develop and maintain an accurate system of projecting cash flow so that temporarily unneeded funds can be invested for terms that maximize interest revenues, and so that the costs of short-term borrowing are reduced or avoided altogether. Become familiar with the yields and terms of various investment instruments that meet legal and policy standards for safety. Employ the school attorney and qualified independent investment counsel to investigate instruments and investment pools with which the district is not familiar or when concerns arise about performance of existing investments.
- Use interfund transfers and loans and the working cash fund in lieu of outside borrowing.
- Judicially use bonds and other tax-exempt credit instruments when cash is needed to fund facilities and other expenses due to enrollment expansion or program need. Keep current with the laws governing the permissive uses, amounts, and authorization processes governing the various forms of short- and long-term debt.

Revenue Controls

- Maintain a system of checks and balances to assure the proper handling of all receipts, especially cash, and separation of the functions of purchasing, payroll, and disbursement of funds. Employ the ABCs of internal control — separate Authorization, Bookkeeping, and Cash control. Ask the district's auditor to periodically review checks and balances and internal control in both the regular and activity funds.
- Conduct internal audits to assure the integrity and accuracy of financial transactions and compliance with law and policy. A large district may wish to establish the position of internal auditor.
- More discussion of internal controls and the annual audit appears in *Chapter 25*.

13 / Calling a Finance Referendum

A referendum may be required to raise the property tax rate for one or more funds, to establish a new tax rate, to raise the revenue limits imposed by the property tax cap, to establish or increase a Debt Service Extension Base (DSEB), or to sell bonds for school buildings, repairs, or for operating funds. Sometimes simultaneous referenda are scheduled for the construction of school buildings and related education and/or operating and maintenance fund tax rate increases.

Except in narrowly defined emergency circumstances, referenda may be held only on four scheduled election dates in each two-year cycle. These are the March primary and November general elections in even-numbered years and the February consolidated primary and April consolidated general elections in the spring of odd-numbered years. (The state held the 2022 primary in June, because pandemic response efforts delayed reporting of the 2020 U.S. Census. It returns to March in 2024.)

However, election laws state that no public question can be on the ballot at a regularly scheduled election at which none of the voters in a school district are scheduled to cast votes for any candidate. This effectively excludes the February consolidated primary date as a referendum opportunity. School boards, therefore, can count on only three election dates in the two-year cycle.

Preliminary planning for a referendum begins more than a year ahead of the election, with the longest lead time required for questions related to the funding of new school sites and buildings. This section outlines some of the considerations for planning for a referendum. School board members and administrators who are contemplating a referendum should consult the resources listed at the end of this chapter for a more complete discussion of pre-election planning and strategies.

Establishing the Need

Whether it involves a new school building or an increase in the tax rate, or both, the referendum question must state precisely the amount of money to be borrowed or the amount of the tax rate increase necessary to meet operating cost needs. Defining these questions requires financial projections and, if a building project is involved, a demographic study and enrollment forecasts. Board of education study and acceptance of these projections is an essential first step in achieving the all-important board unity in the early stages of planning the referendum. If the board is not united, the referendum will likely not gain community support. Consultants and architects can assist in developing financial projections and building cost estimates necessary to size the referendum and determine the ballot language. Involvement of key community leaders and dissemination of study information to constituents are necessary to build community consensus.

Election Formalities

The county clerk or county board of election commissioners administers school elections. School officials should work closely with the clerk to meet full compliance with filing deadlines and publication and posting formalities. Minor errors can invalidate a successful referendum.

The board of education must pass a resolution to place a question on the ballot not less than 79 days before the election date. The resolution must be certified to the county election authority not less than 68 days before the election date.

The school board and superintendent are well advised to call on legal counsel in the early planning stages of a finance election. An attorney can identify the critical dates and procedures for drafting and filing the board resolution calling the election and posting related notices.

If the referendum involves a bond issue, the district will be required to work closely with the bond attorneys who will give approval to the issue. This work will involve ballot language and other paperwork that must be carried out in strict accordance with the law and financial procedures.

In the case of tax rate increases and similar propositions, the regular school attorney may be called upon to guide the district through the legal requirements of the election, including the wording of the question and the required supplementary information to appear on the ballot.

Districts Subject to the Tax Cap

Several laws govern referenda to increase taxes and consequent tax extension practices in tax-capped districts. A taxing agency subject to PTELL may not use other forms of propositions previously authorized in statute, but now only applicable to non-tax-capped districts.

The laws specify exact wording for each of the following types of referenda:
- To authorize a new tax rate, stating its purpose and the amount of the rate.
- To increase the limiting rate, stating the amount of the increase and the resulting maximum rate, and the levy years affected, up to a maximum of four consecutive years.
- To increase the tax rate in the education fund above the limits established by referendum or the School Code, with a commensurate reduction in the maximum rate for the operations and maintenance fund, so that the total tax rate falls within the limit established by PTELL.
- To allow a specified percentage to be used in lieu of the lesser of the Consumer Price Index or 5% in calculating the extension for the levy years identified in the question.

Selection of the question to be posed to voters will depend on the district's revenue needs and other factors. Each option has implications for the amount and timing of new revenue, and for the district's tax rates. Secure help from a financial consultant in selecting the question, and consult the county clerk to determine how a successful referendum will be reflected in residents' tax bills and future property tax revenues.

Supplemental information must be provided for the ballot and election notices for a new tax rate, limiting rate increase, or extension rate increase. Among other information required is the approximate amount of the additional tax on a single-family residence having a fair market value of $100,000 at the time of the referendum. It is important to consult the district's attorney for the exact ballot language and required supplemental information.

Other changes govern the effective dates and phase-in schedule of new tax rates and increased limiting rates approved after March 21, 2006.

The wording of other referendum questions, including those to authorize new bonds, to establish or increase a Debt Service Extension Base, or to raise tax rates of districts not subject to PTELL, is also specified in statute.

Informing and Reading the Community

Two-way communication between the community and school district is essential in building the community consensus necessary to a successful referendum. Referendum communications that are part of an ongoing public relations program will be more effective than "referendum-only" efforts. If the district's internal and external public relations programs are lacking, the time to beef them up is well before the referendum communications are due to begin.

The school board must evaluate public opinion toward the schools and determine what the community can afford and is willing to pay. Reading the local economic and political climate is greatly assisted by communications with business and government leaders early in the planning stages, as well as by analyzing media coverage of the schools. Recent controversies over educational programs or other school issues, labor disputes, or failed referenda in the past few years will have increased the number of potential negative votes and must be anticipated in planning the public relations program.

Community awareness surveys provide valuable insight into attitudes about the schools. If the referendum is tied into a community-wide question such as the construction of a new school, and the consequent redrawing of attendance boundaries and/or shuffling of grade levels, care should be taken to provide opportunities for the entire community to become informed and address the questions. A combination of written surveys and community meetings might be required.

Surveys and public meetings on the subject of the school budget will reveal the public's views on how school money is being spent, as well as unmet aspirations for improvement that can provide additional rationale for a tax rate increase. Consultants can assist in the preparation and analysis of surveys, which can involve interviews of school and community leaders and focus groups as well as analysis of survey data.

The end products of the communication phase include a better-informed electorate, a more precise definition of those needs which the community is prepared to support, and ideas for the campaign theme. The question, "Why do we need the money?" has been answered.

Organizing Campaign Committee Work

Electioneering on behalf of a public policy question at a referendum needs to be handled only by a committee of citizens using private funding. Here are some suggestions to help guide such a committee once it is created and the school board has opted to put a finance question on the ballot.

Once the school board has established the question to be voted upon and selected the election date, a citizens committee can essentially take charge of the campaign organization and work.

It is important that the campaign leadership be representative of all segments of the community, not just the school board and administration. The timetable should allow sufficient time but not too much, so that the campaign peaks just before the election. Sneaking the question through at the last minute seldom works.

Pockets of support are identified to be enlisted during the campaign, and potential opposition groups are also brought forward. Some may represent issues that can be dealt with, while others may be opponents who can be counted, but not persuaded to change their minds. Such counting will help define the number of "yes" votes necessary to carry the question as the campaign stage is organized.

Campaigns are organized around the critical functions of voter registration, canvassing, preparation of campaign materials, finance, and Election Day activities. A steering committee and general chairperson develop strategy and schedule and coordinate the work of the subcommittees. A typical steering committee would consist of subcommittee chairs, an administrative representative, and one or two school board members.

It is important to research past voting patterns and to conduct a registration program that identifies and focuses on potential "yes" voters. However, do not combine voter registration with campaign activities. Study of recent elections will reveal persons who do and do not vote regularly and determine the number of votes needed for approval.

Cross-referencing voter lists with parent lists will identify parents who are not registered to vote. Some may be new to the community, or recent citizens. Train deputy registrars to assist them in registering in time for the referendum. Target non-voting but registered parents for special attention during the campaign. Don't forget 18-year-old students, recent graduates, parents of preschoolers, employees, and other known school supporters. Offer assistance to potential "yes" voters who require absentee ballots.

The effective campaign employs short and simple messages, focusing on why the money is needed and benefits to the children and community. If a building referendum, for example, will fund a central school or renovations and additions in several schools, make it clear that there is "something for everyone" in the community. Communications should be consistent and targeted to their audiences. Simple graphics speak louder than words. Voters will want to know the impact on their tax bills; it is common to tell the effect on the "average" home in the community. It is useful to assemble public relations materials from successful referenda in your area.

A kick-off event is an effective way to begin the campaign. Subsequently, information can be distributed through mailings, door-to-door distributions, signs, the media, public events, endorsements, and paid advertising. Identified "yes" voters call for special attention, including telephone and door-to-door canvassing. Meetings sponsored by the referendum committee and parent organizations provide excellent opportunities to inform school patrons about the referendum and the benefits it carries for their children.

School staff members should limit their comments to the facts when on compensated time and express support for the referendum only when off school grounds and not at a school function — stating that they are not speaking as a part of their school duties and are not on compensated time. Again, administrators should be extra cautious in such situations.

Election Day Procedures

Election Day procedures to maximize "yes" votes resemble those used by candidates for public office, and include phone banks to remind "yes" voters to go to the polls, poll watchers, rides, child care for parents, surveys of voters, assembling and acting on voting and polling data during the day and, hopefully, a victory party followed by recognition and thanking of leaders and workers.

If the question fails, debriefing and evaluation of the campaign will provide important information for organizing the next one. Accept the results of the democratic process, avoid damning the voters, modify plans and campaign approaches as required, analyze the vote, and prepare to begin anew.

Impact of Ethics Laws

Considerable caution is required to separate referendum-related expenditures from those of the board of education. Campaign finance reporting requirements may apply; the necessary information can be obtained from the county clerk. Crossing the line between public business and electioneering provides opponents with powerful ammunition in addition to constituting a violation of the law. Printing and mailing of advocacy material should be performed off school premises, and the school attorney consulted if there is a question as to whether a referendum-related activity can be construed to constitute illegal advocacy. A clear policy should be established with respect to contributions from school vendors and other commercial entities to the referendum campaign.

Two statutes govern referendum communications, and the inconsistencies between them suggest caution in planning communications and conducting campaign activities. Those two statutes are the Election Interference Prohibition Act and the State Officials and Employees Ethics Act. "Organizing Campaign Committee Work," on page 81, provides an overview of how a privately funded citizens committee might approach the referendum. School administrators must be careful to ensure that their official actions — i.e., those carried out during "compensated time" — are impartial and treat opponents and proponents with an equal hand. Work in support of passing a referendum must be carried out by members of a citizens group or school board members and staff acting on their own time and without district resources.

Getting Started

"Answers to FAQs Regarding Referendum Activities Conducted by School Officials," published by the Illinois Council of School Attorneys, is a useful resource for administrators and board members and also describes the possible inconsistencies in the Election Interference Prohibition Act and the State Officials and Employees Ethics Act. It is available from the Illinois Association of School Boards. Workshops and conference programs on conducting a referendum are offered by a number of professional associations, including the Illinois Association of School Business Officials and the Illinois Association of School Boards. Various public finance consulting firms and banks also provide assistance in planning and conducting referenda. School law firms include in their presentations and workshops the applicable legal requirements for referenda, and should be consulted for guidance throughout the process.

Part Two

14 / The Structure and Development of the Expenditure Budget

The first section of this chapter describes the structure of the expenditure and budget summary sections of the Illinois Official School District Budget Form for Fiscal Year 2022-2023. It is intended to guide the user in reading and using the budget form. However, a full treatment of school financial accounting is beyond the scope of this book. Account codes for non-expenditure disbursements such as transfers, and balance sheet account codes required for recording transactions and financial reporting are not included.

Consult the budgeting and accounting regulations that are available from the Illinois State Board of Education at www.isbe.net. Start with the publication, Mechanics of the School District Budget. The codes for classifying expenditures are found in "Part 100 Requirements for Accounting, Budgeting, Financial Reporting and Budgeting". First-time users may also want to consult "The School District/Joint Agreement Budget Instructions for New Users."

The second section describes some general approaches to developing budgets from which administrators choose depending on their management philosophy, the program or service being budgeted, and the financial setting during which budgeting is taking place.

Why Schools Have Budgets

The school budget serves many purposes. It fulfills a School Code requirement for a plan for the receipt and expenditure of money, and is a prerequisite for spending school funds. It provides a minimum level of financial information for the use of the district as well as state and federal government agencies. It justifies the levy of property taxes and defines the account structure for classification of revenues and expenditures.

The budgeting process is a leadership, planning, and communication challenge for the school board and administration. It is an annual opportunity to bring together the district's instructional programs and support services, weigh their resource requirements for the near-term and long-term, compare these costs to the district's goals and available resources, and make decisions to increase or decrease resources to specific programs and services. These decisions require a planning and communication process that fits the decision-making philosophy of the district, as practiced by its board of education, administration, and staff leadership. Defining this process is a critical first step in developing the budget, especially when a new administration takes over or when difficult priority decisions must be made.

Effective budget decisions can be made centrally or at the school site level, or a combination of both. They can reflect formulas established by the superintendent and business manager, or arise from program initiatives and proposals developed by principals and teachers. Commonly, they result from both. Recent years have seen a trend towards increased collaboration amongst administrators including principals. As districts address the increasing needs of students, budgeting decisions must be made in consultation with many stakeholders. The central office role is to establish procedures and general allocations to guide the decentralized process and to play a major role in budgeting for building services, capital improvements, and transportation. Whether centralized or decentralized, a budgeting process will work best when it matches the

Table 16

ISBE Budget Form

Here is a small segment excerpted from the ISBE school district budget form for estimated disbursements and expenditures. The form is a grid created by arraying the various types of expenditures across the top and school programs down the side. Forms may be downloaded from the ISBE website at www.isbe.net.

ESTIMATED DISBURSEMENTS/EXPENDITURES

Description	Funct. #	(100) Salaries	(200) Employee Benefits	(300) Purchased Services	(400) Supplies & Materials	(500) Capital Outlay
10 - EDUCATION FUND (ED)						
INSTRUCTION (ED)						
Regular Programs	1100					
Tuition Payments to Charter Schools	1115					
Pre-K Programs	1125					
Special Education Programs (Total of Functions. No. 1200-1220)	1200					
Special Education Programs Pre-K	1225					
Remedial and Supplemental Programs K-12	1250					
Remedial and Supplemental Programs Pre-K	1275					
Adult/Continuing Education Programs	1300					
CTE Programs	1400					
Interscholastic Programs	1500					
Summer School Programs	1600					
Gifted Programs	1650					
Driver's Education Programs	1700					
Bilingual Programs	1800					
Truant Alternative & Optional Programs	1900					
Pre-K Programs - Private Tuition	1910					
Regular K-12 Programs - Private Tuition	1911					
Special Education Programs K-12 Private Tuition	1912					
Special Education Programs Pre-K Tuition	1913					
Remedial/Supplemental Programs K-12 Private Tuition	1914					
Remedial/Supplemental Programs Pre-K Private Tuition	1915					
Adult/Continuing Education Programs Private Tuition	1916					
CTE Programs Private Tuition	1917					
Interscholastic Programs Private Tuition	1918					
Summer School Programs Private Tuition	1919					
Gifted Programs Private Tuition	1920					
Bilingual Programs Private Tuition	1921					
Truants Alternative/Opt. Ed. Programs Private Tuition	1922					
Total Instruction (without Student Activity Funds 1999)	1000					
Total Instruction (with Student Activity Funds 1999)	1000					

district's management culture and administrative style. Put succinctly, "You budget like you manage and you manage like you budget." *Chapter 15* further discusses budgeting philosophies, timetables, and techniques.

Change is a fact of life in every school district. Public school enrollment is decreasing at the national level. While the COVID-19 pandemic may have impacted public school enrollment, sub-populations of school districts are also changing, along with needs and expectations for public school providers. There are curricular changes, technology needs for instruction and administration, and needs for building repairs and additions. Parents and teachers demand greater voice in significant decisions. In times of change, simply building next year's budget on top of this year's allocations will not suffice. Rather, a collaborative process extending over the entire school year is required, thereby making budgeting a major leadership opportunity for both building and central administrators alike. If a sound, creative, and energizing process of planning and communication has taken place, the final budget should contain no surprises to the staff, the public, and especially the board of education.

The Structure of the Budget Document

This section should be read along with the expenditure portion of the school district budget on the form provided by the State Board of Education. The form can be downloaded from www.isbe.net. ISBE also publishes a booklet, Mechanics of the School District Budget, which serves as a useful guide to understanding the structure of the budget. It contains charts and schematics of the account structure, sample budget pages, legal requirements for budgeting, and a glossary of budgetary and accounting terms. Administrators responsible for budget construction and administration should keep the current edition of this document for handy reference.

Each budgeted expenditure is assigned to a cell representing fund, function, and object. A small segment of the ISBE expenditure budget form appears in *Table 16* on *page 84*. It illustrates the expenditure categories. Each fund has its own section of the budget. The nine major funds, their numerical designations on the state budget form, and uses are:

- (10) Education — For instruction-related items and transactions not covered in another fund
- (20) Operations & Maintenance — Costs for the upkeep and maintenance of buildings and grounds
- (30) Debt Service — Payments on bonds and other long-term debt.
- (40) Transportation — Costs associated with student transportation.
- (50) Municipal Retirement — The district's share of required IMRF and Social Security payments if a separate tax is levied for this fund.
- (60) Capital Projects — Used when needed for expenditure of construction bond funds, tracking large-scale capital projects, or other long-term financing agreements and construction grants. Note: Separate sub-funds for each debt issue and capital project are required; the sub-funds are consolidated into single Debt Service and Capital Project funds for budgeting purposes.
- (70) Working Cash — Repository of funds from interest or a tax or bond issue to provide cash reserves for school districts. No expenditures are made from this fund. Note: See *Chapter 11* for information on allowable interfund loans, transfers, and abatement of Working Cash Fund moneys.
- (80) Tort Immunity — Payments for risk management activities, including but not limited to liability insurance and legal judgments against a district. Note: See *Chapter 3* for information on allowable uses of the Tort Liability Fund. In the interest of greater accuracy and transparency, the budget form now provides for Tort Fund expenditures to be spread among several accounts in the various function categories.
- (90) Fire Prevention — For eligible code-required and state-approved building projects.

The functions or activities to which expenditures are charged are represented by the rows. Each function has its own number, assigned according to a "chart of accounts" specified in Section 23 Illinois Administrative Code, Part 100 (IAC). The numbering system for the functions recognizes six general categories of expenditures and account series, as follows:

- (1000) Instruction — teaching of pupils and teacher-pupil interactions.
- (2000) Support Services — administrative, technical, logistical services.
- (3000) Community Services — provided to community or a segment thereof.
- (4000) Payments to other districts and governmental units for services such as special education.
- (5000) Debt Services — for specific debt repayment obligations.
- (6000) Provision for Contingencies — identifies amounts for contingencies.

Each category includes the instructional programs and support services for which budget appropriations are made. Four digits including the function category are used to categorize the expenditure function. For example, regular K-12 school instructional expenditures are numbered 1100 and building administrative services are coded 2410.

Many districts expand their budget documents beyond the state form to include statements of strategic planning goals, program enrollments, school improvement plans, narratives describing revenues and expenditures, organizational charts, budget process descriptions, financial projections, and more. Examine some of these budgets to select possible enhancements to your district's budget. Standards for expanded budget documents may be obtained from the Association of School Business Officials International's website or www.asbointl.org. The Meritorious Budget Award and other publications on budgeting are also available on that website.

The "objects" or types of expenditures are shown on the budget form in numbered columns, headed as follows:
- (100) Salaries — gross salaries for district personnel.
- (200) Employee Benefits — fringe benefits paid by the district on its employees' behalf.
- (300) Purchased Services — payments for personal services rendered by non-employees.
- (400) Supplies and Materials — amounts for material item of an expendable nature.
- (500) Capital Outlay — amounts for acquisition of fixed assets or additions to them.
- (600) Other Objects — amounts for goods and services not classified above including dues, fees, and out-of-district tuition.
- (700) Non-Capitalized Equipment — capital assets costing more than $500, but less than the capitalization threshold adopted by the school board.
- (800) Termination Benefits — payments made for unused sick or vacation days upon termination or retirement.

The eight categories of expenditures are totaled for each function (line) in column 9 of the state budget form (omitted from the segment in *Table 16*).

The second and third digits add detail to the object classifications. For example, general supplies are classified in 410, textbooks in 420, and library materials in 430. The chart of three-digit object numbers is found in the IAC.

Examine the cells formed by the intersection of each line and column of the district budget on the state form. A white cell is a legal budget classification; a shaded cell represents a classification that is not permitted by law or state regulation. Now you understand the origin of the expression, "Stay out of the gray area," a warning by and to accountants to classify revenues and expenditures correctly!

The district may expand its chart of accounts to include additional classifications and account numbers for each school building, grade level, high school department, and even the subject area and level of individual courses. Nine is the minimum number of digits required to code an expenditure — two for the fund, four for the function, and three for the object. Numbers not listed in the program accounting manual may be used if the description falls within the relevant classification. Prefixes and suffixes may be used to identify schools, departments, courses, and other units where cost breakouts may be desired. Identification of schools is increasingly important within a district's accounting structure since the implementation of the Every Student Succeeds Act (ESSA). The Act requires that the school district report school-level expenditure data annually. Districts that do not account for ESSA revenues and expenditures at the school level should consider adding this dimension to their chart of accounts.

Additional numbers permit the preparation of reports to assist administrators and teachers in monitoring their budgets, a necessity for decentralized decision-making. However, each additional category creates complexity and opportunity for error in classifying expenditures for budgeting and accounting. Like the budgeting process, the account structure should reflect the district's management philosophy.

Reading and Using the Summary Sections

The state budget form begins with a summary section. An excerpt from the summary section is shown in *Table 17* on *page 88*. Study of this section is essential to understanding the district's financial condition at the open and close of the school year. For each fund, the opening fund balance and the year's revenues, other financing sources and uses, expenditures, and projected closing fund balance are shown. A separate summary of cash transactions compares cash and investments at the beginning and end of the year and describes the expected use of interfund loans, warrants, and notes during the budget year. As with other state budgeting and accounting reports, the district's Activity Fund transactions and balances are now included in the summary section (but not in the portion excerpted in *Table 17* on *page 88*).

Analysis of changes in the operating fund balances and cash position, combined with an analysis of monthly cash flow (described in *Chapter 10*) reveals whether borrowing may be required during the school year, and whether steps must be taken to adjust revenues and/or expenditures in budgeting for the following year. The corresponding lines on the district's Annual Financial Report, filed with the State Board of Education following the close of the fiscal year, are a measure of fiscal health used by the state to determine the need for oversight of a district's finances.

A report at the end of the budget shows the operating surplus or deficit for each operating fund. Assuming the budget is prepared using the Excel formulas within the state form, that page will reveal whether a deficit requires the district to submit a three-year deficit reduction plan to ISBE along with the budget. The form includes space for a brief narrative and supporting projections. See *Chapter 15* and ISBE's *Mechanics of a School District Budget* for further information on the balanced budget requirement.

Required addenda to the budget include a worksheet showing the change in budgeted administrative costs from the previous year's estimated actual expenditures, and a report of public vendor contracts of $1,000 or more. A self-checking balancing sheet checks key cells to assure that selected items are in balance before the budget is finalized.

ESSA Site-Based Expenditure Reporting Now Required on School Report Cards

Rules established for the federal Every Student Succeeds Act (ESSA) require that the Illinois School Report Card shows additional expenditure information for the district and each school. The information includes the per-pupil expenditure of federal, state, and local funds, including actual personnel and non-personnel expenditures for the preceding fiscal year disaggregated by source of funds.

ISBE has prepared illustrations of the required data and how it might be visualized in the report cards by various graphical techniques.

General Budgeting Techniques

There are a variety of techniques for developing budgets. Financial administrators employ several of them, selecting those that fit state requirements, the program or service being budgeted, the district's management philosophy, and the financial setting in which the budget decisions are taking place.

- **Incremental budgeting** is performed by applying an inflation rate to items in the previous year's budget. Incrementing assumes a static program, and that each item will continue to receive the same relative slice of the budgetary pie. It is undemocratic but quick and serves well for long-term budget projections.

- **Line-item budgeting** considers and prioritizes each budgetary item. The line-item technique obscures the costs of individual programs in favor of highlighting individual salary, supply, and capital items. It is best suited for budgeting a relatively static program within a centralized budgeting philosophy or as part of an intensive effort to reconsider or reduce every possible cost.

- **Student-based funding (SBF)** allocates resources to schools based on individual student characteristics and needs. The goal is to increase equity of funding. The means include a system of weighted student formulas and greater decision-making power to the schools to align resources with student needs. This approach is manifested in the Illinois Evidence-Based Funding budgeting model.

- **Zero-based budgeting (ZBB)** is a product of a period of government downsizing and fiscal restraints in the 1970s and 1980s that produced "sunset laws" and gave birth to anti-tax measures. It requires annual justification for each program or expenditure. Since many school programs are mandated by law or otherwise entrenched in practice, zero-based budgeting is useful primarily to select from among competing new programs, or to develop portions of a budget. Principals might use it with their staff to make decisions on allocations for instructional materials and equipment.

- **School-site budgeting**, also known as building-based budgeting, is a method by which a school, under the leadership of its principal, allocates budgetary resources with as few externally imposed rules and assumptions as possible. It requires new behaviors on the part of administrators, staff, and parents; requires considerable time; and can raise issues of inter-building equity. School-site budgeting is discussed in more detail in *Chapter 23*.

- **Equity-based budgeting** is a newer methodology that considers students' needs prior to allocation of funds. While most districts account for student needs relating to English Language

Table 17
Budget Summary
Here is an excerpt from the summary section of the ISBE budget form.

A	B	C	D	E	F
Description	Acct #	(10) Educational Fund	(20) Operations & Maintenance	(30) Debt Services	(40) Transportation
ESTIMATED BEGINNING FUND BALANCE July 1, 2023					
RECEIPTS/REVENUES					
LOCAL SOURCES	1000	0	0	0	0
FLOW-THROUGH RECEIPTS/ REVENUES FROM ONE DISTRICT TO ANOTHER DISTRICT	2000	0	0		0
STATE SOURCES	3000	0	0	0	0
FEDERAL SOURCES	4000	0	0	0	0
Total Direct Receipts/Revenues					
Receipts/Revenues for "On Behalf" Payments	3998				
Total Receipts/Revenues					
DISBURSEMENTS/EXPENDITURES					
INSTRUCTION	1000	0			
SUPPORT SERVICES	2000	0	0		0
COMMUNITY SERVICES	3000	0	0		0
PAYMENTS TO OTHER DISTRICTS & GOVT UNITS	4000	0	0	0	0
DEBT SERVICES	5000	0	0	0	0
PROVISION FOR CONTINGENCIES	6000	0	0	0	0
Total Direct Disbursements/Expenditures		0	0	0	0
Disbursements/Expenditures for "On Behalf" Payments	4180				
Total Disbursements/Expenditures					
Excess of Direct Receipts/Revenues Over (Under) Direct Disbursements/Expenditures		0	0	0	0

Learners, Special Education and low income within their budget, this methodology provides a more thoughtful accounting for all students' needs, as some may not fall within the most common demographic categories.

These techniques are not mutually exclusive. A budget official might employ an incremental technique for non-instructional budget lines when no decisions on staffing supply or service level increases or decreases are to be made. In the same district, principals might work with teachers and department heads to "zero base" faculty proposals for new curriculum materials, courses, or other expenditures, and select the worthiest for inclusion in the budget. Regardless of the methodology or combination thereof, the budget should reflect the strategic goals of the district.

A useful guide to making budget allocation decisions is contained within Illinois' Evidence-Based Funding (EBF) state aid system, which went into effect in 2017-18. It is described in *Chapter 6* and contains over 20 evidence-based benchmarks or best practices in staffing classrooms and support functions and allocating money to non-personnel items. While the benchmarks, or elements, were compiled to drive state budgetary decisions on state and local revenue sharing for each district, they provide persuasive information to the school budgeting process, in considering student characteristics, class sizes, ratios of support personnel to total students, and dollars for instructional supplies and other items. Portions of the EBF elements are shown in subsequent chapters on budgeting instructional and other services to illustrate how they can provide a research basis for budget decisions.

Likewise, decentralized and centralized management philosophies lie on a continuum which administrators must occasionally slide along to fit a district's economic circumstances. A flexible philosophy and knowledge of several techniques for making budget decisions will assist both building and district-level administrators to develop budgets that meet the needs of the educational program and support services as a district's economic circumstances rise and fall over the years.

Multi-Year Budgeting

At the same time they discuss and record budgetary decisions for the coming year, many school districts are developing detailed budgets for future years as well. These multi-year budgets go beyond the projections of historical trends that are used for long-term "fiscal overview" projections described in *Chapter 10* for revenues and *Chapter 19* for expenditures.

Multi-year budgets record the resources required to implement elements of a long-term strategic plan. They project the costs of new educational initiatives to meet specific needs and any savings from discontinuing current programs. They reflect cost increases and decreases from projected enrollment changes. They include the costs of facility renovations and repairs as developed for the long-term capital program.

Of course, the multi-year budget also includes estimates of revenue required to meet the projected costs and the planning required to raise revenue in a sufficient amount.

The numbers in a multi-year budget can be recorded in a matrix similar or identical to the ISBE annual budget form used for the current year. Presentation for discussion and communication should be organized according to purpose. One grouping might project the cost of maintaining the "basic" educational program, including personnel costs. Additional groupings would project the costs of specific components of the strategic plan scheduled for implementation in each year. Such a presentation will facilitate the decisions that will face the district in the future in the likely event that the costs of meeting all desired plan components exceed the funds available.

Performance Budgeting – A Technique for Hard Times

In his book, *School Budgeting for Hard Times* (Corwin, 2011), William K. Poston, emeritus professor of Educational Leadership and Policy Studies at Iowa State University, discusses techniques for making tough budget decisions in today's era of restricted or declining resources. In the lead chapter on Performance Budgeting, he states its purpose is "to tie measured performance, or achievement of established outcomes or objectives, into the decision-making process. ...The aim is to implement a process that results in a planned budget based on the measured and defined educational needs and accomplishments of a school system ... performance budgets are generally highly collaborative in nature and definitely lead toward decentralized decision making." The remainder of the book is a guide to implementing a performance-based budget.

Such a budgeting process places the board of education, superintendent, and financial administrator at the intersection of money and learning, where measures of effectiveness meet limits on resources and require tough decisions on expenditures. Add in community preferences, legal directives, equity issues, and faculty inputs that accompany school budgeting, and you have an exciting and potentially treacherous process that poses challenges to leadership, but holds out promise for improved schools.

15 / Budgeting Calendars and Communications

Legal Steps in Budget Adoption

Although budgeting takes place throughout the school year, Illinois law establishes dates for the formal consideration and adoption of the budget by the board of education. The deadline to adopt a school budget in Illinois is September 30, long after key expenditure decisions are made and the new fiscal year begins. Legal requirements for preparing and adopting a budget are found in Section 17-1 of the Illinois School Code for all districts except Chicago Public Schools, for which they are found in Sections 34-42 through 34-82. Requirements are spelled out in ISBE's *Mechanics of a School District Budget*.

The first step required by law is formal designation by the school board of a person to prepare the budget (typically the district superintendent or designee). The budget is adopted in tentative form during the spring or early summer. It must then be placed on public display for not less than 30 days after publication of a notice in a newspaper circulated in the district, announcing its availability for inspection and giving the date of a public hearing. If no newspaper is published in the district, the hearing notice must be posted in five of the most public places in the district.

The final budget, reflecting revisions and corrections in revenue and expenditure items, must be adopted by the board of education by the end of the first quarter of the district's fiscal year. Since the common fiscal year beginning date is July 1, the budget adoption deadline is September 30. The budget may be amended during the year by board action, again following a public notice and hearing.

The district must file with the county clerk, within 30 days of adoption, copies of its budget and an estimate, certified by its chief fiscal officer, of revenues, by source, anticipated to be received by the district during the fiscal year. Care should be taken that a signed copy of the official district budget, on the state form, is filed, and that a separate certification of revenues is signed by the chief school business administrator, superintendent, or other administrator responsible for financial oversight.

All districts must electronically submit a budget on the official ISBE form to the State Board of Education within 30 days of local board adoption, or by October 31, whichever is earlier. The law requires that the budget be balanced. If the budget is not balanced, the district must adopt and file with the state board, with the budget, a plan to achieve a balanced budget within three years. This requirement is the only penalty for an unbalanced budget, although repeated unbalanced budgets may reduce the district's state financial profile score to the level at which ISBE monitoring or intervention could occur.

A deficit reduction plan is required if the board adopts or amends a budget in which the total direct expenditures in the operating funds (Educational, Operations and Maintenance, Transportation, and Working Cash) exceed total direct revenues by an amount equal or greater than one-third of the total estimated ending fund balance. In other words, a plan is required if the estimated fund balance is less than three times the operating fund deficit. The calculation worksheet and plan format are found on the ISBE School District Budget Form.

The requirement to submit a deficit reduction plan may also be triggered by the State Board of Education finding that the district is in financial difficulty. Such a finding may be issued if the district issues teacher orders to pay wages, tax anticipation warrants, or notes against second-year taxes while current year warrants or notes are outstanding, or when other short-term debt is also issued under the above circumstances. A financial difficulty finding may also be issued if, for two consecutive years, the district's expenditures and other financing uses in the four funds exceed the revenues and other financing sources plus the funds' opening balances.

Districts that maintain websites are required to post a copy of the budget for the current year, itemized by receipts and expenditures. While posting the state budget form fulfills this requirement, an opportunity exists to post additional information that is understandable by residents, and to employ graphics to help carry the message.

Board members, superintendents, and financial administrators should keep current with laws governing budget formalities, as departure from the laws can be grounds for "tax objections." These are legal actions which are expensive to defend and damaging to lose or settle. The novice administrator is best guided by an attorney through the formal budget adoption cycle.

Workshops on basic and advanced budgeting and accounting are offered by the Illinois Association of School Business Officials. Additional programs specifically for board members are offered by the Illinois Association of School Boards, Information regarding these offerings may be obtained at www.iasbo.org and www.iasb.com.

Budget Planning and Communications

"Never surprise a board of education." Experienced superintendents frequently give this advice to novice administrators, and for good reason. Administrators are granted considerable authority for operating the schools and for developing and overseeing the planning process that produces the annual budget. However, boards of education retain the legal responsibility for the smooth operation of the school district, including its financial soundness. Board members rightly demand to have voice as well as vote as decisions are made on programs, personnel policies, and major expenditures that will affect the district's budget and long-term financial picture.

Schools are among the most conservative of government institutions. Their programs reflect long-standing practices and the expectations and values of the community and teaching profession. That conservatism is being severely tested by challenges to the effectiveness of the schools, changes in the student population, the promises of technology, and a trend towards more active — even militant — involvement by the school's clientele in its decision-making processes.

Modern budgeting, therefore, is much more complex than developing and recording numbers on a state budget form and performing the legal budget adoption rituals. Instead, budgeting is a planning and communication process and challenge that extends throughout the school year and may involve not only the board and administration, but staff, parents, and even students.

This chapter outlines a model calendar for timely expenditure budget decisions and illustrates the communications between administrators and boards of education that are necessary at critical points in the annual expenditure budgeting process. Each district's calendar will reflect its own timetable and process for budgetary communications and decisions during the

---

Model Expenditure Budgeting Calendar

Fall
- Project enrollments and teaching staff.
- Develop revenue estimates for following year.
- Identify capital projects for the following summer
- Update long-term revenue and expenditure projections.

Fall/Winter
- Cost-out and decide on new programs or expenditure reductions.
- Develop allocations for instructional supplies.
- Consider priorities for textbooks, equipment, building repairs, buses, and other capital items.

Winter
- Begin process of teacher assignment and update staff budget.
- Refine next year's revenue projections.
- Compile a total expenditure budget and compare with revenue.
- Make decisions on major expenditures as bids are received.

Spring
- Make remaining decisions on instructional program changes and related budget items.
- Adjust salary budgets in line with staff numbers and contract negotiations.
- Update revenues as tax revenue and state aid information becomes available.
- Revise the compiled budget for updates and changes.

Summer/Early Fall
- Formal budget consideration, public hearings, and adoption take place.
- File budget with county clerk(s) and ISBE and place on district website.
- Begin fall budgeting activities for the following year.

school year. If these processes reach decisions during the time periods in the model calendar, they will be timely for staff employment and purchasing decisions for the coming year. The text box on *page 91* provides a summary of the model expenditure budgeting calendar.

As Soon as School Opens

Budgeting for the coming year begins with determining student and staff numbers, which can be projected as soon as opening enrollments are known. The first step is to project the following-year enrollments for each school and for the whole district.

The projected enrollments become the basis for calculating the number of teaching positions that will be required. This calculation, when combined with projection of salaries and benefit costs for the coming year, will constitute a substantial portion of the instructional budget. The need for additional teachers, or for reducing the number of teachers, will become apparent. If enrollment is growing, it is good budgeting practice to round up when counting the numbers of students and teachers for the following year, but not to contract for new teachers until the students are actually enrolled. If the students do not materialize by budget adoption time in the fall, the tentative budget can be reduced at that time.

Budget estimates for support staff, such as teacher assistants, secretaries, custodians, and other non-instructional personnel, can also be made in the fall. Support staff counts tend to be relatively stable over the years; salary projections for constant numbers of personnel will suffice for early budgeting unless support staff increases or reductions-in-force are required.

At this point, an estimated "no change" budget for the coming year can be constructed by adding to the staff budget the current year's budget for services and expendable materials. Now is the time to compare projected revenues with the cost of maintaining the existing program to determine if reductions must occur, if new initiatives must come at the expense of reductions in other areas, or if such additions are affordable without corresponding reductions. The enrollment, staff, and financial projections should be discussed by the board of education in preparation for the decisions to come. Boards with standing committees may conduct these preliminary budget discussions in finance, personnel, and/or education committees.

Later in the Fall and Early Winter

This is the time to look at non-personnel expenditures. Determine what funds are available for new instructional materials and to meet the inevitable cost increases in materials and services. Remember to allow for changes in enrollment and especially for increases in special education and English language program costs due to program changes or enrollment increases. Decide if allocations to each school, grade level, or department for supplies, materials, and services are to be increased, held constant, or decreased in favor of other programs. It will be necessary to decide what inflation rate will be used if an increase in materials is budgeted. Cost increases are outpacing revenue increases in many districts. The tax cap inflation rate, which limits the district's major source of revenues, has recently been far below the inflation rate of educational materials.

Major non-personnel expenditures must be budgeted, such as purchases of computer equipment and the costs of curriculum changes, including textbook adoptions. Adoption costs of technology-based instructional packages, including computers, software, teacher training, equipment maintenance, and other investments call for a multi-year budget. The costs of such packages are higher than those associated with textbook purchases alone. Implementation might take place in a single year or be spread over several years. Either way, accurately budgeting these expenditures involves "life cycle costing" which considers the initial purchase, training, maintenance, annual licenses, and replacement costs. Some of these costs recur and must be budgeted each year that the package is in use. Curriculum adoptions are major decisions that affect educational program planning. Therefore, it is timely for the board of education to discuss the rationale and financial implications of the decision by the middle of the year. Boards especially want to be involved in decisions with curricular impact and those concerning major expenditures.

Late fall is the time to develop a preliminary budget for major building repairs, remodeling, and equipment needs for buildings and transportation. Planning for these items must be underway by early winter to allow for specification development, bidding, and evaluating bids. When actual costs are known, the projects can be prioritized and contracts awarded on a schedule to allow for the completion of projects and acquisition of equipment in a timely way. This is a good time for a report to the board of education on the state of the buildings, and on needed major repairs for the coming years, with immediate priorities identified.

In the calendar described above, the major planning assumptions for the budget have been placed before the board of education by the middle of the school year. The board may not be able to consider and make decisions on all of them by this time, but the budget planning agenda will have been laid out and the necessary decisions identified.

One way to organize these discussions is to develop revenue and expenditure assumptions that summarize historical understandings about the budget, along with current information pertaining to programs, revenues, and expenditures. Such premises might include statements like the following:

Sample Revenue Assumptions
- The tax cap will limit revenue to less than the needed amount.
- The board intends to adopt a levy in December that will be sufficient to capture the maximum revenue when it is extended during the following spring. If a member or members request that the topic of maximizing or reducing the levy should be discussed before its adoption, long-term revenue and expenditure projections should be reviewed several months ahead of the levy decision. The preparations should also include options such debt service restructuring or levy abatement, described in Chapter 11. The district's financial consultant can assist in preparing for this discussion.
- Some increase can be expected in the level of state funding (depending on the district's "funding tier" under the new Evidence-Based Formula.)
- There is a need to identify alternative sources of revenue, i.e., grants, user fees, etc.
- Long-term revenue projections are to be developed to guide consideration of a referendum to increase tax rates.

Each assumption can be expanded to include expected amounts of tax revenue, state and federal aid, legislative proposals under consideration, and the types of borrowing options available.

Sample Expenditure Assumptions
- Although enrollment is increasing, maintaining present class sizes will be considered a major priority throughout the budget process.
- Hiring decisions will seek to create a wide range of experience among faculty members.
- Supplies and materials budgets will increase relative to the Consumer Price Index as used for property tax cap calculations.
- Special education programs are to be reviewed to ensure that each student is receiving the most appropriate education at the most effective cost.
- The district's commitment to technology is ongoing.
- Funds for maintenance of the buildings will be provided to protect this important capital asset.
- Custodial contract negotiations will affect the budget.

As with the revenue assumptions, each expenditure premise can be detailed as necessary. Each item represents a board of education decision that is required before budget planning, staffing, and purchasing can proceed.

In the Spring and Summer

As updated revenue information becomes available and expenditure decisions are made, the results are recorded in a continuously updated budget. It reflects final staff needs, hiring decisions, the outcome of contract negotiations, and purchases. At this point, budgeting becomes a matter of compilation in the business office rather than decision-making. Although unexpected revenue changes and unforeseen expenditures due to enrollment increases, unanticipated special education costs, or emergency building repairs can affect the budget at the last minute, the well-developed and communicated budget will contain no surprises by the time of its formal adoption in the fall.

16 / Budgeting the Elementary School

This chapter describes a process for budgeting expenditures for an elementary school district and its individual buildings. The techniques are "process-neutral," in that they apply in centralized or decentralized management situations and are necessary to developing an accurate description of the costs of the school program.

Illinois Enrollment Trends

The 1990s saw a dramatic change in school enrollment patterns in many areas of the state. For almost two decades enrollment decreases, reductions in force, and school closings had dominated school planning. Subsequently, the so-called "baby boom echo," generational housing turnover, a rising number of immigrant families, and development of new housing in the "outer ring" of the state's metropolitan areas contributed to large increases in enrollments in many districts. The housing market slump that began in 2008 slowed the rate of growth in districts where new construction had taken place as families were locked into their current residences and were unable to "out-migrate" to new homes.

As the economy recovered, changes in school enrollments have been uneven, and rates of enrollment change vary widely around the state. Each community has its own pattern. Enrollments in some districts are increasing slowly, or have remained in the low range to which they fell during the "baby bust" years. Other communities have experienced an increase in the percentage of their students who are immigrants and in need of intensive language instruction. Chicago Public Schools have seen an overall decline in enrollment, with uneven changes among the city's racial and ethnic groups and neighborhoods. Some districts where the "housing bust" led to closing some unneeded buildings during the recession have since reopened them as young families again moved in.

In the wake of the coronavirus pandemic, statewide public school enrollment has declined an estimated 7.5% since 2019.

Statewide enrollment trends from the Illinois School Report Card are illustrated in *Figures 8* and *9* on the *next page*. They show a 132,223 student or 6.64% drop in P-12 enrollments from 2,001,548 in September 2018 to 1,869,325 in September 2022. Grade K-3 cohort sizes in 2022 were in the 125,000-127,000 range, while those in the upper grades were in the 146,000 to 156,000 range, signaling a continued long-term decline in statewide enrollment. Other Fall 2022 statistics and trends of note include:

- The student body is made up of 46% white, 17% Black, 27% Hispanic, 5% Asian, and 4% American Indian, Pacific Islander, and mixed-race children.
- 46.5% of students are considered low income, a decrease from the 48.1% of students identified as low income in 2021.
- 17% receive special education services through an Individualized Education Plan (IEP).
- 13.7% of Illinois students are considered English Language Learners.
- 7.8% experience at least one transfer in/out of the school between the first school day of October and the last school day of the year (mobility rate), not including graduates.
- 2% do not have permanent or adequate homes.
- 91% is the average statewide attendance rate.
- 22% of students miss 5% or more of school days per year without a valid excuse, and are classified as "chronically truant," a 4% increase over 2015.

Projecting School Enrollments

It is essential for administrators to be able to discern and project the population trends in their districts and in each school attendance area. Inaccurate

Figure 8
Total Enrollment

Year	Enrollment
2022	1,869,325
2021	1,887,316
2020	1,957,018
2019	1,984,519
2018	2,001,548

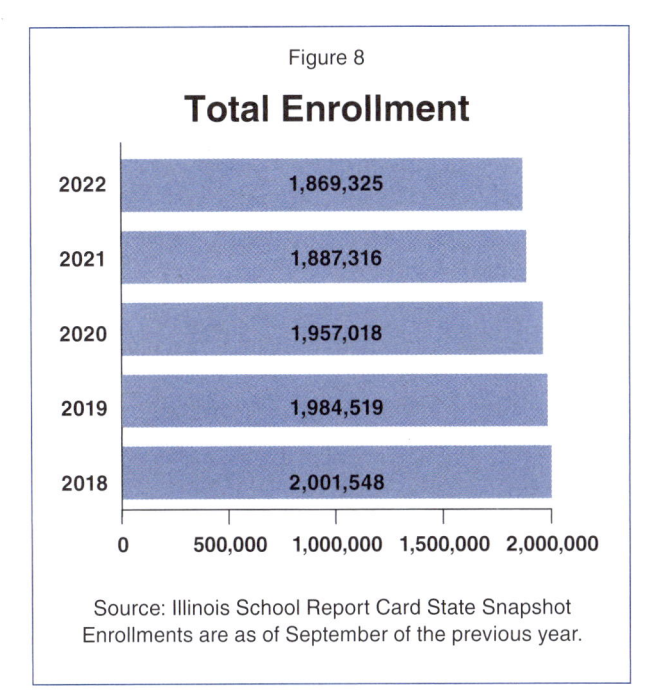

Source: Illinois School Report Card State Snapshot
Enrollments are as of September of the previous year.

Figure 9
2022 Grade Snapshot

Grade	Enrollment
PK	76,645
K	124,808
1	128,801
2	127,437
3	127,217
4	129,338
5	133,597
6	135,399
7	140,813
8	145,466
9	157,008
10	149,133
11	146,066
12	149,597

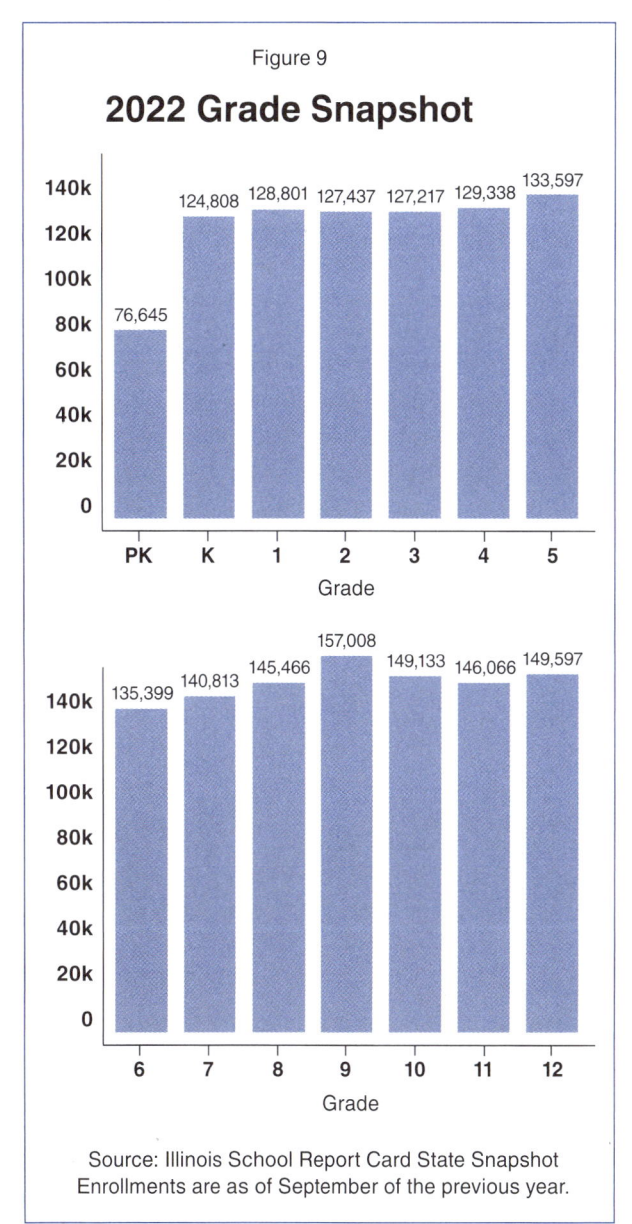

Source: Illinois School Report Card State Snapshot
Enrollments are as of September of the previous year.

projections can quickly lead a district into financial difficulties, classroom shortages (or overbuilding), and a loss of confidence by the community in the schools' leadership. Trending recent changes will suffice if the school's student population is stable or changing slowly. Demographic consultants can research factors related to population changes, apply them to a particular community, and project trends and enrollment ranges for future years.

Both short- and long-term projections for elementary schools are more difficult than for high schools, because they must anticipate future births and deal with the fact that many parents relocate as their children approach school age. Demographers use a variety of techniques to develop long-term enrollment projections, selecting their tools according to the characteristics of each community.

The most common approach is the "cohort survival" technique. Cohort survival is a method for analyzing recent change trends and projecting them into the future. The simplest form of cohort survival projections measures the changes over the past three to five years in each class-age group (cohort) as it moves through the grades, projecting those rates of change into the future. Simple cohort survival projection yields accurate year-to-year projections for individual buildings and the district unless there are housing developments or other factors causing rapid population changes.

Like all projection techniques, cohort survival is less valid beyond three years, and long-term enrollment projections must be updated frequently. Demographers develop ranges of long-term projections, showing what will happen if present trends continue, if the rate of children enrolling and remaining in the district increases, and if the rate of new enrollees and returning students decreases.

A variation of the cohort survival method goes beyond total district and building projections to forecast trends for subpopulations of the district, such as language-ethnic groups, children from low income families, and special needs students. Such reports are used by districts with diverse student populations to refine planning for special needs students and to project the total number of students in neighborhoods impacted by ethnic groups with higher birth rates.

A demographics consultant should be helpful in projecting subpopulation trends, as patterns in birthrates, immigration, and migration in these groups must be analyzed.

Some demographers utilize area economic data as a projection tool. Especially useful for large districts, this provides insight on trends in building permits for construction and employment. The results are typically used to account for economic changes that may impact school enrollments. A study for a suburban Chicago high school district by consulting demographer Jerome McKibben, Ph.D., combine the district's cohort survival history with "an assessment of the impact of factors such as fertility rates, housing patterns, mortgage rates, mortality rates, census data, migration patterns, unemployment rates and the dynamics of local private schools, while also taking elementary school feeder data into consideration." (*Glenbrook High Schools District 225 Enrollment Forecast Update, November 2016.*)

Table 19 illustrates the simple cohort survival method applied to grades K-3 of an elementary school district. The first step is to go back five years to compute trends.

Table 18
Five-Year Enrollment Trend

School Year	Kindergarten	Grade 1
5 years ago	438	455 (not added)
4 years ago	470	467
3 years ago	464	460
2 years ago	470	464
1 year ago	557	562
Current year	486 (not added)	486
Totals	2,399	2,439

Next, "cohort survival" ratios are computed for each grade transition (kindergarten to first grade, first grade to second, and so on). Inspection of the table shows that some kindergarten classes grew from the fall of the kindergarten year to the fall of first grade. The entering class of five years prior grew from 438 to 467, as the number of children entering the school was greater than the number leaving. However, the entering kindergarten class of four years prior, with 470 students, decreased to 460 by first grade. The class of three years prior remained at 464 students, where the classes of two and one year prior changed greatly in opposite directions as they went through the kindergarten to first-grade transition.

The "transition ratio" for each grade is computed as follows, using the kindergarten to first-grade transition as an example:

Over the five grade transitions, 2,399 kindergartners became 2,439 first graders. The ratio of first grade to kindergarten enrollments was 1.017, or a growth rate of 1.7%. This is the K-1 transition (cohort survival) ratio. Similar calculations are used to compute the historical ratios for each grade-to-grade transition. The ratios may be more or less than 1.00; it is common for schools and districts to show different patterns for different grade levels, reflecting moving patterns of families as the children grow older. Changes of 5% or more indicate a strong pattern of enrollment growth or decline.

The transition ratio is the tool for projecting future enrollments. This district has used a preschool census, community preschool and childcare enrollments, birth data from the Illinois Department of Public Health (and perhaps a demographer) to project its future kindergartens as shown. Applying the 1.017 multiplier to each projected kindergarten yields projected first-grade enrollments as shown in *Table 20 (next page)*.

The process is repeated to generate projections for each grade. Special needs populations can be estimated by taking their percentage of enrollment for recent years, increasing, decreasing, or holding it constant, depending on trends, and applying a percentage figure to compute future years' special population estimates.

As with any statistical procedure, the larger the sample, the more accurate the analysis will be.

Table 19
Five-Year Projected Enrollments

School Year	Kindergarten x 1.017	Grade 1
Current year actual	486	486
1 year hence	496	494
2 years hence	538	504
3 years hence	512	547
4 years hence	523	521
5 years hence	524	532

Cohort survival projections for an entire district will, in the long run, be more accurate than projections for any one year, or for any one grade or building. Principals especially should be alert for changes in their population trends that suggest modifications in cohort survival projections for their schools, to produce the most accurate and useful projections for staffing and other budgeting activities. Principals' research and intuition are essential to developing reliable enrollment projections.

Cohort survival projections are most valid where changes in a community's housing stock and/or turnover of homes are occurring at modest rates. They are less useful in times of rapid growth. Therefore, demographers projecting enrollments in districts experiencing a large amount of new housing construction have developed formulas that relate the size of a new home in bedrooms to the numbers and ages of children enrolling in schools.

Use of United States Census data for projecting enrollments is most useful for the few years following its availability every 10 years. If a community conducts a special census between the decennial counts, the results can be valuable to the schools if the special census breaks down child population by age ranges.

Schools report varied success with "child find" surveys to discover preschoolers. Door-to-door surveys miss many young families and others are reluctant to answer mailed questionnaires — or are unable to predict accurately if they will be living in the community when their children enter school. Surveys of local preschools and childcare centers are more useful. Birth data for counties is available from the Illinois Center for Statistics, which is accessed from the website of the Illinois Department of Public Health (www.dph.illinois.gov). From the DPH home page, do a search for IQUERY and select the information on birth rates. Call IDPH's Vital Records Division at (217) 782-6554 to determine whether birth information is available for the communities within your school district. If data by community are not available from IDPH, try the county or municipal health department.

Consider U.S. Census data by community and, if your district includes only portions of a community, by census tract also. Superimpose a district map on the census tract map to determine the tracts that lie in the district. The data on children six years of age and under will give you a preview of the size of future kindergarten cohorts. Compare the number of children counted in the census by age group with the district's corresponding grade level enrollments to ascertain the percentage of the child population attending public school. Apply that percentage to the census counts to reveal the numbers of children in private schools and home-schooled and factor that information into your enrollment projections.

Budgeting for Classroom Teachers

Staff salaries and benefits comprise 80% or more of most school budgets. Timely and accurate staff budgets are essential to the fiscal health and morale of the school. Their preparation is followed avidly by school staff members, and inconsistencies and perceived inequities within and among schools can be grist for parent complaints and lengthy board of education discussions.

Staffing is driven by formulas drawn from preferences for class sizes at different age levels, past practices, and collective bargaining agreements. It can also be influenced by the degree of autonomy granted to principals to develop staff plans. An example of formula-based staffing appears in *Table 21 (next page)*. Assume that the allocations reflect policies adopted by the board of education, past practices, and agreements with the union on average class size. Note that the formula includes provisions for teacher assistants.

The chart demonstrates some of the difficulties of budgeting for classroom teaching staff. In terms of enrollment, there are "nice numbers" and "nasty numbers." Take the second grade in the fictional Home Valley Schools district. Nice enrollment numbers are even or close multiples of an average desired class size range. If an average size of 20 is desired, nice total numbers of students are 40, 62, 81, and 104. They will produce classes close to the desired average.

Nasty enrollment numbers produce larger or smaller class sizes than desired. They are especially

Table 20

Classroom Staffing Guidelines for the Home Valley Elementary Schools Showing Enrollment and Number of Class Sections

Grade	Normal Range	Maximum Size	2 Sections	3 Sections	4 Sections
Kindergarten	18-23	26	27-52	53-78	79-104
Grade 1	17-22	25	26-50	51-75	76-100
Grade 2	17-22	25	26-50	51-75	76-100
Grade 3	18-23	26	27-52	53-78	79-104
Grade 4	19-24	27	28-54	55-81	82-108
Grade 5	19-24	27	28-54	55-81	82-108

Table 21
First Section Projection
Home Valley School — Next Year

Grade	Enrollment	Sections	Average Size
Kindergarten	72	4	18
First	67	3	22.3
Second	51	3	17
Third	64	3	21.3
Fourth	63	3	21
Fifth	42	2	21
Total	359	18	19.9
(Last year)	380	19	20

troublesome in small schools. Take a cohort of 52 second graders. You can make two sections of 26 pupils or three sections of 17-18 pupils. Parents and teachers may object to the classes of 26, especially if class sizes in other district schools run around 20. However, the cost of the third teacher and the possible difficulty of finding a classroom for the third section, not to mention setting a precedent for this cohort as they move through the upper grades, are even more troublesome. Administrators therefore seek flexibility in negotiating class size limits, supplementing large classes with teacher aides, interns, and other support personnel.

First section projections for the coming year can be prepared in the fall, based on projected enrollments. However, if the projections indicate an increase in the number of teachers due to students projected to enroll but not yet enrolled, it is wise to budget the position but not staff it until the children actually appear. If a cohort is expected to decrease sufficiently to drop a position but the children have not withdrawn by the spring, it is prudent to develop a plan to reassign or dismiss the teacher, but to keep the position in the budget until the actual enrollment and staff are known at the end of the summer. Classroom planning should also be flexible.

Budgeting for classroom and special teachers is intertwined with the school's schedule. A new principal should become familiar with the parameters that impact the schedule prior to staff planning for the following year. A fall staffing projection for an elementary school is illustrated in *Table 22 (next page)*.

The principal has two problems in staffing the school for next year. This year's fifth grade of 60 students (not shown on table) required three teachers; they will be replaced by only 42, requiring that a section be dropped. The second problem is more complex and involves a "nasty number." Only 51 second graders are expected next year. Putting them in two sections with 25 and 26 students will result in the largest classes in the school. Perhaps a teacher aide could be employed less expensively than adding a third teacher. Or perhaps a few advanced first-grade students could fill out a combined first and second grades section, resulting in more suitable section sizes for both grades. Having three sections of 17 pupils is educationally and politically more desirable but adds a teacher to the budget as opposed to the two-teacher plan. It will also have ramifications for staffing specialist teachers, as shown in *Table 23* on *page 100*.

Budgeting for Special Education Teachers and Pupil Support Staff

The first section projection serves as a starting point if clusters of special needs students are to join the regular classrooms. Special education staffing traditionally related teachers and support staff to the numbers of pupils in a resource or self-contained program. Current state regulations specify the number of pupils in a teacher's workload according to the severity of students' needs, and a process for developing a district's workload plan. Law and practice call for inclusion of special education with varying needs in "regular" classrooms. These regulations and practices affect the classroom staff plan and increase the amount of information that principals and special services administrators require to complete it. (Note: The applicable rules can be found in The Illinois Administrative Code, Section 226.730 Class Size for 2009-2010 and Beyond.)

Projecting special education enrollments is difficult, and it is common for schools to find themselves under- or over-staffed in this area as the opening of the school year approaches. Children receiving intensive special education services, and enrolled in classes or

Table 22

Projected Specialist Time

Home Valley School
Based on 9 sections per day (45 per week)
Calculated in 30-minute blocks per week

Allotment of Specialist Time in 30-minute Blocks per Week

Subject	Kindergarten	Grades 1-2	Grades 3-5
Music	1	3	2
Phys. Ed.	1	2	3
Art	1.5	2	2

Weekly Sections

Grade	No. of Sections	Music	Phys. Ed.	Art
Kindergarten	4	4	4	6
First	3	9	6	6
Second	3	9	6	6
Third	3	6	9	6
Fourth	3	6	9	6
Fifth	2	4	6	4
Total	**18**	**38**	**40**	**34**
No. days/week		**4.2**	**4.4**	**3.8**

included in regular education classrooms, are, as a group, a more mobile population than other children.

Principals, pupil services directors, and other administrators responsible for special education budgeting and staffing need to communicate regularly with teachers, psychologists, and other knowledgeable staff and to track the program plans of each special needs child. Surprises will occur; a family with several such children will enter or leave the school attendance area, or children will enter the program from another school district. Experienced administrators budget contingency amounts for additional special education staff and tuition that might be required during the school year.

The presence of children whose native language is not English can complicate staff and space planning. Staffing guidelines that are educationally sound and meet applicable regulations are required for such special population classes. Class size ratios will reflect the smaller numbers of students and/or multiple staff assigned to these classes. Further complications occur when instruction is offered in more than one model — for example both bilingual and dual language programs. Efficiency is gained if students from several buildings are combined into like groups. However, parents may resist transferring their children. In such cases, the administration and school board must be the spokespersons for the budget and necessary efficiencies.

Budgeting for elementary school "special" teachers, such as art, music, and physical education, takes into account the number of available weekly teaching periods for these subjects. If there is insufficient need for a full-time special teacher, consider if there are other needed assignments in the school or positions required in another school that can be effectively filled by the specialist. If not, perhaps the position can be budgeted at less than 100%.

A staffing projection for special subject teachers at the Home Valley School appears in *Table 22*. Note that the assignments begin with the specified time allotments for each subject for each grade, as spelled out in the school district's curriculum. Principals must be prepared to resist demands from specialist teachers to exceed these district-determined allotments at times when lower enrollments result in less than full-time assignments.

The budget for many support positions is usually independent of building enrollment. Principals, secretaries, health staff, librarians, psychologists, social workers, speech therapists, and resource teachers are often allocated on a per-school or caseload ratio basis, although non-teaching specialists may serve two or more schools.

ISBE's Evidence-Based Funding elements, shown in *Table 9* in *Chapter 6*, illustrate research-based staffing ratios of effective schools for teaching and non-teaching positions, which provide data with which to "benchmark" a district's own budgets. These comparisons can be a starting point for considering increasing or decreasing these expenditures. Evidence-based allocations for certain non-personnel expenditures, including instructional materials, professional development, and technology are shown in this chapter in *Table 23*.

Under some models of building-based budgeting, a single staff allocation would be created, from which the school's decision-making process would select classroom and specialist positions configured to meet the needs of its population. Such "wide open" staffing arrangements are rare, because practice, contract provisions, and state certification rules speak to traditional arrangements. However, more school systems are permitting limited trade-offs of specialist staff for generalists or specialists from other disciplines.

School-level autonomy in budgeting, where it has been successful, puts an accountability burden on the principal for results. It tests the principal's knowledge of the mix of staff competencies and material resources that make for effective instruction. The focus of the central office shifts from supervision to support in financial management skills and professional development.

An up-to-date budgeting procedure manual is a valuable resource for building and district administrators. Such a manual incorporates staffing formulas and related board policy and negotiated agreements, as well as procedures and allocations for non-personnel items. A new administrator should study it before the budgeting cycle begins. If there is no such manual, review of the budgeting communications and reports of the school for the past year will reveal much of this information. A meeting with the business manager to discuss the budget process will also be valuable.

Budgeting Supplies, Services, and Equipment

Allocation formulas and procedures for non-personnel items follow the budgeting philosophy of the school system and establish the authority of the school to make non-personnel budgeting decisions. In centralized budgeting, common formulas allot money to each grade level and special subject in the district. In a building-based budgeting process, a starting point for allocations to school budgeting units might be the evidence-based allocations suggested in the Illinois school funding formula. They are shown in *Table 24* on *page 103*.

Table 23

Illinois Evidence-Based Funding Guidelines

Per-Pupil Allocations for Selected Expendables and Equipment

Instructional Materials	$190
Gifted and Talented	40
Professional Development	125
Assessment	25
Computer Technology	285
Student Activities	
Grades K-5	100
Grades 6-8	200
Grades 9-12	675

The total allocations for each building would be assigned to grade levels, departments, and other budgeting units during the school's budgeting process.

Under building-based budgeting, principals have autonomy to modify the centrally determined dollar allocations; as long as the building's total allocation is not exceeded. In an even more decentralized form of building-based budgeting, the district office would compute a total building allocation based on each school's enrollment, and the principal would advise the central office how the money is to be distributed among the grade level and departmental budgets.

Some districts begin the budget process without fixed allocations, requiring each school to propose and justify budgets for non-personnel items. The budgets and justifications are reviewed by the central administration or perhaps by the entire administration, including the principals. Limits are then set, considering both the district's revenue situation and the priorities of the entire district and each school. While more democratic in appearance, such a process can lead to differences that are perceived as less equitable than formula-driven allocations.

Curriculum adoption material and technology and other budgetary decisions that follow a curriculum or program study process also require time for staff, administration, and board of education to weigh the need for these items along with other competitors for discretionary budget dollars. Budgets for one-time purchases, such as equipment, technology, and other capital items, often compete for the small amount of the annual budget that is truly discretionary. Such decisions are, therefore, often made last, following considerable administrative discussion and weighing of priorities. Boards of education tend to participate actively in decisions on curriculum changes and capital purchases. Such purchases are often part of a multi-year plan, and it is good practice to budget such items on a multi-year basis. This helps establish their priority position in subsequent years' annual budgets.

The budgeting philosophy for a school should be reflected in the monthly reports that are made available to principals and teachers. Otherwise, communication and accountability on budgetary resources cannot take place efficiently. If the unit of budgeting is the grade level, the accounting system of the district should produce reports showing budgets and expenditures-to-date for each grade, especially for the non-personnel items over which the principal and teachers have control. As budgeting becomes more decentralized, the accounting requirements become more complex. However, budgeting/accounting technology exists to support such decentralization, providing an important measure of accountability and control.

17 / Budgeting the Secondary School

This chapter describes a budgeting process for a secondary school. The budget process in secondary schools, due to their larger size and departmental organization, is characterized by greater faculty participation, especially for non-personnel items. Middle school budgeting follows a process that combines an elementary school and a high school approach. High school budgeting derives from the course of study which, in contrast to the curriculum of elementary and junior high schools, undergoes frequent review and changes in accordance with curriculum changes and student course selections. An example of a process for revision in the course of study appears in the chapter.

Enrollment Projections and Staff Budgeting

If a district contains only one middle/junior high school, drawing from all of its elementary schools, the cohort survival projections used for the elementary grades will likely generate accurate enrollment projections. Special education students counted separately in elementary enrollment reports will need to be factored into planning in accordance with the junior high's programs. Districts with two or more middle schools can aggregate the projections of the feeder schools to each building and should be alert to trends that may signal increases or decreases in enrollment in specific sending schools.

The starting point for high school enrollment projections is the cohort survival projections for the lower grades, which are extended to generate ratios through grade 12. Multi-campus high schools that draw from several junior highs or school districts require regular analysis of geographical trends within the district to determine the need for future boundary adjustments or construction. Adjusting school boundaries is a complex and time-consuming communication process, and the lead time for constructing new facilities can be three years or more.

Depending on the community, there may be a significant number of students who transfer from or to private schools between eighth and ninth grades. Keeping in touch with the district's middle school counselors, parents, and the private middle and high schools will lead to more accurate enrollment projections. Housing and economic factors may influence high school enrollment projections as in projecting elementary school enrollments. The movement of families into or within a high school district may be affected by housing availability within the desired area, home prices, and mortgage rates.

Examples of enrollment projection demographic work are available. Jerome McKibben's 10-year enrollment projection for Glenbrook High School District 225 in north Cook County, consisting of two schools, illustrates a multi-factor approach. It can be found in the agenda materials for the district's March 17, 2014 board meeting by searching for Glenbrook HS enrollment. John Kasarda's 10-year enrollment projections for the nearby New Trier High School District 203 build on the cohort survival method and projections for the sending elementary districts. Three sets of projections are developed based on assumptions on fertility rates, family migration rates, and housing turnover. Kasarda's 2014 report can be found by searching New Trier HS Enrollment Projections.

Projecting high school enrollments to determine annual staffing needs differs in one important respect from the lower grades. In addition to school-wide enrollment, historical projections by department and course are also required for staff planning, since high school teachers are generally certified in only one or two areas. The example presented in *Table 24* on the *next page,* from a hypothetical large high school, shows how the historical enrollment of one department is broken down for budget and staff planning.

Table 24

Historical Enrollment of One Department

Central Valley High School Enrollment/ Staff History — Mathematics Department

Year	Total Students	Class Sections	Staff (FTE)
3 years ago	2,885	125	25.4
2 years ago	2,945	127	25.6
1 year ago	3,019	129	25.8
Current year	3,110	130	26.0

Central Valley High School Enrollment — Freshman Advanced Mathematics

Year	Fall term	Winter term	Spring term
3 years ago	200	180	170
2 years ago	215	190	180
1 year ago	230	205	195
Current year	240	210	200

Since these are first-year students, the numbers in the "average" mathematics class would have increased as students entered from the advanced classes. It is common for enrollments in advanced classes, especially in first-year sections, to decrease and those in average-level classes to increase as students (or parents) who are stretching the limits confront reality.

The first table shows that total mathematics class sections and department staff have increased in approximate proportion to enrollment. This will not always be the case, for enrollment increases and decreases create plateaus when staff adjustments are not possible, and students can or must be scheduled within the same number of sections. Therefore, budgeting secondary school staff focuses on the total school student-teacher ratio, and must be done in concert with development of the school's coursebook and master schedule.

Aggregate enrollment, registration, and staff numbers commonly change at different rates. The total number of students may increase 2.5%, but the total number of class registrations may increase by 4%, reflecting a shift in the average number of courses taken by students in excess of their graduation requirements. Changes in the drop-out rate, trends in summer school course enrollment, and the number of students graduating at the midpoint of their senior year must also be considered in scheduling and staffing, as must special education and other special needs programs for the school's various populations. Combined with the realities of scheduling, this school's 4% increase in section registration might require a total staff increase of 5% or more. This is the figure that the district administration must deal with in developing the school's total staff budget.

Curriculum Change and the High School Budget

Enrollment and staff histories are a starting point for projecting the following year's staff and materials budgets. The budget must also reflect additions and deletions to the course of study. The disciplines taught in today's high school are expanding in scope and in means of differentiating instruction according to student's needs. Growth in staff and material expenditures results. Examination of the offerings for a suburban high school of 1,500 students shows more than 15 options for mathematics, social studies, world languages, English, and science. Each must be scheduled for one or more sections according to student needs, whether determined by achievement-based placement or student selection. Supply, equipment, room modification, and professional development needs accompany each addition.

The point of control over the course of study is the board of education approval process for changes. The decisions are required in the fall, so they can enter into master scheduling and faculty budgeting, assignment, and hiring during the winter. In October 2019, the Niles Township High School District 219 Board considered nine course proposals for 2020-2021 that were recommended by its Curriculum Standards for School Improvement Committee. Four were from the Engineering, Computer, Science, and Business department, and one each from the English, English Learner, Fine and Applied Arts, and Science departments. (Source: October 15, 2019 Board of Education agenda materials.)

The Committee provided for each proposed course a brief description, how the course addressed a documented learning need, how the proposal evolved, how the new course related to other courses in the department, the criteria for student entry, and plans for staff, logistics, and assessment.

Budget Decision-Making at the High School

Secondary school department heads have a greater influence in determining the specifics of the non-personnel budget than is the case for most elementary teachers. District control over the budgets for instructional materials, services, and equipment

Table 25

Home Valley High School Budget Summary*

The staff budget is shown in Full-Time Equivalent (FTE) teachers.
Enrollment = 2,000 students
The supply budget is allocated to departments based on student course registration.

Department	FTE Instructors	FTE Dept. Chairs	Total FTE	Change from prior year	Supplies
Art	2.8	0.2	3.0	0.0	$ 12,500
Business	2.8	0.2	3.0	0.0	$ 4,000
Educational Services	7.5	0.5	8.0	0.5	$ 13,000
English	15.0	1.0	16.0	1.0	$ 12,000
Writing lab	1.0	0.0	1.0	0.0	$ 3,000
Reading lab	1.0	0.0	1.0	0.0	$ 4,000
Family/Consumer science	2.8	0.2	3.0	0.0	$ 21,000
Foreign language	11.5	0.5	12.0	-0.5	$ 7,600
Industrial technology	2.8	0.2	3.0	1.0	$ 9,000
Mathematics	15.0	1.0	16.0	1.0	$ 5,000
Vocal music	3.0	0.1	3.1	0.0	$ 4,000
Instrumental music	2.6	0.1	2.7		$ 16,000
Physical education	8.5	.5	9.0	-0.5	$ 9,500
Driver education	1.5	0.0	1.5	0.0	$ 4,000
Health	1.5	0.0	1.5	0.0	$ 3,800
Science	15.0	1.0	16.0	1.0	$ 32,000
Social studies	14.0	1.0	15.0	1.0	$ 7,800
TPI/ESL	2.0	0.0	2.0	0.5	$ 3,000
Subtotal	**110.3**	**6.5**	**116.8**	**5.0**	**$171,200**
Activity Director	0.5	0.0	0.5	0.0	$ 6,000
Inclusion Facilitator	1.0	0.0	1.0	0.0	$ 3,500
Chapter I Director	0.5	0.0	0.5	0.0	$ 2,300
Deans	2.0	0.0	2.0	0.0	$ 3,000
Guidance	7.0	1.0	8.0	0.0	$ 20,000
I.M.C.	2.0	0.0	2.0	0.0	$ 35,000
Nurse	1.0	0.0	1.0	0.0	$ 2,800
Social Workers	2.0	0.0	2.0	0.0	$ 2,800
Subtotal	**16.0**	**1.0**	**17.0**	**0.0**	**$ 75,400**
School total	**126.3**	**7.5**	**133.8**	**5.0**	**$246,600**
FTE/Staffing ratio	15.8		14.9		
Principal/APs/AD	3.0		3.0	0.0	$ 85,000
Athletics					$ 75,000
Grand total	**129.3**		**136.8**	**5.0**	**$406,600**

* Ed Hoster presented this table format at a Loyola University class in 2004.

may be exercised by determining the total amount for each campus. Principals assume responsibility for allocating the total budget among the school's various departments and priorities. The school's administrative team and department heads may act as a group in making or advising on such allocations.

In a more centralized approach, each department makes its annual budgetary case to the principal and district office, which must sift through the priorities and make budgetary decisions. In either case, decisions on major expenditures, especially curriculum changes and capital items, usually require board of education discussion and approval. Even in a centralized budgeting approach, decision-makers are advised to consult with department heads who have knowledge of the increasingly varied and changing high school curriculum and its needs for specialized materials and equipment.

The principal and curriculum administrator play a critical role in long-term budgeting for high schools. They are knowledgeable of the big picture — trends in department curricula, total enrollments, student course selections, accreditation standards, college admissions requirements, teacher preparation and competencies, and the many other factors that enter into planning the high school program. It is important, therefore, that they understand the school district's total financial picture, the costs of the school's various programs, and especially the cost implications of changes, both those proposed internally and those imposed externally.

A secondary administrator or department head new to budgeting responsibility should examine the supporting documentation and communications behind several recent years' budgets as a guide to building a timetable, database, and procedures for future budgeting. Examination of practices in other schools is useful, especially when the new administrator is undertaking a change in the school's budgetary decision philosophy. The National Association of Secondary School Principals (www.nassp.org) offers publications on budgeting and related secondary school management activities.

As with the elementary schools, the elements of the Illinois Evidence-Based Funding model, shown in *Table 9* in *Chapter 6*, include ratios for teaching staff, counselors, administrators, and support staff and dollar allocations for instructional materials, technology, student activities, and other budgetary components. Representing the practices of successful schools, they are useful benchmarks for evaluating the secondary school budget and identifying changes for future consideration.

A Sample High School Budget

Table 25 on *page 104* illustrates a high school department staffing plan and supply budget. The format also lends itself to a district with multiple schools, displaying comparisons of staffing ratios and supply budgets among the schools.

18 / Budgeting and Managing Non-Instructional Costs

This chapter discusses the budgeting and cost management of building operations, security, transportation, food services, purchasing, insurance, and administrative costs. Tables at the end of the chapter provide budgetary benchmarks that will enable the reader to compare a district's budget for instructional and non-instructional services to the FY 2020 cost survey of the National Center for Education Statistics (www.nces.ed.gov). Helpful resources on support services are included in Appendix A. The sections on building operations, transportation, and food services include information on how these services and their costs have been affected by the COVID-19 pandemic.

Cleaning and Maintenance

Controlling building operating and maintenance costs requires active management to assure that the money available for building care is best spent to preserve and protect the building structures and systems. On average, 9-10% of the total budget for operating the school program is expended for building cleaning and maintenance, supplies, and utilities. While age and condition of the buildings may cause these expenditures to consume a higher percentage of the district's funds, the averages are useful benchmarks with which to assess the quality and efficiency of the building care program.

A quality building care program will provide the proper allocation of personnel between cleaning and maintenance. In a well-cared-for school, daily care of buildings and grounds requires about 40% of the budget for building operations. Repairs and maintenance require about 20%. Utilities average 33%. Supplies and equipment require about 7%.

Quality building management requires attention to selection, training, standards, schedules, supervision, and safety. Buildings and grounds directors and principals should work together to determine the standards and selection criteria for new staff. Principal involvement in interviewing applicants and selecting personnel for custodial positions will pay off in establishing positive working relations among the custodians, faculty, and principal.

Training for day and evening staff should include an orientation to their areas, duties, techniques, and schedules for caring for each type of space and safe work practices, including mandated training on asbestos and toxic substances. Supervision involves observations and evaluations during their initial weeks, and regularly scheduled evaluations thereafter.

Prepare cleaning schedules for each area and type of room showing the schedule for rooms cleaned several times during the day (bathrooms and entryways), and for those cleaned on a daily, weekly, monthly, quarterly, or annual basis. Invest in quality equipment and supplies. Even well-trained custodians will be inefficient when equipment and supplies do not match the materials to be cleaned in their areas.

Document the schedule and techniques for critical tasks that, if neglected, can cause severe and expensive problems. An example is the cleaning or changing of filters and maintenance of motors in heating/cooling equipment. These tasks are subject to neglect, unless they are described in schedules specifying the frequency when they are to be performed. Poor maintenance of filters and motors is a common and preventable cause of heating/cooling system failure. Custodians can do much of this work if they are trained in how and when to do it.

The staffing guidelines of the American Physical Plant Association (APPA) shown in *Table 26* on *page 107*, provide a benchmark for measuring the needed

Table 26
Cleaning Staff for a 75,000-Square-Foot Building

Description of Area	Square Feet in Building	Cleaning Level	APPA Sq. Ft./FTE for Area Type	FTE Staffing
Bathrooms and Kitchens	7,500	1 Orderly Spotlessness	8,500	.88
Entrances and High Visibility/Need Areas	8,000	2 Attentive Cleanliness	16,700	.48
Classrooms and Normal Use Spaces	47,500	3 Ordinary Cleanliness	26,600	1.79
Mechanical, other	2,000	4 Safe and Adequate	39,500	.29
	75,000	Total Staff for Building		3.45

Total daily hours @8 hours/FTE 27.6

Average square feet/FTE 21,739

Source: Adapted from recommendations of the American Physical Plant Association (APPA) and a presentation at the 2017 IASB/IASA/IASBO Joint Annual Conference by Kerry Leonard and Ken Roiland.

---

levels of custodial staff. They are expressed as the number of square feet cared for by a full-time custodian. Districts can adapt the benchmarks to suit their resources and expectations and the characteristics and uses of the buildings.

The number of staff is determined by designating the level of cleaning required for each area on a scale, ranging from:
- Orderly spotlessness (level 1) appropriate for kitchens and bathrooms;
- Attentive cleanliness (level 2) for preschool, kindergarten, and special needs classrooms;
- Ordinary cleanliness (level 3) for other classrooms and large areas; and
- Safe and adequate cleanliness (level 4) for storage areas and mechanical rooms.

The total daily hours required for the school are then calculated based on the area for each type of space, as illustrated in *Table 26*. The hours are then divided between day and evening schedules and are assigned to workers.

On average, a full-time custodian can clean from 20,000-25,000 square feet of an elementary school to a standard that is acceptable to most stakeholders. The benchmark for high schools, with larger spaces that lend themselves to more efficient cleaning, ranges from 25,000 to 30,000 square feet per worker. Where a school falls on this range will depend on such factors as the cleaning standards established by the district, the age of the students, and the types of surfaces (especially floors that may require more or less cleaning time), and the quality of the training, equipment, and supplies that are furnished.

Day custodians will clean a smaller area, since they have responsibilities for lawn and playground care, responding to student emergencies, and assisting in the lunchroom. Evening custodians will clean the bulk of the building's space. Where budget constraints require that custodians service larger areas, consideration can be given to cleaning lightly used rooms on a less-than-daily basis.

Supplies and equipment comprise 10% of the average Operations and Maintenance budget. Careful attention to the safety, quality, appropriateness, and inventory of supplies and equipment is necessary. Equipment and supplies must be matched to the materials on which they will be used. Otherwise, they will not achieve the desired results and flooring and whiteboards may be damaged. Standardization of quality products among schools and central purchasing and distribution will work to contain supply expense. To protect the integrity of the district's purchasing process, building personnel should be instructed on procedures for purchasing and dealing with salespeople and cautioned not to order outside them.

Illinois law (105 ILCS 140/10 et seq.) requires schools to use environmentally safe (green) cleaning products, "when it is economically feasible," posing a challenge to facility managers to comply with the law, respect community and staff opinions on "green cleaning," and control the cost of cleaning supplies.

Outsourcing custodial services may reduce labor costs, but issues of supervision, compliance with standards, and efficiency must be considered when evaluating the pros and cons of contracting. The post-pandemic labor market has required contractors to increase wages and benefits which has reduced the cost differential between district-employed and contracted personnel.

Some districts will use district-employed staff during the school day and employ contract cleaners for evening work, perhaps employing a night supervisor in high schools and other buildings with heavy evening use by student and community groups. Other districts outsource building services management along with cleaning and maintenance or as a stand-alone service while retaining district-employed workers. As with all other contracts, defining specifications and standards of performance when the services are bid is critical to gaining cost savings from contract cleaning without harming the condition of the building.

In preparing bid specifications for contract services, specify hiring standards and procedures that are comparable to those practiced by the district. Clearly specify the requirements and responsibility for conducting required criminal background and reference checks and reporting findings to the district prior to employment. While contractors may have employed personnel that they have placed in non-school assignment and intend to assign to the school, do not assume that their pre-employment checks comply with the laws and policies affecting the school. Insist that the contractor have on-site management, have a district administrator perform regular inspections with the contractor's manager, and have a short-notice termination clause in the contract if performance turns out to be unsatisfactory. Also be aware that Illinois law places limits on contracting of non-instructional services to third-party vendors when the work is currently performed by a district employee. Consult an attorney if such action is being contemplated.

Skilled maintenance by district staff and contractors consumes about 20% of the average building operating budget, approximately half of the amount required for cleaning. The APPA guidelines for staffing for maintenance suggest levels for different quality levels and functions required of maintenance staff. Highly trained staff adept in trade skills and performing preventive maintenance and repairs of complex equipment might be service 50,000-75,000 square feet per worker. They would be compensated at a higher rate than general maintenance workers performing work requiring less skills, including caring for outdoor parking and athletic facilities. Such workers might be staffed at one position for each 100,000-150,000 square feet of building space, depending on the size of the outdoor facilities to be maintained.

Heating and cooling equipment and controls are increasingly complex and computer-driven, with specialized repair requirements best performed by an outside company. Custodians can train to perform minor electrical and plumbing repairs and lock work, but major projects require expertise and equipment not found in most school maintenance departments.

Maintenance-management programs and software are available to assist building directors in scheduling preventive maintenance, prioritizing and assigning work orders, and accounting for staff time and supplies. Use of such programs facilitates efficient use of the maintenance budget.

Work often performed by skilled maintenance staff can be less expensively performed by "general maintenance workers" and includes such tasks as installing cabinets or shelving, painting, classroom equipment repair, and transporting items between schools. Purchasing ready-made classroom fixtures, deferring painting until it can be performed by summer staff, or employing delivery drivers or using bus drivers between runs frees up maintenance staff for the work that keeps a building and its systems functioning well.

Some principles apply to managing maintenance in both large and small facilities.

- Preventive maintenance (PM) is preferable to and less expensive than emergency repairs and should be scheduled for each building component.
- Heating, ventilating and air conditioning systems, roofs, and fire safety systems are priorities for PM.
- Playgrounds, athletic areas, laboratories, and communication and security systems require regular safety inspections.
- PM requires training, supervision, and inspection to assure its performance.
- Contract outside firms as opposed to using district staff for less frequently required service of components and systems.
- Develop a cadre of locally based quality firms which will respond quickly to emergencies.
- Plan for maintenance when designing facilities and replacing building equipment.

- Continuously update maintenance plans and priorities.
- Pay special attention to safety and security for off-hours users of school buildings and grounds.

Tools for Managing Cleaning and Maintenance

The following publications will help the school district develop policies and standards, organize work, and train staff:

- The U.S. Environmental Protection Agency at www.epa.gov (search for schools) offers information on identifying and remediating many types of building problems, including air quality, pest management, and environmental issues.
- Operations and Maintenance Best Practices Guide, available as a download from the U.S. Department of Energy Federal Energy Management Program at www.energy.gov, describes computerized maintenance management systems, the pros and cons and techniques of various types of maintenance programs, predictive maintenance technologies, the commissioning process, and other topics. The agency's website also contains information on project financing sources and other topics pertaining to energy use.
- Planning Guide for Maintaining School Facilities, published by the National Center for Education Statistics is available at www.nces.ed.gov/pubs2003/maintenance.

Utilities

Utility budgeting involves the uncertainties of predicting the weather and the volatile market for electricity and heating fuels. Energy, utilities, and trash disposal average 30% of the budget for building operations. Keeping and studying records of utility consumption by building by month will identify operating inefficiencies or equipment malfunctions that contribute to higher costs and may identify a safety hazard. Records will also assist the building budget administrator in projecting costs for the coming year. If energy expenses are excessive, consider using a consultant who will train the staff on conservation measures and identify procedural and equipment changes that will reduce utility costs. The New Guide to Operating and Maintaining Energy Smart Schools can be downloaded free of charge at www.energy.gov.

Costs of electricity and fuel fluctuate with national and world market conditions as well as with climate variations. Good budgeting practice includes looking at climate and consumption data and utility expenses over a 3-to-5 year period and building in contingency amounts in the event of unusually hot or cold weather or a sudden spike in prices.

Joining a cooperative may reduce utility costs. One statewide cooperative is the Illinois Energy Consortium. It is an energy purchasing program sponsored by the Illinois Association of School Boards, Illinois Association of School Administrators, and Illinois Association of School Business Officials. Information can be found by contacting one of the sponsoring member associations.

Repairs and Replacement of Building Systems

A comprehensive plan for major repairs and replacement of building systems is the guide for the annual budget for capital maintenance. It is the product of an audit of the condition of a building's major systems. The facility audit identifies needed repairs, their costs, and anticipated schedule over the coming 3-to-5years.

Table 27 on page 110 shows the anticipated life of a building's systems.

Maintaining the Building Structure and Site

An inspection schedule and plan for repairs and maintenance of the building interior and external structure completes the information for the maintenance budget.

Interior components:
- Walls
- Ceilings
- Windows, doors, and hardware
- Carpet and hard flooring
- Built-in fixtures and equipment
- Stairs, elevators, and lifts

Exterior components:
- Foundations
- Masonry, brick, and block walls
- Structural steel
- Concrete slabs, walks, and driveways
- Roofs and soffits
- Drainage and sewer treatment systems
- Lawns and turf, including artificial turf on athletic fields
- Playgrounds
- Fences
- Trees and shrubs

Table 27

System Design Life in Years

Plumbing	HVAC	Electrical	Low Voltage	Fire Protection
Pumps, water heaters 20	Heating, ventilation and cooling equipment 30	Service, switches 35	Fire alarm devices 15	Pumps 20
Distribution pipes 35	Distribution pipes, ducts 35	Distribution, panels 35	Fire alarm wiring 25	Backflow preventer 30
Waste pipes 40	Terminal devices 25	Terminal devices 20	Communications 20	Piping 40
Fixtures 25	Controls and automation systems 15	Lighting 20 Wiring 45	Technology 10	Sprinklers 20

Source: Presentation by Kerry Leonard and Kenneth Roiland to the Annual Conference of the Illinois Associations of School Boards, Administrators and Business Officials, November 23, 2019.

Each year's inspection report will identify the work to be budgeted for the near term. A priority ranking system will assist in refining the budget to identify immediate need and work that can be postponed. Such a system might prioritize work as: 1) necessary to student safety and building integrity; 2) required to meet environmental law or building codes; 3) necessary to meet educational program requirements; 4) preventive maintenance; 4) projects to reduce annual utility and maintenance costs; and 5) aesthetic improvements.

Because the needs of several buildings may be contained in the plan, the decision on the maintenance budget requires that the board be informed of the administration's recommendations on the priority projects at each location. Some board members may have expertise in building matters and need to be heard during the budget discussions. Others may question the priority ranking based on interbuilding equity. It may be helpful to begin the discussion with a proposed total capital budget for the year, and to organize the discussion according to the priority ranking system described above.

The capital plan is a dynamic report, updated and discussed annually with the board. As projects for the year are selected, budgeted, bid, and completed, the report is revised to reflect needs not yet met, and new needs identified during the most recent facility audit. Thereby, the board and administration are creating a continuously updated five-year plan and budget. A decision can then be made if meeting priority needs can be funded by annual revenues or if a borrowing or other financing plan is required.

The management of building and grounds care and maintenance has become increasingly complex and professionalized. Building and grounds director positions are hard to fill, and some districts are developing in-house talent drawn from their cleaning and maintenance staff. The Illinois Association of School Business Officials has developed training programs for facilities specialists that cover the technical, financial, legal, and personnel requirements of these positions. Information on the program can be found at the Illinois ASBO website, www.iasbo.org.

Transportation

On average, transportation costs consume 4-5% of the total operating budget. There are wide variations; rural districts' transportation costs run higher, while small suburban districts may transport only a few students on two or three buses and spend far less.

Transportation costs are increasing at a rate greater than inflation. A nationwide shortage of drivers has resulted in higher wages and benefits. Fuel costs rose sharply in early 2022 when war in Europe curtailed petroleum shipments. Vehicle costs also increased. A standard-sized bus equipped with seat belts costs $90,000 or more. Larger-capacity "transit-style" buses with flat fronts can run $125,000 or more. A 27-passenger bus equipped with a wheelchair lift costs around $60,000.

Transportation is funded by a combination of state aid, property taxes, and student fees, with the mix varying widely according to the type, size, and property wealth of the district. State aid is calculated on an equalizing formula based on the number of students who live more than 1.5 miles from school or who live within areas that have been approved by the district and state as "hazardous" for walkers. A district may also be reimbursed for bus service to students who would otherwise traverse areas with a pattern of criminal gang activity.

State aid for transportation ranges from $16 for a wealthy district up to 80% of eligible costs for a district with a low tax base. Costs for transportation of students attending vocational programs and for transportation of students with disabilities are reimbursed at up to 85% of eligible costs.

Transportation taxes in non-tax-capped districts are limited by state-specified tax rates. (See *Table 4* in *Chapter 3* on *page 21*). In tax-capped districts, where a single limiting tax rate applies to the operating funds, the total rate must be apportioned among all the operating funds, including transportation. Because property tax receipts and state aid are insufficient to cover transportation costs and in the interests of pupil safety and parent convenience many districts offer fee-supported transportation to students who live within 1.5 miles of school. Rising costs have caused some districts to increase the proportion of transportation costs funded by fees, which can run several hundred dollars a year per child.

The following procedures will assist the transportation administrator to keep the program within its budget.

- Fill the bus and reuse it as many times a day as possible. Begin with an analysis of the efficiency of the present program. A benchmark for efficiency is 60%-70% of capacity. If a 65-passenger bus (at three to a seat) is running to an elementary school with only 25 passengers, look for options to consolidate the route with other underutilized buses. It can cost $50,000 or more in personnel and vehicle costs to put a bus and driver on the road for a year. Each bus run, vehicle, and driver saved is a substantial reduction in the budget.
- Examine trip pairing and double runs to reduce costs per student and increase bus utilization. Staggered starting and closing times at two schools permit additional trips for much less cost than adding vehicles and drivers. Double runs where buses make two runs to a school in the morning and two in the afternoon also save money but create supervision problems and increase costs. Offering early morning and late afternoon trips for students participating in activities will take some ridership pressure away from other runs.
- The most efficient transportation system serves elementary, middle, and high schools with the same vehicles. Contracting transportation maximizes the opportunity for efficient vehicle utilization when buses are used by more than one district, although it will impose scheduling restraints.
- Utilize drivers efficiently. When the labor market permits, hire as many drivers as possible on a part-time basis, with a cadre of full-time drivers to cover noon-hour kindergarten and field trips. Offer full-time drivers employment in other roles when they are not required to transport students. This will make them eligible for insurance and other benefits and increase retention.
- Save fuel by using the smallest suitable vehicle for trips with fewer riders, including noon-hour kindergarten trips, inter-school shuttles, and travel by clubs and small teams. Train operators in fuel-efficient driving and enforce regulations limiting engine idling.
- Control special education transportation costs. Special education students can cost four to ten times more to transport. The transportation administrator should work with the special education staff to develop cost-sensitive guidelines for when special transportation is necessary and work to maximize vehicle utilization within reasonable riding time limits.
- Charge school budgets for field trips and sports and extracurricular activity trips. Many of these costs will pass through as participant fees, reducing the drain on scarce budget revenues. Consolidate such trips where possible to reduce costs.
- Consider frequent, even annual, vehicle replacement, or leasing as opposed to purchasing buses. Districts that keep their buses only for the warranty period reduce maintenance costs and can make do with fewer spares, since breakdowns are infrequent. Leasing also provides greater flexibility in adjusting fleet size to ridership and reduces the impact on the capital equipment budget when several buses must be replaced.
- In 2022 the annual lease cost for a 71-passenger bus was in the range of $16,000; a 22-passenger bus could be leased for about $11,000 a year. Joint bidding with other districts and purchasing under a state contract may reduce acquisition costs.

- Consider electric buses. Districts that have tried them are reporting higher reliability and lower maintenance costs. The buses can provide emergency power to schools when they are not in use, and return electricity to the grid, lowering utility costs. While the cost of an electric bus is more than a petroleum-fueled one, grant programs exist to assist with the cost of conversion. Check out current costs, funding sources and the experience of "early adopting" schools before deciding. The Illinois Energy Consortium (IEC) collaborates with several manufacturers and bus dealers to bring electric school buses to price parity with diesel.

The Illinois State Board of Education offers manuals on transportation operations, including vehicle specifications, driver qualifications and training, route safety information, and special needs transportation. The manuals can be obtained at www.isbe.net/transportation.

Safety and Security

School safety and security has a nexus in almost every area of the school budget and is a priority for all school districts.

State law requires school districts to have a threat assessment team and a board policy on targeted school violence prevention. A state School Safety Working Group issued recommendations to make schools safer, including communication and information sharing, hardening of school facilities, response protocols, and training for staff. Recommendations from the School Safety Working Group of the Illinois Terrorism Task are available from the Illinois Emergency Management Agency website, ready.illinois.gov. A comprehensive school policy on school safety is included as part of the Illinois Association of School Boards PRESS policy subscription service.

Grants may be available from the State Board of Education (ISBE) to support school security improvements, including professional development, safety-related upgrades to school buildings, equipment, and facilities. Additionally, school districts can use revenue provided by the County School Facility Occupation Tax for school security personnel, such as school resource officers, and mental health professionals. Additional information on the County School Facility Occupation Tax can be read in *Chapter 9*.

Based upon the recommendation of the Federal Commission on School Safety in 2018 (www2.ed.gov/documents/school-safety/school-safety-report.pdf), the U.S. Departments of Homeland Security, Education, Justice, and Health and Human Services created a central school safety clearinghouse website at www.schoolSafety.gov to share actionable recommendations to help schools prevent, protect, mitigate, respond to, and recover from emergency situations. Topics include bullying/cyberbullying, student mental health, school climate, threat assessment, emergency planning, security, recovery, and drills.

There are four ways to improve security: 1) upgrade building or site features; 2) add electronic security devices; 3) increase personnel; and 4) improve school climate. The best solution is often a mix of two or more of these measures. The list below identifies low-cost means to protect property and improve security. The comprehensive list of cost-saving measures was developed in 2008 by the National Clearinghouse for Educational Facilities (ncef.org) under a grant from the United States Department of Education.

- Prepare facility emergency information for administrators and first responders and keep the information current. Building maps including the location alarm, utility shutoffs, fire hose boxes, and other features are part of this information.
- Clearly define school property with signs, vegetation, and fencing.
- Trim shrubbery, remove trees, and relocate trash containers to eliminate hiding places and provide a clear field of sight throughout the school grounds.
- Prevent access to windows and roofs by trimming trees and relocating objects that can be used as climbing devices, including dumpsters and light posts.
- Secure roof hatches, access panels, skylights, etc. from the inside.
- Ensure that fire hydrants and hose connections are visible and unobstructed.
- Inspect the buildings and grounds and make immediate repairs to damage inside or outside the building. This demonstrates respect and helps prevent the spread of vandalism.
- Inspect regularly and repair outside lighting and its controls. Reset lighting during the year as necessary based on times of sunrise and sunset.
- Keep bus and car access separated from building and play areas by curbs, removable bollards, or gates that allow emergency vehicle access. Clearly mark and separate visitor parking in an area visible from the school, preferably the office.
- Clearly mark and give directions to the main office where you require visitors to report.

- Screen fresh air intakes; when designing the school, locate them at least 12 feet off the ground.
- Identify, light, tie down and restrict access to and underneath portable classrooms. Provide them with emergency communications to the school office and outside, as well as the legally required fire alarms.
- Limit use of building entrances to one or as few as possible. Require that all other entrances, including delivery entrances, be opened with a key or fob.
- Inspect all exterior doors regularly; the doors, framing, and hardware take a beating. Consider replacing them with stronger doors and frames.
- Install face plates on exterior doors to prevent jimmying.
- Install fisheye viewers in exterior doors lacking windows or sidelights.
- Institute and enforce strict control of keys and fobs, employee identification cards that open doors and combinations to keypads.
- Require that night custodians, at the end of their shifts, check that all doors are locked by walking around the building and testing them from the outside.
- Only after consultation with the fire department, separate school areas from joint use facilities such as gyms with doors and locking devices, making sure that there are at least two unlocked egress points from all areas.
- Number doors and rooms in a logical, sequential floor-by-floor pattern to aid emergency responders and place those numbers on building maps provided to responders. Consider displaying room numbers on outside windows.
- Remove identifying signs such as "mechanical room" from areas where intruders could create serious problems, but identify the rooms on emergency maps.
- Regularly inspect all windows accessible from street level for damage and faulty hardware and make repairs immediately.
- Be sure that all exterior "emergency windows" are operable and are not blocked by equipment, landscaping, or other obstacles.
- Install motion detectors inside the school in areas attractive to intruders, including offices and technology centers. Instruct occupants in these rooms not to use ceiling decorations or other features that can wave back and forth when heating systems come on at night, triggering a police call.
- Lock unoccupied rooms and spaces during the school day.
- Consider keeping door latches in the locked position so that teachers can secure their rooms by simply pulling doors shut.
- Keep corridors, stairs, stairwells, and exits clear of obstructions and flammable materials.
- Be sure that all decorative materials and classroom furniture (chairs, sofas etc.) are flame retardant. Prohibit teachers from furnishing their classrooms with their home discards, which probably do not meet fire codes.
- Limit displays of teaching materials and artwork to no more than 20% of wall space in the interest of fire safety. Observe a stricter limit if specified by local codes.
- Provide secure controls over corridor, stairway, and restroom lighting.
- Work with your architect and fire inspector to be sure that all spaces in the school requiring two exits have, in fact, two functioning exits. Remodeling, if not properly designed and constructed, can compromise this essential safety feature.
- Routinely check that exit signs are visible and illuminated.
- Check that fire alarms and extinguishers and other fire safety components are in working order and that staff members are trained in how to use them.
- Check that clear and precise evacuation maps and instructions are in each room, and that the maps show at least two evacuation routes.
- Install a panic alarm at the reception desk and within the school office.
- Instruct principals and administrative staff on the location and operation of the shut-off switch for the heating/ventilation system. There may be more than one such system in larger buildings or buildings built in stages over the years.
- Ensure that radio frequency (RF) communication is possible throughout the building. Test this with local emergency responders. Repeaters can be installed to reach "silent" areas.
- Install battery or portable generator backup power supplies for telephones and emergency communications.
- Provide back-up emergency lighting in stairs, hallways, and interior rooms.

In addition to these measures most, if not all districts are adding secure entrances to future construction projects. These entrances should mitigate an intruder's ability to enter the school. Many secure entrances use a vestibule/double entry system that requires visitors to pass through the main office prior to accessing the secondary entrance of the building. This requirement creates a delay that would allot staff additional time to notify the authorities of a potential threat and implement intruder response plans.

> **Upgrading Security and Plans to Respond to a Shooting Event**
>
> In 2022, Highwood-Highland Park District 112 upgraded its security plan following a mass shooting at the July 4 parade in downtown Highland Park. The upgraded plan was incorporated into a successful November 2022 referendum to borrow $111.4 million to modernize the district's schools. The referendum request was increased by $6 million to fund security improvements including:
> - Exterior electronic door sensors/controls – $660.000
> - Repairs and upgrades to interior locks – $3.3 million
> - Posts to divert traffic away from buildings – $380,000
> - Alert systems, panic buttons, strobe lights – $360,000
> - Two-way radio replacements and upgrades – $150,000
> - Security window treatments – $1,600,000
>
> The district also developed a plan to help students and staff during the opening days of school. The plan included:
> - Restriction of media access to students and staff.
> - Therapy dogs during the first days of school.
> - ALICE training (Alert, Lockdown, Inform, Counter, Escape) is to be provided to students on an annual basis.
> - Annual active shooter drills
> - A weekly Social Emotional Learning check-in for all students, with teacher feedback.
> - Regular emails to parents, staff, and community.
> - Communications on social media.
>
> Sources: North Shore School District 112 Community Newsletters (August, and September 2022), and www.alicetraining.com.

Food Services

Child nutrition programs are among the most heavily regulated aspects of school operation, with local health departments, the Illinois State Board of Education, and the U.S. Department of Agriculture (USDA) issuing regulations and auditing the cleanliness of facilities and compliance with rules governing the nutritional and financial aspects of the program

Under normal circumstances the budgetary goal of school food services is a break-even operation from meal receipts and federal and state subsidies. Deficits must be made up from the Education Fund. This fact has given districts special incentive to assure that meal programs meet their expenses from program revenues. Recent increases in food prices and a scarcity of labor have required districts to raise the cost of paid meals and to take measures to increase participation by making the menu more attractive to students. School food services management requires skills that are difficult to find in today's labor market. Many districts contract for food services programs to achieve experienced management and lower food and supply costs from bulk purchasing.

Public Act 12-1101, effective July 1, 2022, exempts food service agreements from the lowest responsible bidder requirement. To qualify for the exemption the district must make a good faith effort to give preference to contracts that: procure healthy food, comply with U.S. Department of Agriculture's nutrition standards, give preference to locally-sourced products, give preference to suppliers who use producers that adopt USDA hormone and pest-management practices, give preference to suppliers who value animal welfare and increase opportunities for businesses owned and operated by minorities, women, or individuals with disabilities. (Source: Franczek.com, July 12, 2022)

The following procedures will assist the district in planning and budgeting the food services program:

Modify menus as necessary to meet student demand and increase sales. Much of the lunch program budget consists of fixed costs for labor and equipment, and additional food sales are money in the bank. Children's tastes vary, and the more diverse the school district, the greater the impact of ethnic group preferences.

Districts must also offer options for children who observe vegetarian and low-fat diets. Bills have also appeared before the legislature that would require any state-operated facility that provides food services to offer halal and kosher food options upon request.

Table 28

2023-2024 School Food Service Program Reimbursement Rate

Lunch Program

	Less Than 60% Low Income	Less Than 60%* + 8 cents	60% or More Low Income	60% or More* + 8 cents
Paid	$0.40	$0.48	$0.42	$0.50
Reduced-Price	$3.85	$3.93	$3.87	$3.95
Free	$4.25	$4.33	$4.33	$4.35

*Requires a one-time menu certification

The maximum price for a reduced lunch is $.40

Breakfast Program

	Non-Severe Need	Severe Need**
Paid	$0.38	$0.38
Reduced-Price	$1.98	$2.43
Free	$2.28	$2.73

The maximum charge for a reduced breakfast is $.30.

* The higher rates of lunch reimbursement apply if 60% or more of the lunches served during the second preceding school year were served free or at a reduced price.

**The higher rates of breakfast reimbursement apply if 40% or more of the breakfasts served during the second preceding school year were served free or at a reduced price.

Consider breakfast programs, especially in schools with early starting times. Since much of the cafeteria labor is in place to prepare lunches, breakfast prices can be established to cover food costs with an increment for supervision and equipment. The Childhood Hunger Relief Act requires districts to operate a breakfast program in each building in which 40% or more of the students are eligible for free or reduced-price lunches. Districts can petition their regional superintendents to opt out if federal subsidies would not cover the costs. Federal School Breakfast Program reimbursements for 2022-2023 ranged from $2.26 to $2.67.

Eliminate unnecessary kitchen equipment. Older school kitchens were built for the menus of 30 to 40 years ago. Large ovens, mixers, and freezers may no longer be necessary to prepare current menus. Some districts construct one or more central kitchens to prepare meals to be delivered to smaller schools. Substantial savings in labor and equipment costs result; however, menu items that do not transport well may have to be eliminated.

Use federal and state subsidies. Rates change every year on July 1 for the coming school year and are available on the website of the Illinois State Board of Education (www.isbe.net). Rates for 2023-2024 reimbursements are found in *Table 28*.

Charge the lunch program for maintenance and utilities required to operate the kitchens, which would otherwise be paid from the Operations and Maintenance fund. That fund, along with other operating funds, is under pressure from higher costs and the constraints of the tax cap.

Benefits and Insurance

Health and dental insurance costs are increasing above the rate of inflation, and increased premiums are expected to put pressure on salary increases when negotiations on new contracts occur. In budgeting health and dental insurance costs, financial administrators must examine provisions of employee contracts to determine how future premium increases are to be allocated between the district and employees. If the agreement calls for a constant dollar payment on the part of the district, the burden of increases falls entirely on the employees. If a percentage division is called for, the premium increase falls on the district. It is important to keep in touch with the district's health insurance representative so that the budget is realistic and to negotiate more favorable premium rates if possible. In negotiating with employee unions, propose policy changes, including increasing co-payments and deductibles, providing incentives for using managed care plans, institution of health reimbursement and savings accounts, and modifications in prescription drug and mental health benefits. Some districts are offering employees wellness benefits and disease management programs.

Group life and long-term disability insurance rates are lower than health insurance rates. Consider offering higher life and disability insurance benefits and encourage employees to sign up for disability benefits to preserve their accumulated sick leave. Also consider long-term care insurance, which is especially important as the average age of teaching staff has been increasing over the past few years.

Property, liability, and workers' compensation insurance premiums experience cycles of increase and decrease. Rates reflect the district's claims experience and the money market. Premiums tend to rise when interest rates are low, since companies earn less on their invested reserves. Periodic reviews of property insurance deductibles may offer premium savings if the district were to assume the risk for minor damage and burglary claims.

Regular appraisals of buildings and property are necessary to assure full protection in the event of a catastrophic claim, as well as to meet current accounting standards. Statement 34 of the Governmental Accounting Standards Board (GASB) outlines these requirements. Information can be found at www.gasb.org.

Health, property, liability, and workers' compensation insurance are offered by groups of districts that self-insure some of the coverage. Among those pools are those sponsored by the Illinois Association of School Boards. Information is at www.iasb.com.

Debt Service

Tax levies for bond principal and interest are calculated at the time debt is issued. A schedule of future levies is filed with the county clerk, who will extend them each year to be sure the funds are available when required. The tax levy form certified by the district has a line at the bottom where the district notes the number of bond issues outstanding for which levies are to be made. County clerks check this number against their records. If the numbers do not agree, the district's and the clerk's records need to be reconciled to assure that the clerk extends the required amount. County clerks will add a percentage to the levy to cover "loss and costs." That percentage can range up to 10%. This assures that funds will be available to meet debt payments, when due, in the event of a shortfall in collections.

Traditional dates for payments on bond principal and interest are June 1 and December 1. Because levy years and fiscal years do not coincide, the financial administrator may want to consult the district's bond advisor in developing the debt service budget.

Administrative Costs

Building and central administrative costs are budgeted separately on the Illinois budget form. Central administration budgets include salaries and benefits for superintendents, assistant superintendents, business administrators, and office staff. Also included are board of education expenses, including legal and audit. Building administrative costs include principals, office staff, supplies, and purchased services contracted for by principals. In Illinois, district and building administrative costs together constitute 9% of the operating budget. Costs that exceed these guidelines may indicate a district that is undergoing growth or undertaking a major reorganization requiring additional leadership to assure the success of the change.

State law imposes "administrative cost caps" which limit the annual increase of certain non-instructional administrative expenses to 5%. Provisions for low expenditure districts and waivers exist in the law (105 ILCS 5/17- 1.5). Certain expenses are exempt; budget makers should be aware of the capped and exempt classifications when constructing central administrative budgets. (See the Administrative Cost Cap Calculation in the Annual Financial Report and ISBE's Mechanics of a School District Budget.

Using Budgetary Benchmarks

It is useful to compare a school district's total budget for the educational program and support services to those of districts similar in type, location, and size. Districts' budgets can be found on their website and are also posted on the ISBE website. Compare the amounts and percentages of the operating budget assigned to the regular educational program, special education, building and district administration, building operations, and

Table 29

Illinois Per Pupil Expenditures by Function, FY 2020

Area Function		
Instruction	$10,819	62%
Student Support	1,312	8%
Staff Support	661	4%
General Administration	658	4%
Building Administration	913	5%
Operations & Maintenance	1,378	8%
Transportation	715	4%
Food Services (a)	407	2%
Other	620	3%
Total	$17,483	100%

(a) Most expenditures for food services are offset by sales and government payments.

Source: *Revenues and Expenditures for Public Education FY 2020, Tables 3 and 4*, NCES Publication 2022-301 at NCES.ed.gov.

transportation. Individual district characteristics and priorities will account for some of the observed differences, but the comparisons may reveal areas for study to determine if resources can be shifted to instruction. State law requires school districts with websites to post their budgets, making it easier to obtain comparative cost data.

Comparing Your Budget to Others

The National Center for Education Statistics, www.nces.ed.gov, publishes a report on total operating expenditures for elementary and secondary education, by function and object. The data provide a useful benchmark for comparing a district's current budget and trends for the major expenditure categories to other Illinois districts. The report excludes expenditures for capital outlay, interest on debt, community services, private school programs, adult education, and others not related to the operation of the K-12 program. Data are shown in *Table 29*.

19 / Expenditure Management and Control

Management of expenditures, especially those not directly related to instruction, is an annual responsibility of the board and administration to ensure that always-limited resources are put to their most effective use to achieve the goals of the school. When times are tough, expenditure management shifts to a higher intensity, and a systematic plan to review and reduce expenditures is required. At such times, board members and administrators must be ready to deal with personal stress.

This chapter offers suggestions for budgetary processes and communications when tough decisions must be made, and for cost-reduction techniques applicable to educational and support services. Other suggestions on cost containment in support services will be found in *Chapter 18*. The final part identifies practices and programs that research shows to be effective and cost-efficient as an additional guide to decisions on resource allocation.

Processes and Communications

- Maintain two-way communications with the community, staff, union leadership, and public. These lines are especially important in times of crisis.
- Educate the board, staff, and community on the school budget.
- Develop team skills and spirit among the administration and board of education.
- Make it clear that budget cuts are the responsibility of the board and administration, not the result of a plebiscite of special interests.
- Hold periodic brainstorming discussions among administrators and with staff to review ways of operating programs more efficiently.
- Make the budget document understandable. A clearly presented budget lends itself to critical analysis as well as citizen understanding and participation.
- Consider community surveys and meetings, but judiciously, and only if you are prepared to act on the results.
- Look for opportunities to share services and facilities with other public agencies, such as park districts, for the mutual benefit of the agencies and their clients.
- Make budget development a year-long process, with time to review each of the major assumptions as they are made and to consider carefully the benefits of new expenditures and/or means of reducing expenditures.
- Keep current on new ideas to reduce costs. *The School Administrator* (www.aasa.org) and *School Business Affairs* (www.asbointl.org) have articles on processes and techniques for budget reduction, and for maintaining a positive climate during times of stressful financial decisions. *The Illinois School Board Journal* (www.iasb.com) features articles from the school board perspective.

Educational Program Expenditures

- Consider the long-term impact of cuts on students and the long- and short-term impact on the budget.
- Perform regular evaluations on programs to examine their costs and benefits, and to seek alternative means of meeting a program's objectives. Use program budget cost data, the results of research and evaluation, and productivity benchmarks in making decisions.
- Look at the big picture from time to time. Are the district's schools organized to make the most efficient and effective use of staff, buildings, and other resources, or is a study of that question in order? A multi-year study of facility needs in North Shore School District 112, in Highwood and Highland Park, examined many aspects of the educational program, school organization, and building utilization, and concluded in a plan to close some buildings while modernizing and meeting needs for infrastructure replacements in the others. The district retained its current grade organization

and designated some buildings as dual-language academies. Some of the study papers describe alternatives accompanied by research findings and extensive decision rubrics. The study papers are available at www.nssd112.org.
- Rank expenditures by priority categories, such as programs mandated by law, services necessary to pupil health and safety, costs for non-mandated programs or other district goals, and those for community services.
- Take the long view when considering the addition of new programs. Project the costs out for several years, being generous with your assumptions on expenditures and cautious in your assumptions about revenue — the same attitude to have when doing long-term budget projections.
- Implement no new programs unless they are replacements for existing ones.
- Seek cuts that eliminate "structural deficits." These are repeating costs or those with built-in annual increases, as opposed to "one-time" savings.
- Establish short-term remediation programs where possible in lieu of placing students in expensive long-term special education, remedial classes, and other non-time-limited compensatory programs. Multi-Tiered Systems of Support (MTSS) is such a monitoring and instruction approach to help students who have difficulty learning.
- Look for redundancy and overlap in remedial programs and cost out and assess the effectiveness of each, selecting the most cost-efficient ones to retain.
- Increase (or avoid reductions in) class size except where present ratios are educationally unsound and resources exist to fund reductions. Class size is the single most powerful medicine or poison in controlling the education budget. Establish and adhere to class size guidelines for each grade and subject. Combine grade levels or use teacher assistants instead of additional teachers where class sizes exceed limits by increments that might not require an additional section.
- Monitor the efficiency of schedules of elementary and secondary schools so that unneeded sections are avoided.
- Place special education pupils with low-incidence handicaps in district-operated programs where possible, gaining educational benefits as well as savings in expenditures for transportation, overhead, and communications required for distant placements
- Educate the staff on special education law and service requirements. Focus, on a case-by-case basis, on seeking lower-cost alternatives. Use the help of the local attorney to seek mediation and avoid expensive legal proceedings.
- Perform especially intensive budget reviews on services that are not directly related to instruction.
- Consider school-based management of selected budgetary resources, to place as many decisions as possible — and as the school is ready to make — close to those who work with children.
- Become familiar with the growing body of research on cost-effectiveness of educational expenditures, and adopt that state of mind when performing budget reviews or considering new programs and other expenditure increases. Start with the book by Lawrence O. Picus, *In Search of More Productive Schools*. Follow the work of the Consortium for Policy Research in Education at www.cpre.org.
- The Illinois Evidence-Based Funding (EBF) model is built on research on effective practices, including class size, staffing ratios for support services, and per-pupil expenditures for non-personnel items that are associated with successful school district. The EBF description in *Chapter 6* includes a summary of this research.
- Lengthen curriculum review and textbook adoption schedules. Consider lower-cost electronic editions, technology-based curriculum packages, and other alternatives to expensive paper texts.

Personnel Costs

Keep current on the market for area salaries in all positions, so that schedules are established and negotiations conducted with knowledge of these markets.
- Exercise control in hiring and in establishing salary schedules. Salary administration requires a balance to meet the district's long-term faculty needs.
  ◦ Salaries for beginners need to be competitive to attract quality candidates, especially in hard-to-staff schools and in specialties such as technology, special education, and English-language programs. Otherwise, most new hires should be brought in at the lowest rate required to meet the qualifications for the position. Career compensation must be sufficient to attract and retain quality teachers, especially in hard-to-staff specialties.

- Revisions in the Illinois Teacher Retirement System establish a Tier II category that advances the age at which teachers can retire with maximum benefits and makes other changes in retirement rules. A teacher hired at age 22 in a district with a 20-step salary schedule to its maximum could conceivably work at that salary level for 25 years, to age 67, receiving only annual adjustments related to the cost of living. Districts are making adjustments in step increments, salary lanes, and schedule length to retain experienced teachers who might otherwise leave for positions with more attractive mid- and end-of-career compensation. Such adjustments must be implemented in such a way as to treat less-experienced staff in an equitable manner.
  - Some of the cost increases from enhancing the salary plan as described above can be offset by reducing the number of lanes and relating them to factors other than credit hours of study. Achieving National Board Certification, performing leadership responsibilities, high levels of classroom performance as objectively evaluated, and serving as teacher mentors and instructional coaches would replace graduate work as a basis for salary advancement.
- A paper, *Do More, Add More, Earn More*, outlining comprehensive teacher compensation reforms, is found at the website of the Center for American Progress, www.americanprogress.org.
- Project the costs of proposed contract terms over a multi-year period to determine their affordability. Establish multi-year adjustments to institute in the early years those components with the lowest cost, postponing higher-cost provisions until later years.
- In projecting teacher and support staff salaries, factor in the effect of 2019 changes in the minimum teacher salary law and the Illinois Minimum Wage law.
  - The teacher law increases the minimum salary in phases to $40,000 in the 2023-24 school year. As the minimum increases, negotiations to raise other salaries to maintain experience increments will be required. The result will be a higher overall percentage increase in the salary budget than market and cost of living factors might otherwise have produced.
  - The Illinois Minimum Wage law increases the $10 an hour 2020 minimum wage in annual dollar increments until it reaches $15 an hour beginning January 1, 2025. Negotiations of districts' support staff salary plans must consider the mandated increases and the effects they will have on rates for experienced staff and on differentials based on wage rates for the different classifications of employees. As with teachers, increases above recent trends will need to be factored into budget projections and staffing plans.
- Exercise control of benefit costs by resisting the expansion of benefits, self-insuring or pooling where cost and risk factors are favorable, and by competitive shopping for insurance coverage. Avoid indexing benefits to salary schedules and percentages of benefit costs. Rather, offer a fixed amount that must be renegotiated in future contracts.
- Use part-time personnel where possible with resulting savings in salary and especially benefit costs. Control overtime and sick and personal leave days.
- Impose and enforce controls on overtime.
- Consider retirement incentives where replacement of experienced personnel with lower-cost beginners is feasible.
- Contract with other schools or private agencies for professional services, including student services that are less frequently utilized.
- Audit payrolls and benefit participation regularly to catch errors, including overpayments and benefits to ineligible persons.

Purchasing and Support Services
- Use the internet as a tool for purchasing instructional supplies and other "commodity" items such as office supplies, paper, custodial supplies, and furniture.
- Use limited authorization purchasing cards, such as the Illinois ASBO-sponsored P-Card, to reduce the time and costs associated with small purchases. Establish procedures and checks to assure that the cards are used for intended purposes.
- Form purchasing cooperatives for supplies and equipment. Solicit donations or low-priced purchases from businesses; form school-business partnerships for mutual benefit.
- Consider using vendor-established purchasing cooperatives to simplify bidding of furniture and other supplies. In such arrangements, a vendor who otherwise might be competing with others

disqualifies itself and assists the district in preparing specifications, securing competitive quotations, and in evaluating them.
- Order in sufficient quantities to gain quantity pricing but take deliveries during the year to reduce storage requirements and retain use of the district's money as long as possible. Eliminate vendors that offer poor services, charge high delivery fees, or are used infrequently.
- Plan equipment purchases carefully, purchase quality equipment, such as computers and machinery, and consider life-cycle costs over the long-term for staffing, maintenance, and replacement.
- Maintain accurate but efficient systems for inventorying supplies and equipment to control hoarding and over-ordering. Freeze allocations for supplies other than basic all-student materials for one or two years to encourage use of existing materials.
- Control the costs of copiers and other equipment and services that require large initial investments and usage charges.
- Decide if one-time expenses, such as for technology improvements, can be "ridden out," perhaps by reducing costs in the subsequent year to restore the fund balance.
- Consider contracting out non-instructional services (building cleaning and maintenance, food services, transportation) to reduce costs and secure specialized professional management of these functions. Consider the same approach with some administrative services. Benchmark these services against accepted norms relating personnel to enrollment and facilities size and costs in comparison with the total budget. Note that the Illinois School Code places numerous restrictions and requirements on subcontracting for non-instructional services. Consult the school attorney before embarking upon subcontracting.
- Examine administrative and non-instructional personnel job descriptions to identify redundant functions, short spans of control, and excess layers of management. Use technology to streamline these functions and to permit management to focus on the instructional program and the most necessary and productive functions of management. Hire generalists rather than specialists where possible and organize work accordingly.
- Invest in energy-efficient building equipment and lighting, and retrofitting or replacing older equipment that is expensive to operate and maintain. Examine the costs and benefits of geo-thermal systems, wind power, and other technologies.
- Avoid short-term solutions, such as cutting back on building maintenance, which will hauntingly return with higher costs in the future.
- Perform efficiency studies of bus routes and consider altering school schedules or joint transportation services with other districts to maximize the use of school buses and drivers.

Research on Effective Practices

The following practices have been identified in the literature as researchers' favorite methods of improving student achievement:

- Recognize that a student's home background is responsible for roughly half of his/her achievement and that high-quality preschool experiences also exert great power on later school success.
- Focus on reading and math, especially acquisition of reading skills in the early primary grades and mastery of concepts before moving to the next level.
- Employ trained tutors to set students on the right academic track, saving money by reducing the need for expensive long-term special education and remedial services.
- Invest in the best available teachers, specialists in their fields, and make them more effective at the beginning of their careers through staff development and mentoring programs. Then continue to invest heavily in intensive professional development. Research shows that quality professional development has an extremely high beneficial effect on student achievement.
- Reduce adult-to-student ratios in the primary grades, especially first grade, through smaller class sizes and/or employment of trained teacher aides. Such measures are effective when teachers are trained to teach in a manner that uses the additional resources effectively, including active engagement of students in language-development activities.
- Consider the beneficial relationship between smaller schools (1,000 or fewer for high school and 500 or fewer for elementary schools) and test scores, student attitudes, student-faculty relationships, and ties to the community. If schools must be larger, consider subdividing them into units to achieve the advantages of smaller schools.

- Increase the amount of time for learning by such means as significant lengthening of the school year as well as the school day by one hour or more. Offer enrichment programs such as before- or after-school activities or turn them over to community groups or private teachers who can work with children outside of the school day.
- Set measurable goals and be accountable by evaluating the success of the school towards attaining them.
- Consider the "whole-school" curriculum; link across grades and subject areas where such organization works towards higher achievement of rigorous and specifically defined goals of skills acquisition.
- Experiment with and evaluate uses of technology in instruction to identify both effective and counter-productive practices.
- Alleviate conditions that inhibit learning by providing meal programs and health services to children whose school progress is affected by poor nutrition and lack of access to preventive medical care. Such services have provided substantial assistance to families impacted by the pandemic and its upset to family incomes and schedules.

20 / Long-Term Expenditure Projections

The purpose of this chapter is to describe methods by which a district can develop expenditure projections to guide its budget planning for future years. It is suggested that it be read along with *Chapter 10* which covers long-term revenue projections.

Developing an Expenditure History

Step 1 for projecting expenditures is development of a cost history for personnel (salaries and benefits), services, materials, capital items, and other costs which do not fall within these categories. The source of this information is the district's Annual Financial Reports, which are completed each summer following the close of the fiscal year on June 30.

An example of a historical expenditure report for the Education Fund is shown in *Table 30* at the end of this chapter. For each object line, calculate the percentage increase beginning with the first year's expenditures and concluding with the current year's budget. For example, the total increase in salary costs over the period from year FY2018 to FY2023 is $6,753,000 or 35%. Dividing the total increase by 5 produces a rounded average percentage increase of 7%. Repeat the process for the other expenditure categories. In the example, it produces average percentage increases of 12% for benefits, 5% for services, 3% for materials, 9% for equipment and 11% for other expenditures. The total budget increase over the five-year period was 38%, which is an average annual increase of 8%.

The table also shows the district's enrollment and Full Time Equivalent (FTE) teaching staff for the past five years. Enrollment increased from 1,750 to 2,000 students or 15% over the five years, which is an average increase of 3%. Accompanying that increase was an increase in FTE of 2%.

Using a similar method, develop expenditure histories for the Operations and Maintenance, Transportation, and Municipal Retirement/Social Security Funds. Beginning in FY2020, these histories will reflect pandemic-related expenditures for personnel, services, and capital items. These "one-time" expenditures need to be considered in determining the percentage to be used in projecting costs for the coming year. Some may become "permanent" while others will phase out as the pandemic's effects on student learning are remediated and as capital improvements to improve school building health are completed. Expenditures that will phase out should not be considered in future year projections.

Projecting Future Education Fund Expenditures

Step 2 is to develop assumptions for projecting expenditures for the coming five-year period. Districts with stable enrollments can prepare projections through trending recent years' expenditures. If enrollments are trending up or down, estimate the effect on staff numbers, and project costs accordingly. In the example, the projected enrollments and teacher counts increase at annual rates of 3% and 2% respectively a year. Enrollment data should consider new birth data and may consider data obtained through the use of a demographer. See Chapter 16 for more on enrollment projections.

Expenditure projections should be revised annually to reflect current information on enrollment, program modifications, personnel count, employee contracts and major capital expenditures. As this chapter is written, the rate of inflation has reached 8%, a level not seen since the 1990s. Annual projections should be updated each year to reflect the then-current rate of inflation and estimates of inflation for the coming five years.

Projecting Expenditures for the Other Funds

Historical costs and projections for the Operations and Maintenance and Transportation funds include salaries and benefits for district-employed personnel and

Table 30

Education Fund Expenditures

Historical Education Fund Expenditures ($ in thousands, % rounded to nearest whole number)

Object	FY18	FY19	FY20	FY21	FY22	FY23	Inc.	Avg.
Salaries	5,000	5,250	5,513	5,898	6,311	6,753	35%	7%
Benefits	600	642	687	769	862	965	61%	12%
Services	300	318	337	347	358	368	23%	5%
Materials	400	412	424	437	450	464	16%	3%
Equipment	200	216	233	252	272	294	47%	9%
Other	700	784	878	940	1,005	1,076	54%	11%
Total	7,200	7,622	8,072	8,644	9,258	9,920	38%	8%
Enrollment	1,750	1,800	1,850	1,900	1,950	2,000	15%	3%
F.T.E.	100	102	104	107	110	112	12%	2%

Projected Education Fund Expenditures ($ in thousands)

	FY23	Inc. %	FY24	FY25	FY26	FY27	FY28
Salaries	6,753	1.07	7,226	7,732	8,273	8,852	9,471
Benefits	965	1.12	1,081	1,210	1,356	1,518	1,701
Services	368	1.05	386	406	426	447	470
Materials	464	1.03	478	492	507	522	538
Equipment	294	1.06	312	330	350	371	393
Other	1,076	1.11	1,194	1,326	1,472	1,633	1,813
Total	9,920	1.08	10677	11,496	12,383	13,344	14,386

Assumptions: Enrollment will increase by 3% each year. Teacher count will increase by 2% each year.

---

services, supplies, and capital items. If building cleaning and maintenance and transportation are contracted, the salaries and benefits for the contracted workers are categorized as services. Historically, annual increases in personnel costs for non-licensed personnel have generally mirrored those for licensed personnel. In recent years, however, increases in inflation, and the effects of labor shortages must be considered in developing projections for ancillary staff including custodial, maintenance, food service, and transportation.

Some districts are replacing petroleum-fueled buses with electric buses. While the cost of an electric bus can be upwards of three times that of a gasoline or diesel bus, they may bring with them operational advantages, cost offsets, and funding opportunities which are discussed in *Chapter 18*. If a decision is made to convert a bus fleet, future-year projections need to be adjusted to reflect the consequent operational and capital expenditures.

Projections for the Illinois Municipal Retirement and Social Security funds will mirror the projections of non-teaching personnel salaries. Projections should also reflect the recent history of the IMRF-calculated employer contribution rate for the district. Projections of debt services expenditures will consist of the obligations determined at the time the debt was issued.

Since there are many uncertainties in projecting revenues and expenditures, it is common for two or three sets of projections to be developed and discussed by the board of education. Each projection reflects different assumptions about revenue trends, enrollment, expenditure changes, and inflation. In presenting projection reports, an accompanying narrative should clearly spell out the assumptions behind each set of projections. Projection data should be presented in tables rather than in detail. Simple graphs should be used to illustrate total revenues, expenditures, and the resulting changes in fund balances. If the projections suggest action to increase revenues, such as a referendum or borrowing, these options should be clearly defined and include a timetable for consideration.

21 / Looking at the Big Picture

Recognizing the Danger Signs

Achieving financial soundness begins with an annual fiscal self-examination. A more frequent review is required if events signal deterioration of revenues or increases in expenditures. The Illinois State Board of Education (ISBE) publishes an annual School District Financial Profile, which places each school district in one of four categories based on calculations of five critical indicators. The method for calculating the index can be found at www.isbe.net/Pages/School-District-Financial-Profile.aspx, as can the profiles of all Illinois school districts.

The indicators, which are calculated from end-of-year data on the school district's Annual Financial Report, are described below. Each of the five indicators is calculated and the results are slotted into one of four categories, with four being the highest. Each of the five indicators is then weighted. The sum of the weighted scores determines the financial strength designation.

The five indicators of financial health are:

- Ratio of fund balance to revenue, which is the result of dividing the ending fund balances by the revenues for the Educational, Operations and Maintenance, Transportation, and Working Cash Funds. The IMRF/Social Security Fund is included only if the ending balance is negative. This ratio indicates the overall financial strength of the district for the prior year and the four previous years and counts for 35% of the overall financial strength score. A ratio equal to or greater than 25% places the district in category four — the highest category.
- Ratio of expenditures to revenue, which is computed by dividing total expenditures for the Educational, Operations and Maintenance, and Transportation funds by the revenues for the same funds plus the Working Cash Fund. This ratio identifies how much a district expended for each dollar received, and counts for 35% of the district's overall score. The calculation also takes into account remaining balances of these funds at the end of the year if the district scores low in the expenditure-to-revenue ratio. This helps the score of a district that is spending accumulated funds for a special project or one that maintains large fund balances. The highest category (four) requires that a district spend less than it receives.
- Days of cash on hand is computed by dividing the total cash and investments on hand by the district's average daily operating expenditures. It provides a projected estimate of the number of days a district could meet expenditures without receiving additional revenues or borrowing money. It counts for 10% of the overall score. Having at least 180 days cash on hand earns category four.
- Percent of short-term borrowing ability remaining is computed by subtracting the amount of tax anticipation warrants from the statutory amount of authority to issue such warrants. It counts for 10% of the overall score. Having 75% or more of borrowing ability earns category four.
- Percent of long-term debt margin available is computed by subtracting long-term debt from the statutory general obligation debt limit. It counts for 10% of the overall score. As with short-term borrowing, having 75% or more of borrowing ability earns the highest category (four).

The overall financial strength score is the sum of the five weighted scores. It ranges from 4.00 down to 1.00. The score places the district in one of four categories, which determine the degree of state intervention in its financial affairs:

- Financial recognition, which is awarded for a score of 3.54 to 4.00, means the district requires little or no review or involvement by ISBE, unless requested.
- Financial review, the result of a score between 3.08 and 3.53, results in a limited ISBE review, including examination of the next year's school budget for potential downward trends.
- Financial early warning, assigned for a score of 2.62 to 3.07, brings close ISBE monitoring and

technical assistance. The district is reviewed to determine if it meets the criteria to be certified in financial difficulty and possibly qualify for a Financial Oversight Panel.
- Financial watch, which results from a score lower than 2.62, results in more intensive state monitoring and financial assistance and review for certification of financial difficulty and a Financial Oversight Panel. See *Table 31* for the Distribution of Districts in 2020 and 2012.
- *Figure 10* below shows an example of the Financial Strength Profile report for Elgin U-46. The report was prepared along with the annual audit and submitted to ISBE for review, including any commentary the district wished to add, and approved by the State Board of Education in the following spring. Districts in EBF Tier 1 are the neediest of funds to achieve adequacy.

Recognition of the early warning signs of financial difficulty and implementation of a remediation plan may prevent the district from reaching even the first level of state certification. It will also provide the time needed for a considered review of expenditure priorities and development of a plan to increase revenue.

The danger signs listed below supplement the financial difficulty indicators currently employed by ISBE. They must be considered together in the overall assessment; for example, adoption of an unbalanced budget is less troublesome if cash balances are high and/or the deficit is due to capital expenses that will not repeat in future years.

- Adoption of an unbalanced budget for two or more consecutive years.
- Expenditures in an unbalanced budget that are "structural" or have repeating increases built in for future years, as opposed to one-time capital expenditures.
- A cash-on-hand position at the opening of the fiscal year that is insufficient, when combined with budgeted revenues, to meet monthly expenditures without short-term borrowing. The threshold depends on the schedule of revenue receipts, but an opening cash position of at least 90 days of expenditures is desirable. The upper limit on the balance is a function of the district's overall financial circumstances and board of education policy.
- Stagnant or decreasing property tax revenues as a result of lack of growth or deterioration in the property tax base.
- Non-compliance with a school board policy on fund balance.
- The district is subject to the property tax cap, especially if new growth is minimal and the district lacks authority to issue non-referendum bonds. This authority, for schools subject to the tax cap, is conferred and limited by the individual district's history of non-referendum borrowing. See *Chapter 11* for more information on borrowing options.
- Employee contracts with built-in increases in salary and benefit expenditures that exceed foreseeable increases in revenues.
- Enrollment is increasing at a rate that requires additional staff.
- Shortages of space are developing that require construction of new facilities, especially if a referendum will be necessary to fund the new facilities.
- Building maintenance expenditures are rising as a result of deferred maintenance, the age of the schools, and obsolescence.
- The district has engaged in repeated short-term borrowing for program operations and is approaching its legal debt limits, or is using "teachers' orders" as part of its financing strategy.
- Voters have turned down a recent proposition to increase the education fund tax rate or to borrow money for program operation.
- One or more major sources of revenue, other than property taxes, is showing a trend of major decreases, including state aid or grant funds.

Figure 10
Financial Strength Profile of Elgin U-46

Indicator and Weighting	Data Year 2021	Data Year 2020
Balance/Revenue 35%	1.40	1.40
Expend/Revenue 35%	1.40	1.40
Days Cash on Hand 10%	.40	.40
Short term Borrowing 10%	.40	.40
Long term Borrowing 10%	.30	.30
Total Weighted Score	3.90	3.90
Designation	Recognition	Recognition
% of Adequacy/EBF Tier	61% Tier 1	Not shown

- Financial mismanagement has occurred, including non-emergency expenditures without budgetary authority, budgeting and payroll errors resulting in higher than budgeted expenditures, and misappropriation of funds.

Focusing on the Big Picture

The events above are warning signs, not indicators of financial doom. Districts in financial distress normally get that way over a number of years. While they may budget and spend with restraint, revenues do not keep up with even modest spending increases. Deficit budgeting is not uncommon; even the most well-managed district will probably experience a deficit at some time.

It is essential that the superintendent, business official, and board of education be able to interpret the school district Annual Financial Report (AFR). The AFR is an audited statement of operations for the previous fiscal year, along with a statement of the district's fund balances. It contains a number of queries designed to signal impending financial difficulty, which may activate the state review procedures described above. Information on ISBE's website describes the purpose and components of the report.

Inexperienced administrators will want the auditing firm to assist in analyzing the AFR for signs of financial difficulty and to suggest necessary actions for the coming year. The most necessary of these actions is initiation of long-term planning to increase revenues and prompt communication to the board of education, staff, and community of the district's financial outlook and options to restore financial health. The Illinois Association of School Business Officials (www.iasbo.org) offers human resources, including experienced business manager mentors and certified public accountants that are available to assist superintendents and financial administrators in interpreting financial and audit reports.

Illinois schools are blessed with a number of "safety valve" measures that enable them to engage in short-term borrowing in hopes of a brighter revenue picture. These measures are described in the section on borrowing in *Chapter 11*.

Some of these measures provide cash for only a few weeks or months, until infusions of tax revenue are received. Then the borrowed money must be repaid. Other measures allow a school to borrow money to build a cash balance and repay it with new taxes. If the district resists the temptation to spend this borrowed money quickly, the cash cushion generates interest revenue and prevents an occasional unbalanced budget from creating a fiscal crisis and program curtailments. It is important in interpreting financial reports to be aware of the extent to which cash balances include borrowed money.

Table 31

School District Financial Profile Ratings

Distribution of Districts

Designation	Fiscal Year 2020	Fiscal Year 2021
Recognition	728	749
Review	101	74
Early Warning	16	14
Watch	6	14
	851	851

Source: Illinois State Board of Education

Annual Financial Report – Supplemental Reports

Deficit Reduction — If the result of the annual audit reflects a deficit, the district shall, within 30 days after acceptance of the audit report, submit a deficit reduction plan. The deficit reduction plan is required when the operating funds result in direct revenues being less than direct expenditures by an amount equal to or greater than one-third of the ending fund balance. That is, if the ending fund balance is less than three times the deficit spending, the district must adopt and file with ISBE a deficit reduction plan to balance the shortfall within three years unless such a plan has already been required and completed in the annual budget form. (105 ILCS 5/17-1)

Improving Fiscal Efficiency — All school districts and joint agreement entities are required to report attempts to improve fiscal efficiency through shared services or outsourcing as defined in the Annual Financial Report (AFR). The report must be approved by the school board and published on the school district or joint agreement website, if any. (105 ILCS 5/17-1.1)

Source: Illinois State Board of Education, School Business Services Memorandum, June 2012

Table 32
FY 2019 Education Fund Balances

HISTORICAL SUMMARY AND FUND BALANCE ($ in thousands)

	Year 4	Year 3	Year 2	Year 1	Last year	Current budget
Opening balance July 1	$2,866	$7,261	$7,509	$7,588	$7,364	$6,700
7/1 balance/expenditures	40%	95%	93%	88%	80%	68%
Revenues	7,595	7,870	8,151	8,420	8,594	8,796
Expenditures	7,200	7,622	8,072	8,644	9,258	9,920
Operating surplus (deficit)	395	248	79	-224	-664	-1,124
Transfer from W.C. fund	4,000	0	0	0	0	0
Ending balance, June 30	7,261	7,509	7,588	7,364	6,700	5,576

In anticipation of a trend of deficits, the district closed its Working Cash Fund into the Educational Fund at the end of prior year 4, thereby increasing the fund balance by $4 million. The revenue and expenditure projections were developed by trending as illustrated in *Chapters 10* and *20*.

PROJECTED SUMMARY AND FUND BALANCE ($ in thousands)

	Current budget	Year 1	Year 2	Year 3	Year 4	Year 5
Opening balance July 1	$6,700	$5,576	$3,949	$1,767	$-1,388	$-4,861
7/1 balance/expenditures	68%	52%	34%	14%	-10%	-34%
Revenues	8,796	9,059	9,334	9,260	9,918	10,228
Expenditures	9,920	10,686	11,516	12,415	13,391	14,449
Operating surplus (deficit)	-1,124	-1,627	-2,182	-3,155	-3,473	-4,221
Ending balance, June 30	5,576	3,949	1,767	-1,388	-4,861	-9,082

Discussion of the AFR, along with multi-year financial projections, may lead the board of education to conclude that a referendum will be necessary. Time must be allowed for a careful process of planning and conducting a referendum to increase tax rates, for usually only three such votes may be held in each two-year election cycle. Information on referendum planning is found in *Chapter 13*.

Table 32 and *Figure 11* summarize the educational fund revenue and expenditure projections that were detailed in earlier sections of the book. A complete analysis would involve developing tables for all of the operating funds separately and together. *Table 32* includes a shaded line showing the relationship between the opening (July 1) balance in the fund and the budgeted expenditures for the coming year. This percentage measure is a quick guide to determining whether the district may have to engage in short-term borrowing to meet its obligations during the school year and to the need to increase its permanent revenues and/or reduce expenditures. Notice how the district, which closed its Working Cash Fund into the Educational

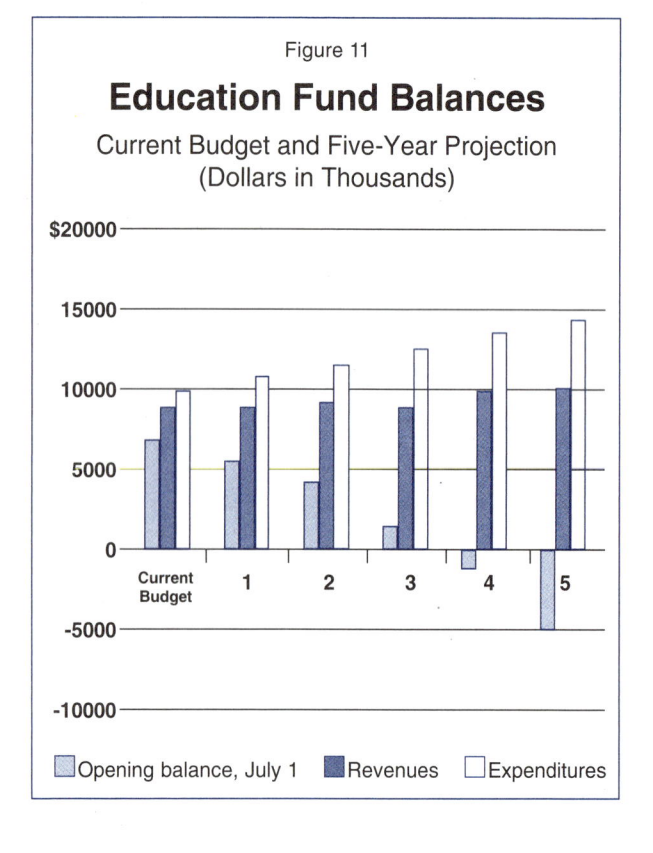

Figure 11
Education Fund Balances
Current Budget and Five-Year Projection
(Dollars in Thousands)

Table 33
Financial Profile Ratings Compared with EBF Tiers

EBF Tiers	Recognition	Review	Early Warning	Watch	Number of Districts
Tier 4	130	8	2	0	140
Tier 3	53	4	1	0	58
Tier 2	270	60	13	4	347
Tier 1	253	41	8	4	306
Total	**706**	**113**	**24**	**8**	**851**

Resources as a Percentage of Adequacy
Tier 4-100% or more
Tier 3-90-99%
Tier 2 -75-89%
Tier 1-Less than 75%

Source: Illinois State Board of Education

Fund at the end of prior year four, has drawn down the large balance as its deficits rose.

Over the coming five years shown on the graph in *Figure 11* rising enrollments and costs that will increase at a greater rate than revenues will reduce the fund balance to the point that borrowing will be necessary beginning in year three, and negative fund balances will occur beginning in year four. The projections serve as an early warning that planning is required for a tax referendum, working cash bond sale, or for other measures to balance the budget and build up the fund balance. The simplified format of the table and graph helps convey this message to the board of education and members of the public.

EBF Adequacy and the Financial Profile

ISBE publishes statistics showing the number of districts falling within each financial strength category according to their resources as a percentage of their adequacy amounts, as calculated under the Evidence-Based Funding (EBF) formula. (See *Chapter 6* for a description of the EBF formula.) That percentage determines the amount of new EBF funding to each district. Districts whose resources were furthest from adequacy (less than 75%) were placed in Tier 1 and received the most new money on a per-pupil basis. Districts with 100% or more of their adequacy amounts available from local resources were placed in Tier 4 and received minimal EBF money. *Table 33* shows the Fiscal Year 2021 statistics.

The comparison of a district's available local resources to its cost to fund an adequate program suggests a new dimension to the profile rating, one that relates funding ability to educational program needs. Were such a dimension to be incorporated into the future profile ratings, it would become a true "School District Resource Strength Profile."

22 / Looking Ahead

Four interrelated forces are changing budgeting practices and documents. These changes will enable participants in the budgetary process and users of the budget document to better interpret and utilize financial information for the benefit of children. The principal and the budget administrator will develop a new relationship that requires new knowledge, philosophies, and skills. The four forces are:
- Changes in educational programs
- Decentralization of school management
- New external demands for information
- Changes in school funding systems

Changes in Educational Programs

The starting point for the school budget is the educational program. Changes in curriculum content and approaches will impact the processes and structures within which future budgeting takes place.

Results-oriented schools will require that costs be related to new initiatives and ongoing programs. The costs of curricular and organizational innovations will need to be identified and tied to anticipated and actual results. This will require development of expanded budget communications and formats. Cost breakouts of broad budgeting categories may be required, along with comparisons of costs and benefits of traditional and innovative — and competing — approaches to improving school performance. The budget administrator will need to be conversant with curricular changes and their implications for personnel and non-personnel costs, as well as the educational benefits sought by investments in change.

Changes in various compensatory education programs will require corresponding changes in account structures. There is renewed emphasis in special education on keeping children in the classroom program. This has made the accurate costing out of special education services even more difficult to accomplish. Changes in the long-standing structure of these accounts will be necessary to facilitate allocation of resources in the schools and to strengthen the case for adequate external funding of services for special needs children. The budget administrator will require knowledge of programs and accounting to achieve these changes in account structure.

The diversity of our student bodies requires not one but several approaches to language instruction. A single "bilingual" account is no longer adequate to reflect the costs of different approaches with different philosophies and outcomes. Like special education, many of these approaches are "overlays" on the regular classroom setting, and their funding is shared among local, state, and federal levels. Accurate comparative cost identification is a must.

Changes in community priorities and resources will continue to require data to make difficult financial decisions. Rare is the school district that has not made decisions to discontinue programs due to revenue shortfalls or a desire to implement new programs. These tough and very public decisions are often challenged by the communities served. The Great Recession and the resulting shortfalls of local and state revenue required extensive budget reductions, even among districts that were considered as having strong financials beforehand. Budget administrators learned to take the lead in developing processes and documents that anticipate the need for such decisions to provide accurate cost breakouts of programs and services, that withstand review in times of financial stress.

Decentralization of School Management

Current thinking in educational management emphasizes decision-making at the school level by principals and staff who work with students and know their needs. Many models of school reform focus on the individual school and encourage a decentralized process of creative mixing and matching of school and community resources to achieve the school's stated aims for students.

In the process, it may be necessary to let go of certain long-standing beliefs about budgeting and financial management, and to develop new methods of internal communications on financial matters. Given well-established building goals and training in making and evaluating financial decisions, there are certain "rules" that may no longer be useful and may even be counterproductive to cost-effective budget management.

These old rules can be replaced with new ways. Why not allow schools to carry over unexpended balances (and deficits) to the next year in order to encourage staff to make thoughtful, long-term decisions on expenditures of discretionary funds, rather than "dumping" money to preserve future allocation levels? Providing incentives to conserve utilities and reduce other overhead costs by allowing the funds to be expended for direct student benefit may require cross-fund budgeting procedures but may also provide a rationale for the eventual consolidation of the operating funds.

Encouraging schools to shop for cost-effective support services, and allowing them to expend the savings, may work to reduce the costs of building, transportation, instructional support — and even some business services that are now provided or allocated centrally.

"Whole-school" staffing approaches, which allocate total staff based on overall and special needs enrollments and leave it to the school to determine the best uses of each staff member, have profound implications for budgeting structures and teacher contracts. There is a growing body of evidence that certain non-traditional, all-school reform models that employ such staffing procedures are able to achieve their goals within acceptable costs.

These forces have profound implications for the budgeting role of the budget administrator, shifting it from the maker of allocation decisions and enforcer of budgetary rules to that of colleague and teacher of the building leadership team. The end is the making of wise, data-driven decisions on the optimal allocation of resources to achieve the school's goals.

To function under such forces, the budget administrator will need a solid grounding in curriculum trends and educational leadership techniques, as well as flexibility in developing and interpreting budgetary/accounting systems for and with the building leadership. He or she will increasingly be called upon to integrate educational performance data into budgetary and other financial communications to internal and external audiences.

New External Demands for Information

Illinois' program accounting and budget structure was developed in the 1970s, partly in response to the needs of government funding agencies and school systems to track revenues and expenditures for a large number of then-new grant programs. Many districts have elaborated on the "minimum" account structure in state accounting manuals to provide detailed cost breakouts for departments, grade levels, locations, and specialized educational programs and support services.

Just as program budgeting evolved in response to external demands for information, new external demands will influence the type of information contained in budgets and other financial presentations. In analyzing school performance and developing strategies for improvement, school performance information will be considered along with financial data. There is a growing body of educational-economic research focusing on relating educational costs to program effectiveness. It underlies Illinois' Evidence-Based Funding (EBF) formula. State and federal funding agencies are stating their intent to tie funding levels to adoption of higher standards and to implementation of practices that research has shown to be associated with improved student achievement. Reference points for higher standards may no longer be those of other districts and states, but rather those of other nations whose students excel in international assessments.

Standards for exemplary practices and documents for budgeting and financial reporting require information on educational plans and accomplishments, as well as financial information related to these plans. Achieving the Certificate of Excellence in Financial Reporting requires preparation of a Comprehensive Annual Financial Report that combines data and analysis of finances, students, educational program factors, district-wide and school-level program plans and achievement. The Certificate of Excellence and Exemplary Budget programs are administered by the Association of School Business Officials, International, www.asbointl.org.

Such a document is an impressive communication to boards of education, district management, and staff, and also to important external audiences such as municipal bond rating agencies. The budget administrator must not only be familiar with educational program planning data but also able to help interpret it to both internal and external audiences — to speak in the language of the educator as well as that of the financial specialist.

Changes in School Funding Systems

In many states, now including Illinois, the focus of school finance reform has become "adequacy" as well as "equity." At both the state and district level, the question, "How much is enough?" is being asked. Whether adequacy is addressed in the courts, the legislature, or by individual boards of education, the demand exists for accurate research on the costs of successful programs for students with a variety of needs.

Research on the comparative costs and effectiveness of "whole-school" reform models is essential to selection of a model in districts where reconstitution of the schools, their program, and its management is being attempted. Some of this research informed the Illinois EBF formula. These developments have implications for the account structure and management of future budgets and for internal and external communications about them.

At the state level, data will be required on the costs of providing an adequate and effective education to students displaying various characteristics. Legislatures will require such data to make decisions on funding levels for "general" and "categorical" programs. The report of the Wisconsin School Adequacy Initiative at www.cpre.wceruw.org provides powerful information for state policy-makers and local school officials on which to base decisions on the productive allocation of resources. It also has informed Illinois' EBF formula.

While many states, including Illinois, are gathering and using data on such costs, the present budgetary account structure is proving inadequate to identify accurately the full costs of the complex programs required by many of today's students. "How much is enough?" cannot be answered without better information on "How much does it cost — and for whom — and to accomplish what?"

At the local district level, account structures and reporting must be sufficiently flexible so to provide answers to new questions. Imagine a "child-based" system of allocating resources to diverse elementary schools in the throes of an all-school reform effort. For one school, it may be necessary to align the budget to identify the costs of meeting curriculum standards for "normal" and "gifted" children, and to identify the costs of serving bilingual special needs children from poverty-impacted families. Another school will require a different array of cost breakouts and allocations. On the revenue side, local and external funds may need to be tracked to the school level — or even to the individual student.

Now combine statewide, adequacy-based school reform with a budget structure that focuses on the unique characteristics and needs of an individual building's student population. Might we see state aid formulas combining general and categorical elements to develop allocations for each building in the state? Business managers and principals would partner in determining the most cost-effective means of budgeting state and local funds to meet the needs of that school and the standards of the district and the state.

The Future Role of the Financial Administrator

Will the school district as it exists today still be necessary in 2030? Imagine largely state-funded education, with allocations to individual schools, in adequate amounts, determined by research-based formulae recognizing the school's unique population makeup. Continue to imagine state-collected property taxes on regional commercial and industrial property being distributed directly to individual schools. Both of these proposals have been advocated by school finance reformers. What if they were combined? What remains for the local district if its revenue raising and distribution functions are taken over by the state?

Decentralization of school decision-making is a central theme of the school reform movement. Reformers advocate a greater role for parents in school policy determination and emphasize the role of the principal as the key decision-maker in the school. They also point to the school as the appropriate site for delivery of an array of social services to children and their families.

What work would remain for a school district business manager if the revenue raising and allocation functions were reduced, especially if schools were to elect to purchase some support functions from somewhere other than the district office?

There will always be a need for someone to teach principals and their staffs the skills of financial management and control and cost-effectiveness analysis in decision-making. The ideal context for such teaching is the budget process — that year-long activity that bridges planning, financial management, and evaluation of results. In some cities, business managers are now assigned full-time to high schools and to clusters of elementary and middle schools. The role of the future school business manager is, then, that of teacher and leader, mediating between the worlds of finance and education.

Part Three

23 / Financial Responsibilities of the School Board

While school business officials, superintendents, and other administrators handle budgeting responsibilities, the role of the school board includes policy development and a calendar of board financial actions.

The school board's responsibilities for the school district's financial performance can be outlined as follows:

1. **Establish clear expectations for maintenance of the school district's financial health.** The school district's financial health should reflect values of the school board and community. Board intentions reflected in policy should clarify such issues as:
   - Does the school board insist on fund balances or is it willing to carry or accumulate debt in order to provide desired services? Are there limits on fund balances or amount of debt?
   - Does the board require minimal levels of cash flow so that obligations can be met in a timely manner?
   - On what kinds of expenditures is the school board willing to use its reserves, if any exist, or to engage in short-term borrowing?
   - Does the school board require standards beyond those required by law for such matters as financial reporting, auditing, or protection of assets?

2. **Establish desired outcomes and priorities that need to be reflected in the budget.** The school board is the voice of the community in determining who gets what benefits and at what cost. The school board should satisfy itself that the budget it adopts reflects its expectations for the school district to the extent feasible.

3. **Establish related expectations of the administration in its construction of the budget.** Ask the superintendent to explain the following:
   - What are the assumptions on which revenue and expense projections are based? Do they seem reasonable?
   - Does the proposed budget produce the balance — surplus or deficit — that the board intends or finds acceptable?
   - Does the spending plan serve the priorities and objectives of the district?

4. **Establish policies and limitations on staff authority governing budget preparation, purchasing, protection of assets, and related business procedures.** The school board needs to be assured that:
   - Its policies adequately govern school district financial and business management procedures, including budgeting, purchasing and bid letting, payment of bills, investing of funds, and other standard fiscal practices necessary to safeguard school district moneys.
   - Procedures are in place requiring the segregation of duties of district personnel so as to establish checks and balances in the receiving, banking, and recording of funds and in requesting, making, and recording of payments.
   - The district is in compliance with school board policies and administrative procedures.

5. **Monitor month-to-month financial performance — income and expense — in relation to the financial plan represented in the budget.** Ask the superintendent to provide the following information each month:
   - A summary of income and expense in comparison with budgeted amounts, along with an assessment of whether the district will end the year where the board expected it to be.
   - An updated balance sheet to show how the district's financial status is being affected by current financial activity. Is the district increasing or decreasing its fund balances and how does this relate to the district's financial health?

- Evidence that cash flow is adequate and the district is paying its bills in a timely way.
6. **Monitor the district's financial health, both current and long-term.** Ask the superintendent at least once each year to provide more in-depth information reflecting the district's financial health, including:
    - Cash flow trends.
    - Accumulation of deficits or surpluses.
    - Long-term projections of income and expenditures — five years or more — to show where the district might be headed.

7. **Stay abreast of other financial issues affecting the district.** Members of the school board need to understand a variety of issues that can become vital to the district's financial health from time to time, including:
    - Trends in student enrollment and how they affect costs and income.
    - Internal financial controls.
    - Tax increment financing districts, existing and proposed.
    - State mandates and financial aid.

24 / The Essential Role of School Board Financial Policy

Developing Finance Policies

A school board fulfills its governance responsibilities for maintaining a financially strong district only through a comprehensive set of policies that direct and guide the staff. Every district has a policy manual that governs personnel, the curriculum, student matters, and the board's own operating procedures. Policies reflect the board's expectations regarding the direction of the district and make those expectations known to the community, staff, parents, and students. Many policies are required by the state; but because there are fewer policy mandates in finance than in other areas of governance, the finance section of the policy book is often the slimmest. With that said, financial governance is a critical function for school boards.

Clearly stated, finance policies deliver a message from the board to the administration and public of the principles to which the district will adhere in maintaining financial health. Financial policies assure all stakeholders of the integrity of the district's fiscal management. These policies are most effective when they focus the board's attention on the major issues of financial governance, rather than on day-to-day business office operations.

It is not difficult to develop or expand financial policies. School boards should begin with the most pressing needs. Are there topics that have led to confusion and misunderstanding in the past? Has the financial health of the district changed in recent years? What plans have been made to prepare for the anticipated funding cliff that will occur in 2024? Has there been a significant change in the leadership team? School boards should collaborate, consult, and network with other districts to gain insight and share ideas. While obtaining insight from others is helpful, every district must then adapt their policies to the district's specific circumstances. The board attorney and district auditor may also suggest topics for consideration and potential policy changes. The Illinois Association of School Boards' PRESS policy service offers sample policies in all areas of governance that are in compliance with state and federal law. *Chapter 23* provides a useful outline of needed financial policies.

Regular maintenance of policies is as important to the smooth functioning of a school district as is regular maintenance to an automobile. A section-by-section review of the complete policy book every three or four years is strongly recommended to orient new board members to the policies, identify new policy needs, and identify those that require revision to reflect the district's needs, the law, and current practice.

The next section displays some issues on which district staff might benefit from policy guidance.

School Board Policy Topics

Policies for governing the district's financial and operational affairs, of course, must be in compliance with state and federal laws. In addition, each school board should make its expectations known in each of the following general areas:

- Guideposts for maintaining financial health, including fund balance size and the acceptable uses of borrowing.
- Standards for accounting, reporting, and protection of the district's property.
- A schedule for budget development and responsibilities and guidelines for budget management.
- Requirements for long-term budget projections.
- Rules for bidding and purchasing, banking, and investments.
- Provisions to assure adequate internal controls in handling funds, payroll, accounts payable, and other business operations.

- Standards for managing the business office, building operations, transportation, food service, and other support services.
- Specifications for the content of monthly financial reports and how they should describe current results and relate them to the board's financial goals for the year.

To ensure adequate standards in all of these areas, the school board can adopt needed finance policies on the following topics:

- Role of School Board in Financial Matters
    - Balancing costs and benefits, income, and expense
    - Protecting district assets and ensuring compliance with laws
    - Delegation of authority to manage finances to the superintendent
    - Regular monitoring of current financial performance and future outlook
    - Board member attendance and expenses at conferences and workshops
    - Insurance and indemnification of board members
- Role of Superintendent
    - Developing the budget in accordance with law, priorities, and resources
    - Preparation of regular reports on financial condition and compliance matters
    - Reporting information on pertinent local, state, and federal developments
    - Maintenance and supervision of sound financial and business practices
    - Authority to enter into contracts to an established limit
- Accounting and Reporting
    - Basis of accounting and content of monthly financial reports
    - Capitalization of fixed assets as required by accounting standards
    - Scope of annual audit; process for appointment of auditor
    - Activity and imprest fund limits; authority for disbursements and reporting
    - Authority for waiver and reduction of student fees
- Budget Development and Administration
    - Establishment of goals representing mission and vision of board and community
    - Responsibilities and communications timetable for budget planning
    - Budget transfer authority of superintendent and reports to board
    - The superintendent's authority to approve spending within budget limits
    - Process for approval of major expenditures not in the budget
    - Authority to enter into contracts and expend funds to a designated limit to protect the schools and their occupants in times of national health emergencies
- Bidding and Purchasing
    - Dollar limits on non-bid purchases (may be more stringent than those in the law)
    - Bid advertising and evaluation procedures and award criteria
    - Administrative relations with bidders and vendors, including gift acceptance policy
    - Avoidance of conflict of interest for a board member or employee
    - Authority for approval of construction change orders
    - Establishment of cooperative purchasing agreements
- Long-Term Planning
    - Schedule for development and discussion of long-term projections
    - Standards of fiscal health
    - Fund balance adequacy and maintenance
    - Acceptable borrowing purposes, means, repayment terms, and sale procedures
    - Investment instruments and provisions for protection of funds
    - Emergency preparedness
- Standards for Business Management and Control
    - Process for acceptance of gifts to district from individuals and others
    - Relationship with district foundation, booster clubs, and similar organizations
    - Segregation of duties of district personnel and provisions for checks and balances
    - Standards for the operation of building services, transportation, and food services
    - Responsibility of the superintendent to develop detailed procedures for implementing the operations governed by board policies
    - Use of copier and procurement cards
    - Responsibility for supervision and custodial responsibility for the Activity Fund
    - Limits on Activity Fund balances and transfer of balances in inactive accounts
    - Recovery procedures for insufficient fund checks and debt recovery

Developing a Fund Balance Policy

A realistic and supportable fund balance policy is a critical step toward financial health. Board members and all stakeholders must understand why maintaining a healthy balance in the district's major funds is essential and the circumstances under which the board would be willing to draw upon its reserves.

The overriding rationale for maintaining a good fund balance is to reduce the necessity to borrow and/or curtail programs during times of fiscal stress. Moreover, the interest on invested funds builds up revenues. Reserves enable the district to meet needs arising from enrollment increases and higher costs for mandated programs, both of which can increase sharply as high-need students enter the district. Moreover, any district can be adversely affected by reductions in the property tax base, emergency building repairs, or higher-than-anticipated union contract settlements. Such events can cause reserves to diminish or disappear. When they do, reserves need to be rebuilt to avoid the costs in time, money, and creditworthiness that result from frequent short-term borrowing.

Furthermore, the end-of-year operating fund balance in relationship to total revenues is a heavily weighted component of the Financial Strength Profile score calculated by the Illinois State Board of Education (illustrated in *Chapter 21*). The size of the fund balance and the number of days' cash on hand account for 45% of the total score, underscoring the importance of reserves in measuring fiscal strength. The profile components provide useful criteria and targets for boards to consider as they establish or review their policies, set limits on the annual budget, consider borrowing options, and set short- and long-term financial goals.

A fund balance-to-revenue ratio of at least 25% will give a district the highest score on that component of the ISBE Profile. However, it may not be a realistic target if the district is carrying a deficit or very low balances and is in adverse fiscal circumstances. In such circumstances, a 10-15% balance would be a more realistic target. Where property taxes are often delayed, or enrollment and expenditures are increasing faster than revenues, a higher figure may be required.

Creating a fund balance where none exists (or almost none) will require budgeting for a surplus for one or more years. The board must decide how the necessary revenue will be raised and/or what expenditures are to be reduced. Will the board use working cash bonds or other borrowing measures to build up reserves? What is to be the schedule for reaching the target balance?

Fund balance is a sensitive topic on which community input may be advisable — and employee unions will likely watch the discussions closely as well. School-oriented community members will understand the need for an adequate balance; others may question why the board feels it must invest their money for them. The answers will be more convincing if the fund balance policy reflects clearly stated needs and goals, good research, and an objective opinion by the outside auditor.

The auditor can interpret the district's history of cash needs and its schedule of receipts and expenditures. He or she also knows the practices of the firm's other clients and can speak to the need to reserve funds for unexpected expenditures. The firm's stamp of approval on the policy may help the board convince

---

Fund Balance Policy Statements for the School Board to Consider

The school board will maintain fund balances adequate to:

_____ ensure the school district's ability to cover its obligations in a prompt manner when there are delays in the receipt of revenue;

and/or

_____ ensure the school district's ability to maintain acceptable levels of service in spite of unforeseen expenses or reductions in revenue.

For a district with a fund balance deemed adequate:

The school district will maintain year-end fund balances representing _____ % of the annual expenditures for the Education Fund, Operations and Maintenance Fund, Transportation Fund, and _____ Fund.

For a district with fund balances deemed not currently adequate:

The school district will seek to establish year-end fund balances representing _____ % of the annual expenditures for the Education Fund, Operations and Maintenance Fund, Transportation Fund, and _____ Fund. To achieve this end within _____ years, the district will budget _____ % each year as surplus in each fund.

Fund balances will be used to cover temporary or one-time needs and will not be used to fund recurring expenses.

Note: Every school board is advised to review new or revised policies with its attorney prior to adoption.

skeptical members of the community and the staff of the district's need for reserves. As it develops its policy, the board may want to have on hand policies from districts with comparable resources and good financial health scores. If a bond issue is in the offing, the board will want to know the fund balance criteria used by the rating agencies. The district's financial consultant can assist in researching those criteria.

The Fund Balance Policy Statements on *page 137* will get the discussion started. Notice that the policy starts with statements of purpose and intent. A district's target will reflect the local community's economic, political, and educational considerations. If the district is starting from a satisfactory point, the policy might incorporate that point as the goal for the future. If the fund balance is not adequate, the policy sets a target and a schedule to reach it by designating a percentage of the operating fund revenues each year to build up the balance in each fund.

How much is enough? If the budget is balanced, projections call for an increase in tax revenues, tax collections are timely, the local economy is healthy, and enrollment is stable, a balance, not including early taxes, in the range of 15-20% might be adequate. If circumstances are otherwise, the board may wish to increase the balance, over time, to 30-35% or higher. Where the late fall distribution of second-half property taxes is common, higher balances may be called for to avoid borrowing costs. The board should ask the administration to prepare a multi-year cash flow projection to validate the sufficiency of the target figure.

Reserves dedicated to future capital needs, as opposed to cash flow requirements, should be clearly identified in the district's financial reports and not included in the fund balance calculation. Business-oriented community members will respect the need for such funds — provided that the goals and timetable for implementing the program have been developed and communicated appropriately.

When finished, the fund balance policy and its rationale should be communicated to stakeholders, including the community and staff. Include the policy and its rationale in new board member orientations and communicate it to a new superintendent or business manager. Information necessary to monitor the policy should be incorporated into the district's budget communications and monthly financial reports. It is important to remember and state upfront that the standards described in the policies — whether to spend, save, or borrow, are based on what the board believes is best for the district and the students.

Regularly reviewing the fund balance policy in light of the district's current program needs, budget, planned capital improvements, and economic outlook will suggest either reaffirmation or revision of the district's present target.

25 / The Board's Financial Duties and Calendar

The board of education is responsible for performing many duties necessary to securing and expending district funds. Among them are adoption of the annual budget and tax levy, reviewing and approving the annual audit and financial report, awarding contracts for goods and services after competitive bids and proposals, authorizing budget transfers and borrowing as required, overseeing the investment of school funds, and approval of monthly financial reports and expenditures. Some of these responsibilities occur only once each year — for example, the review of the audit. Some, such as the adoption of the budget and tax levy, must follow specific calendar requirements. Some occur monthly, including review and approval of expenditures. Some occur only as needed, including borrowing, which is done in a series of steps prescribed by the requirements of the borrowing instrument.

This chapter includes an annual calendar of the board's financial duties and sections devoted to five duties essential to maintaining financial health and the integrity of the financial operation. They are the appointment and bonding of the School Treasurer, the maintenance of a system of checks and balances, the oversight of the Activity Fund, the annual audit, and selecting banking services. Many other responsibilities are described in earlier chapters, including the process and timetable for preparing the budget and the tax levy, interfund transfers, and borrowing. A valuable companion to this book is *Illinois School Law Survey* by the late Brian A. Braun. That book, available from IASB, details the legal requirements that govern many of the board's financial duties.

The School Board's Financial Calendar

This section is adapted from the IASB book, *Coming to Order — A Guide to Successful School Board Meetings*, and from *A School Board Member's Handbook*, published by Hodges, Loizzi, Eisenhammer, Rodick & Kohn (2021), where a comprehensive calendar of monthly board actions can be found, including required actions and publications with respect to personnel, finance, labor, students, and other areas. Not all required actions with a financial component appear in the list below.

Each year, the board and superintendent work together to establish the master agenda calendar for the coming year. The calendar includes actions and reports that must be completed during the year to meet legal requirements, keep the schools in business, and provide the board with information necessary for planning. This chapter identifies those requirements of a financial nature and assigns them to the months when they are commonly considered or are required by law to be acted upon.

Some school law firms publish schedules of required actions during the year in their newsletters and other publications. They can also advise on deadlines, the content of required notices, and other legal requirements. It is good practice for one administrator to be assigned responsibility for monitoring the board's master agenda calendar to assure that actions and subsequent publications and filings take place on schedule.

Monthly Topics
- Review financial reports containing
  - Monthly and year-to-date information on revenues and expenditures compared to the budget for the year, and an explanation of variances between the budget and actual figures;
  - Activity Fund revenues and expenditures, showing information for each of the accounts within the fund;
  - Information on investments, showing the type of instrument, purchase date, term, principal amount, current market value, and yield.
- Approve bills for payment.

Budget Planning and Adoption

June, July, and August –
- Discuss, adopt, and display a tentative budget at least 30 days prior to adoption of the final budget.
- Schedule the public hearing on the budget.
- Direct the publication/posting of the notice of the public hearing.

August and September –
- Hold the budget hearing and adopt the budget by September 30.
- File the budget with the county clerk(s) within 30 days of its adoption.
- File the budget with the Regional Office of Education
- File the budget with ISBE
- Post the approved budget on the district's website.

October and November –
- Review opening enrollments, recent trends, and projections for the coming five years.
- Review financial projections as a basis for discussion of the tax levy and budget assumptions for the coming year.
- Begin discussion of budget planning assumptions, including revenue changes, enrollment projections, staff needs, program modifications, capital plans, salary and benefit costs, and allocations for consumables and equipment.

December and January –
- Review a report of the condition of the buildings, describing major maintenance needs, life-safety work, and program-related building project requirements for the coming three to five years. Identify priority projects for inclusion in the following year's budget and authorize solicitation of bids accordingly.

February and March –
- Review updated enrollment, class sections, and staff projections.
- Take actions on personnel, including hiring, dismissal, and reassignment.
- Authorize the superintendent to prepare the following year's budget.

April, May, and June –
- Take action on personnel in accordance with needs.
- Review updated revenue projections in preparation for discussion of a tentative budget.

The Tax Levy

October and November –
- Discuss needs for property tax revenue in each fund, following discussion of financial projections.
- Review the latest available information on assessed valuation and rate limits in tax-capped counties and identify decisions pertinent to the coming levy action.
- Discuss and adopt an estimated tax levy not less than 20 days prior to the adoption of the certificate of levy.
- If required, direct publication of the Truth in Taxation notice not more than 14 days, nor less than seven days, before the required hearing, and schedule the levy hearing.

December –
- Conduct the levy hearing, adopt the certificate of levy, and file it with the county clerk(s) by the last Tuesday of the month.
- Certify compliance with or the inapplicability of the Truth in Taxation Act (even if no notice and hearing were required) and include the certification with the levy filing.
- Publish an additional notice if the adopted levy was increased from the amount published in the Truth in Taxation notice or was in an amount that increased a proposed levy that was below the threshold level required for the notice.

February, March, and April –
- In tax-capped counties, upon notice from the county clerk (schedule varies by county), review tentative levy distribution and fund rates and adjust distribution as needed and permitted.
- Adjust fund levies in accordance with referenda approved subsequent to approval of the tax levy in December.

Other Actions

September, October, and November –
- Review the audit and Annual Finance Report and file with the regional superintendent.
- Publish the Statement of Financial Affairs and file with ISBE.
- Prepare required compensation reports for IMRF and certificated employees, including administrators, and arrange for their publication on the district's website by the required dates.

December, January, and February –
- Approve textbook purchases.
- Authorize and act on bids for time-critical equipment deliveries and summer building projects.
- Review cash flow projections to determine if short-term borrowing will be necessary prior to the end of the fiscal year.
- Solicit proposals for the annual audit if a change in auditing firm is under consideration; otherwise, obtain and approve quotation from current firm.

March, April, May, and June –
- Authorize superintendent to apply for federal and state grants.
- Authorize the annual audit.
- Designate surplus supplies and equipment for sale or donation.
- Act on employment of certified, classified, and administrative staff.
- Keep current on salary and benefit settlements in market area.
- Act on extra-duty stipends for the coming year.
- Approve new employees as recommended by the administration.
- Adopt and publish the Prevailing Wage Resolution.

July and August –
- Act on change orders for construction projects as necessary.
- Approve contracts and salaries that are not settled in the spring.
- Approve board member expenses for attendance at conferences for the coming year.

Maintaining Checks and Balances

It is absolutely essential that board policy requires internal checks and balances. While there is likely no way to prevent theft or fraud where the perpetrator is committed and persistent, effective procedures can certainly discourage it and eventually should detect it.

As an example, the receiving of money (especially cash), recording the receipt, and depositing the money in the bank should be viewed as separate jobs and never assigned to one person. Even the smallest district must identify at least two people who can act as a check and balance in handling cash.

Adhering to standards set forth in the Illinois Administrative Code (Part 100- Requirements for Accounting, Budgeting, Financial Reporting and Budgeting) and in state law can go a long way toward thwarting dishonesty. In addition, the Illinois Association of School Business Officials and the Association of Business Officials International are excellent sources for policies and procedures designed to protect district assets.

Student Activity Funds

While activity funds appear ripe for dishonesty, theft is not the problem encountered most frequently. That honor belongs to disagreements and miscommunications regarding uses of assets and the financial condition of the organization they belong to.

Illinois law requires the local school board to establish policies governing student Activity Funds. Good school board policies and administrative procedures should accomplish the following:

1) Clearly delineate who is responsible for oversight of Activity Fund accounts. Usually this should be the school's principal.
2) Require the district or school administration to adopt prudent procedures that:
   - Provide for different employees to oversee different aspects of money handling and record-keeping;
   - Require monthly reconciliation of accounts between treasurer and club leaders and sponsors;
   - Encourage tracking of trends in revenue and expenses in each account;
   - Encourage first-hand observation of how money is being handled to ensure compliance with required procedures;
   - Ensure that activity leaders and sponsors are working from realistic financial plans or budgets;
   - Ensure that training is facilitated annually for new staff involved with the processing of activity funds.
3) Require the superintendent to present assurances at least once a year that Activity Fund procedures are in compliance with the law and board policies.

Effective in May 2020, ISBE adopted new rules for accounting for Activity Funds beginning with the FY 2021 budget and Annual Financial Report. Consult the Program Accounting Manual, 23 ILL. Admin. Code 100 and ISBE's Anatomy of a School District Budget for regulations and procedures governing the handling of Activity Fund accounts and accounting for fund transactions in the Annual Budget and Financial Report.

The Annual Audit

An independent audit should play a key role in protecting school district assets. Illinois school districts

Internal Controls Protect District Funds

Anyone with a true intent to steal can probably devise a way to bilk anyone — including a school district — out of money. Fortunately, school boards have a number of policy options and safeguards that they can put in place to lessen the likelihood that someone will abscond with district funds.

School boards can get themselves into a difficult situation either by not having good financial policies and procedures in place, or by failing to follow those policies once created. Typical safeguards include a good set of checks and balances, following bidding procedures, and putting good reimbursement procedures in place.

Checks and balances

When it comes to checks and balances, school boards might look first at their policies and administrative procedures on money handling. One of the simplest procedures may be one of the most effective at deterring the theft of money, according to Tim Custis, a certified public accountant with Gorenz & Associates in Peoria, as well as a school board member for Washington SD 52.

His advice: The person collecting the money should not be the same person who deposits that money and records the transaction. The bigger the district, the easier it is to separate collection, recording, and deposit duties, Custis said, but even the smallest district should be able to identify at least two people who can act as a check and balance against each other when handling cash.

"Most people are very honest," Custis said of the school employees his firm deals with during annual school audits. "They act hurt when we point out that having only one person handling receipts and deposits could be a problem. But we tell them it's for their own protection."

Cash transactions themselves can be a problem, he said, because they don't leave the paper trail you have with a check or a credit card transaction. As an example of what not to do, he pointed to a district that had been paying athletic officials in cash from gate receipts. A better procedure, he said, is to write a check ahead of the event and then have the official sign off when it is received. That way, the district has two ways to show that the payment was made and received.

Gate receipts, concession stand money, and pop machine money — all of which generate cash — as well as registration fees where large amounts of money are handled in a short space of time pose a temptation for someone with an eye to steal. Custis suggests that taking care to note beginning and ending ticket numbers for an event, having a second person check the numbers against the money, and then getting the money deposited that night — or at least the next morning — are all good procedures that will help deter theft and minimize errors. Consider using an outside ticketing service for events that generate a large amount of admissions revenue.

What's often missing in the checks and balances equation is someone who questions that something doesn't look quite right. To whom should an employee report a suspicion that someone might be stealing cash? Would they be telling the person who might be taking the money? In that case, it might be wise to tell the school board president.

Activity accounts

Activity accounts handled by a booster club or a student group also can be problematic, Custis said. Huge amounts of money can travel through these accounts with the district having little oversight — especially for accounts maintained on the building level.

According to the Illinois School Law Survey, school boards "1) must establish rules and regulations governing conditions under which school classes, clubs, and associations may collect or acquire funds in the name of any school, and 2) provide for the safeguarding of such funds for the educational, recreational, or cultural purposes they are designed to serve."

If an account is opened by the band parents to purchase new uniforms, and if the school district knows about the account, then the district may be responsible if someone absconds with the funds, Custis said. Additionally, the purchase of those uniforms needs to follow proper bid procedures if the cost is more than $50,000. That's something that's often overlooked when purchases are made by adjunct groups, but still under the auspices of the district.

To keep activity funds on the up-and-up, Custis recommends they be handled through the central office, with policies and procedures that might allow checks to be written every two weeks to expedite any payments that might need to be made.

Conducting the audit

Obviously the most well-known check that finances are on the up-and-up is the annual audit. By law, each school district is required to have an audit done annually and the district superintendent should have a report from that audit by October 15. (105 ILCS 5/17-1)

continued

> Audits must be done using "Government Audit Standards," Custis said, "which means that we have to review internal controls and procedures to be sure that the district has done things properly." That's in addition to what most people associate with an audit — that is, making certain all the funds and columns of numbers balance.
>
> Once completed, the audit report includes a letter known as "Independent Auditor's Report on Internal Control over Financial Reporting and on Compliance and Other Matters Based on an Audit of Financial Statements Performed in Accordance with Government Auditing Standards." It's a lengthy name, but this letter, Custis said, "will reveal any violations of laws or regulations found during that audit, as well as reveal any internal control deficiencies identified."
>
> Additionally, the auditor will issue a separate letter, referred to as the "Communication with Those Charged with Governance." This letter will provide information about any problems encountered during the audit and potential suggestions of how controls might be improved.
>
> Bill Phillips, assistant professor for educational leadership at the University of Illinois-Springfield, said this letter is an important piece of information that not all board members get to see because it first goes to the superintendent.
>
> "Board members should make sure that they see all of the information that comes out of the audit," Phillips said, "including that letter."
>
> Even better, he said, is to ask the auditor to make a presentation to the entire board, rather than just hand the audit over to the superintendent.
>
> Audits look closely for fraud because of the "Statement of Auditing Standards 99" that went into effect for any audit of financial statements for periods beginning on or after December 15, 2002.
>
> In essence, Custis said, standards require auditors to ask more questions about fraud and suspicious activity, such as, is someone all of a sudden living a lifestyle that is way above what his or her salary should be able to afford?
>
> In asking questions, auditors also can find out if certain employees always insist they are the only ones who can handle certain procedures, refuse to have anyone trained as back-up, and never take a vacation. Those circumstances should trigger a red flag that something might be amiss.
>
> "The onus is put on auditors," he said. "Now the public expects us to be looking for fraud." However, he noted, more fraud has been identified since these standards have been implemented.
>
> Source: Adapted from an article in the November-December 2005 issue of *The Illinois School Board Journal*. It was updated in 2014 by Tim Custis, CPA of Gorenz and Associates, Ltd. in Washington, Ill.

are required by state law (105 ILCS 5/3-7) to be audited using Government Auditing Standards. This means that an independent auditor must look at the books and records of the district and evaluate a) whether internal controls have been established and followed; and b) whether the school district has complied with the many regulations and grant requirements imposed by various state and federal agencies.

An audit is designed to test transactions (not look at every transaction) to determine if they have been properly recorded and if proper procedures were followed in collecting and recording transactions. An audit also tests grant expenditures for appropriateness under a grant agreement. These tests of controls and procedures enable the auditor to provide the board and administration with some reasonable assurance that the district's financial statements as presented are fairly stated.

The school district will receive a "Report on Internal Control Over Financial Reporting and on Compliance Based on an Audit of Financial Statements Performed in Accordance with Government Auditing Standards." This report should reveal any deficiencies found during the audit, state that none were noted, or reference a separate letter that identifies internal control or compliance issues that need to be addressed, but that did not result in material deficiencies. The school board needs to see and review this report from the auditor and, in fact, probably should receive an oral presentation of the report at a board meeting.

The school board should understand that, while most auditors will write the financial statements for their client school districts, those statements are the district's responsibility. The auditor's responsibility is limited to providing assurance that those statements are "fairly stated in all material respects" and that internal controls and compliance with laws and regulations have been tested.

Just because these areas have been tested and nothing was found does not provide proof that everything was handled correctly. It is the board's responsibility to establish policies and procedures that will promote the proper recording of transactions and encourage compliance with laws, regulations, and grant agreements.

For more insights into internal controls and the annual audit, see "Internal Controls Protect District Funds," on *page 142*. Information on the audit process and components can be found at www.isbe.net. Select A-133, Single of Audit of Federal Grants on the site map.

The Treasurer's Bond

A school district may inadvertently allow its treasurer to post an inadequate bond. One cause may be the incorrect calculation of the penalty required.

Illinois statutes require the school treasurer to post two types of bonds. The first is a surety bond that every school treasurer must post "before entering upon his duties." (105 ILCS 5/8-2) Pursuant to Public Act 103-0049, "the penalty of the bond shall be determined by the school board in an amount no less than 10% of the amount of all bonds, notes, mortgages, moneys, and effects (instead of providing that for those school districts that have a designation of recognition or review according to the State Board of Education's School District Financial Profile System, the penalty of the bond shall be determined by the school board in an amount no less than 10% of the amount of all bonds, notes, mortgages, moneys, and effects and that for all other school districts, the penalty of the bond shall be 25% of all bonds, notes, mortgages, moneys, and effects)". The penalty may be increased or decreased to accommodate changes in the value of financial instruments under the treasurer's control, but it can never be less than the requirement as stipulated above. The bond must be approved by the governing school board or township trustees and filed with the regional superintendent of education.

The second bond is required before the treasurer can accept possession of the proceeds of a bond issue and will normally be required before bond counsel will give approval to the issuance of bonds. This bond must be equal to 25% of the amount of the bond issue and must be approved by the governing school board or board of township trustees. (105 ILCS 5/19-6)

The penalty required of the second bond is usually easy to determine as the amount of a bond issue should be clearly known in advance. The first bond that is required of all treasurers requires a calculation of the highest amount that is likely to be under the treasurer's control at any one time. This bond, however, need not duplicate coverage of the special bond required for a bond issue.

Selecting Banking and Investment Advisory Services

The banking and investment advisory world has changed greatly over the past 20 years and especially since 2008, when federal authorities closed many large and small banks. The locally owned community bank, in towns where it still exists, faces competition from branches and drive-through offices of out-of-town banks. Schools may choose between banks and investment pools to park their short-term cash and purchase certificates of deposit. Banks, in turn, play in a worldwide money market and invest their local deposits nationwide and overseas as well as locally.

Schools' banking needs and procedures are also changing, as is banking technology. Revenues, including those received electronically, must be accurately recorded and safely invested, with funds available when needed to pay employees and vendors. Payroll and accounts payable transactions must be processed in a timely and reliable manner. Cash and credit card transactions must be handled, and the banking needs of student and staff organizations served. Access to credit markets is needed when borrowing is necessary. Schools desire to minimize banking costs, improve operational efficiency, and improve investment returns, while maintaining close working relationships with their bankers and supporting local businesses where possible.

Depending on the resources available in the local community and board of education practice, school districts may decide to use the only bank located in the district, share the business among all of the local banks, use one bank and rotate the business, or select one bank through competitive bids or requests for proposals (RFPs). In his article "School Boards as Borrowers and Lenders," written in 1981 for the *Illinois School Board Journal*, Ross Hodel provided insights into the four ways of selecting a bank that are as useful today as they were 40 years ago:

- Using the only bank in the district establishes long-term relationships (as long as the bank exists and its officers remain) and keeps the district's business local. However, it can lead the bank to be complacent in serving the district's needs, and there is no assurance that the services are being acquired at the lowest cost.
- Sharing the business among several banks avoids charges of favoritism and treats all local banks the same. However, since each bank incurs costs in establishing the customer relationship and handling paperwork, the cost to the school district may be

greater. Complacency can still occur, because sharing makes the district a smaller customer, and cash pooling is made more difficult.
- Rotating the business among banks facilitates cash pooling, avoids charges of favoritism, and may keep all banks somewhat happy. However, costs must be duplicated when funds are shifted, and disruption is possible. Long-term relationships are less likely to be established.
- Periodic competitive bidding of banking and investment services removes politics from the selection process, assures the lowest possible cost, encourages bidders to develop new services, and avoids the disruptions of frequent changes in financial relationships. Specifications must be developed and, as with other bids, the selection process could raise objections from unsuccessful bidders.

An unstable banking and financial scene requires district officials to pay even more care to the requirement that deposited funds be collateralized. Districts may not always be able to place collateralized deposits in a given bank, especially during times when several agencies receive their property tax revenues, and the supply of funds available exceeds the bank's ability to use them. At such times, direct purchase of insured U.S. Treasury issues, investment pools, and non-local banks may be advisable.

26 / The Financial Responsibilities of the Superintendent

Financial Responsibilities of the Superintendent

The district superintendent is responsible for ensuring that financial performance conforms to state laws and school board standards. Hopefully, many of the duties and tasks associated with that achievement can be delegated to a school business official or other capable staff members who can carry out operational tasks that are critical to the smooth operation and financial stability of the district.

Below is a list of essential competencies and responsibilities for the superintendency. Its purpose is to assist the board and superintendent in establishing performance goals for the district's financial management and evaluating those responsible for achieving them. Because more than one administrative staff member may share financial responsibilities with the superintendent, the goals can be collectively referred to as those of the superintendent's office.

- Financial Management Leadership
  - Demonstrate an attitude and teach techniques of service leadership.
  - Prepare the budget in a manner consistent with the district's management philosophy.
  - Maintain effective control over budgeted revenues and expenditures.
  - Develop and update financial projections, both near-term and long-term.
  - Develop and apply internal controls, separation of functions, and internal audit procedures.
  - Supervise central office/business staff, including training and evaluation.
  - Use office and business management technology that is reliable and efficient.
  - Develop and maintain standards for operations and maintenance, transportation, food services, and other operational areas necessary to support a school system.
  - Develop and monitor a business office calendar of key functions.
  - Comply with board policies, law, and ethical standards governing business operations.
  - Contribute to community relations program, cooperative planning, and programming.
  - Contribute accurate financial information and expertise to the collective bargaining team.
  - Contribute perspective and data to employee benefits and other financial aspects of human resources administration.
  - If appointed school board secretary, perform legal and other duties accurately.
  - Maintain positive relations with board members, central administrators, faculty, and staff.
  - Be knowledgeable in seeking out grants and other outside funding opportunities.
  - Undertake professional growth and development in school finance and related areas.
- Long-Term Planning
  - Understand and help school board members understand the district's financial position, including the annual audit, Annual Financial Report, bond ratings, and the like.
  - Prepare long-term financial projections under different assumption models.
  - Know community and student body demographics and economic trends.
  - Have a philosophy and method for adding and subtracting expenditures.
  - Give attention to long-term planning for facilities, including preventative maintenance.
  - Know the techniques for carrying out a successful referendum campaign.
  - Know how to use cost and evaluation data as guides in decisions on priorities.

- Lobbying
  - Develop and maintain a network of local, state, and even national officials.
  - Educate the school board on key issues and help the board develop a position and lobbying role.
  - Keep current on Illinois legislative and State Board of Education developments.
  - Make personal contacts on key issues.
- Climate and Morale
  - Educate employee groups to understand financial issues and collaborate on solutions.
  - Pay attention to team building and spirit; be cognizant of administrator and staff workloads.
  - Develop ways of dealing with personal stress
  - Keep the organization focused on the purpose of financial management — the educational program.

The Role of the Financial Administrator

The management and control of the district's financial and support services operations require specialists in accounting, payroll, reporting, budget preparation and oversight, and many other school business functions. These functions are required regardless of the size of the district. In addition, supervising building and grounds care, transportation, and meal services requires knowledge of these functions, including numerous compliance requirements.

In larger districts, these functions are overseen by administrators with such titles as Assistant Superintendent for Business, Director of Business Services, Chief Financial Officer or Controller, Chief School Business Official, or other titles which designate the level of knowledge, responsibility, and independence of the business administrator. In small districts, the superintendent may exercise these responsibilities with the help of one or more administrative assistants. The table below illustrates typical titles and the corresponding scope of responsibilities and qualifications.

Certain documents require that the signature of the "Chief School Business Official (CSBO)" be affixed, and use of that title on other items conveys a high degree of expertise to the reader. One administrator, either the superintendent or an administrator overseeing the business management functions should be designated as CSBO by board action, and employ a dual title in official documents — e.g., Assistant Superintendent for Business/CSBO, Business Manager/CSBO, etc. The title should also be included in board appointment and reappointment actions and in the administrator's contract. The CSBO designation is earned in the process of obtaining the license for that position in line with requirements established by the Illinois State Board

Table 34

Choosing a Title for the School Business Official

Typical Titles	Scope of Responsibilities	Typical Qualifications
Assistant Superintendent for Business of Finance	Oversees, supervises and/or is a key decision maker for all finance and operational aspects of a school district.	• Professional Education License with Chief School Business Official (CSBO) endorsement* • Master's Degree Required
Business Manager or Director	Oversees and/or supervises some or all financial and operational aspects of a school district	• Master's Degree Required • CSBO preferred*
Chief Financial Officer or Comptroller	Oversees school finance and accounting functions and/or performs specific tasks (some operational oversight may apply).	• CPA or Master's Degree in Finance of Accounting

*To comply with TRS Guidelines, please add/CSBO to the title of any position requiring a CSBO endorsement.

Source: *Hiring and Training a School Business Official*, Illinois Association of School Business Officials

of Education. They can be found at www.isbe.net/licensure. A licensed person serving as CSBO is a member of the Illinois Teachers Retirement System.

Some smaller districts have found success and savings in administrative costs by combining their business and support staff management with one or more neighboring districts. Such arrangements are known as "Shared Services" and exist between a high school district and its feeder districts or among small districts. They are facilitated by having common vendors and service providers, including student and administrative software, transportation, food service, and auditing. Additionally, regional agencies can provide a variety of administrative services to the districts within the region.

The Illinois Association of School Business Officials also offers conferences, webinars, written material, and professional designation programs to develop and advance the skills of employees who perform and supervise business functions. Training is offered in finance, facilities management, technology, office support staff, payroll, and bookkeeping.

Appendix A / Resources

This section describes resources that informed the content of this book and are recommended for further information. The internet provides valuable portals to information on school governance, financial management and operations, and the political and legal environment for school finance in the United States. Many of these sites feature links to other related sources. These websites are provided for information only, and their inclusion is not intended as an endorsement of their sponsors' positions, products, or services by the author or publisher.

Internet Resources
The internet provides valuable portals to information on school governance, financial management and operations, and the political and legal environment for school finance in the United States. Many of these sites feature links to other related sources. These websites are provided for information only, and their inclusion is not intended as an endorsement of their sponsors' positions, products or services by the author or publisher.

Accounting Standards
Governmental Standards Accounting Board, www.gasb.org

Administrative Associations
American Association of School Administrators, www.aasa.org
Association of School Business Officials International, www.asbointl.org
Illinois Association of School Administrators, www.iasaedu.org
Illinois Association of School Business Officials, www.iasbo.org
Illinois Principals Association, www.ilprincipals.org
National Association of State Directors of Special Education, www.nasdse.org
National Association of Elementary School Principals, www.naesp.org
National Association of Secondary School Principals, www.nassp.org

Associations of School Boards
Consortium of State School Boards Associations, www.cossba.org
Illinois Association of School Boards, www.iasb.com
National School Boards Association, www.nsba.org

Bond Counsel and Rating Agencies
Chapman and Cutler, www.chapman.com
FitchIBCA, www.fitchratings.com
Moody's Investors Service, www.moodys.com
Standard and Poor's, www.standardandpoors.com

Education News and Research
American Educational Research Association, www.aera.net
Education Week, www.edweek.org

Federal Agencies
Department of Agriculture Food, Nutrition and Consumer Services, www.fns.usda.gov
Department of Education, www.ed.gov

continued

Department of Transportation, www.transportation.gov
National Center for Education Statistics, www.nces.ed.gov

Grant Information
Federal Procurement Data System (FPDS), beta.SAM.gov is the successor to the Catalog of Federal Domestic Assistance
Chronicle of Philanthropy, www.philanthropy.com
U.S. Department of Education, www.ed.gov

Illinois Agencies
Governor's Office of Management and Budget, illinois.gov/agencies/agency.gomb.html
Illinois Department of Revenue, tax.illinois.gov
Illinois State Board of Education, www.isbe.net
Property Tax Appeal Board, www.ptab.illinois.gov
Illinois State Treasurer, www.illinoistreasurer.gov
Illinois State Comptroller, www.illinoiscomptroller.gov

Legislative Information
Legislative Reports – Illinois and Federal, www.iasb.com/advocacy/legislative-reports
ED-RED, www.ed-red.org
Illinois General Assembly, www.ilga.gov

Multi-State Governance Organizations
Council of Chief State School Officers, www.ccsso.org
Education Commission of the States, www.ecs.org
National Association of State Boards of Education, www.nasbe.org
National Conference of State Legislatures, www.ncsl.org

Parent Organizations
Illinois PTA, www.illinoispta.org
National PTA, www.pta.org

Communications Resources Including Referendum Planning
Illinois School Public Relations Association, www.inspra.org
National School Public Relations Association, www.nspra.org

School Finance and Tax Policy Research and Reform
Advance Illinois, www.advanceillinois.org
Association for Education Finance and Policy, www.aefpweb.org
Center for Special Education Finance, www.csef-air.org
Center for Tax and Budget Accountability, www.ctbaonline.org
Consortium for Policy Research in Education, www.cpre.org
Taxpayers' Federation of Illinois, iltaxwatch.org
Wisconsin Center for Education Research www.wcer.wisc.edu
Association for Learning Environments, www.a4le.org
Government Finance Officers Association, www.gfoa.org
Healthy Schools Campaign, www.healthyschoolscampaign.org
National Association of State Directors of Pupil Transportation Services, www.nasdpts.org
National Education Access Network, www.schoolfunding.info
Institute of Child Nutrition, https://theicn.org
National School Plant Management Association, www.nspma.org

National School Transportation Association, www.napt.org
Reimagine America's Schools, www.reimagineschools.us

Publications
Educational Facilities Planning: Leadership, Architecture and Management
	by C. Kenneth Tanner and Jeff Lackney. Pearson, 2005.
Financing Education in a Climate of Change, 13th edition, by Vern Brimley, Jr.,
	Deborah A. Verstegen and Rulon R. Garfield. Pearson, 2020
Handbook of Research in Education, Finance and Policy, 2nd edition, edited by
	Helen F. Ladd and Margaret E. Goertz. New York, Routledge, 2015.
Improving Student Learning When Budgets are Tight by Allan R. Odden. Thousand Oaks, CA, Corwin, 2012.
Planning Educational Facilities for the Next Century, 4th edition by UCen I. Earthman. R&L Education, 2013.
The Principal's Guide to School Budgeting, 2nd edition by Richard D. Sorenson
	and Lloyd M. Goldsmith. Thousand Oaks, CA, Corwin, 2013.
School Budgeting for Hard Times by William K. Posten, Jr. Thousand Oaks, CA, Corwin 2011.
A School Board Member's Handbook by the attorneys of Hodges, Loizzi,
	Eisenhammer, Rodick and Kohn, LLP, 2021.
Winning Grants Step-by-Step, 5th edition, by Tori O'Neal-McElrath, 2019.

Publications of the Illinois Association of School Boards
Coming to Order, A Guide to Successful School Board Meetings, 3rd edition, by IASB Staff, 2023.
Illinois School Law Survey, 17th edition, by Brian A. Braun, 2022
Understanding School Finance, by IASB Staff, 2022.

Appendix B / Bibliography

Chapter 1
Center for Tax and Budget Accountability (April 2023) *Analysis of State Operating Fund Budgets for FY2023*. Retrieved from ctbaonline.org.
Education Week. (February 2023). *Quality Counts, FY2021 report*. Retrieved from *edweek.com*.
Governor's Office of Management and Budget. *Illinois State Budget FY 2024*.
National Center for Educational Statistics. (January 2023). "Revenues and Expenditures for Public Elementary and Secondary Education, School Year 2017-2018, Table 1".

Chapter 2
23 Illinois Administrative Code, Part 100
Illinois State Board of Education. (undated). Mechanics of a School District Budget: A Guide to Understanding the Illinois School District Budget Process. Retrieved from https://www.isbe.net/Documents/mechanics.pdf
Mitchell, Tamara. Assistant Superintendent for Business and Financial Services, Joliet PSD 86.

Chapter 3
Dalianis, Ares. Partner, Franczek P.C.
Hodges, Loizzi, Eisenhammer, Rodick and Kohn (May 2007). "The Extra Mile". Retrieved from https://hlerk.com/the-extra-mile-may-2007/
Illinois Department of Revenue (2004). "The Illinois Property Tax System".
Illinois Department of Revenue (June 2014). "Informational Bulletin FY2014-16". Retrieved from www.revenue.state.il.us/publications/bulletins/2014/FY-2014-16.pdf

Chapter 4
Ares Dalianis (Spring 2018). "Adequacy Referendums". *IASBO Update*, p. 28-31.
Hennessy, Elizabeth. Managing Director of Public Finance, Raymond James.
Illinois Department of Local Government. "The Property Tax Extension Limitation Law, a Technical Manual". Retrieved from http://www.tax.illinois.gov/Publications/Local/Government/PTAX1080.pdf

Chapter 5
Brian Braun (2022) *Illinois School Law Survey, 17th edition*. Springfield, Illinois Association of School Boards.
Center for Tax and Budget Accountability. (April 2023) *CPPTRR and K-12 Funding in Illinois; the Intersection of Taxes and Educational Policy*. Retrieved from *CTBAonline.org*.
Illinois Department of Revenue. *Fiscal Year 2023 Estimate for Replacement Taxes*. Retrieved from Illinois.gov/rev/localgovernments/replacementaxestimate.

Chapter 6
Center for Tax and Budget Accountability. (October 10, 2017). "An Analysis of SB 1947 (Public Act 100-0465): The Evidence-Based Funding for Student Success Act," Retrieved from https://www.ctbaonline.org/reports/analysis-sb-1947-public-act-100-0465-evidence-based-funding-student-success-act
Governor's Office of Management and Budget (February 14, 2018). "Illinois State Budget, Fiscal Year 2019".
Illinois State Board of Education (February 14, 2018). "FY2019 Budget Comparison to Governor's Recommendation".
Illinois State Board of Education. (Spring 2018). Understanding Evidence-Based Funding. Retrieved from https://www.isbe.net/Documents/EBF_Presentation_Detailed.pdf
Michelle Mangan. (2011). An Evidence-Based School Finance Solution for Illinois. Retrieved from

http://illinoisvision2020.org/wp-content/files/Funding_EvidenceBasedSummary.pdf

Michelle Mangan and Michael Jacoby (Summer 2006). "Redefining Equity and Adequacy: An Evidence-Based Model of School Funding". *IASBO Update*, p. 32-39.

Chapter 7

Illinois State Board of Education (February 2023.) *FY 2024 Budget Book*. Retrieved from ISBE.net.

Illinois State Board of Education (May 2023.) *FY 2024 Approved Budget*. Retrieved from ISBE.net.

Mitchell, Tamara. Assistant Superintendent for Business and Financial Services, Joliet PSD 86.

Chapter 8

Alice Armstrong (July/August 2008). "Struggling to survive in the grant 'jungle.'" *The Illinois School Board Journal*, p. 14.

Department of Education. (undated). FY 2019 Education Budget Fact Sheet. Retrieved from https://www2.ed.gov/about/overview/budget/budget19/budget-factsheet.pdf

Mitchell, Tamara. Assistant Superintendent for Business and Financial Services, Joliet PSD 86.

Chapter 9

Brian Braun (2022. *Illinois School Law Survey* (Seventeenth edition). Springfield, Ill: IASB

Franczek, PC.(2011). *Frequently Asked Questions About School Fees*. Presentation at Annual School Law Conference.

Illinois Department of Revenue. *How is the County Schools Facility Occupation Tax Distributed?* Retrieved from https://www2.ed.gov/about/overview/budget/budget21.

Illinois State Board of Education. *School Fee Waivers and Verification Process*. Retrieved from *ISBE.net*.

William H. Phillips and Deanna Sullivan (July/August 2008). "Taking new initiatives with county sales tax". *The Illinois School Board Journal*, p. 10-13.

Chapter 11

Brian Braun (2022). *Illinois School Law Survey* (Seventeenth edition). Springfield, Ill: IASB.

Chapman (August 2022). *Borrowing Alternatives for Illinois School Districts*.

Harding, Kyle. Partner, Chapman and Cutler LLP.

Hennessy, Elizabeth. Managing Director of Public Finance, Raymond James.

Hodges, Loizzi, Eisenhammer, Rodick and Kohn (2021). *A School Board Member's Handbook*.

Chapter 12

Linda Dawson (November/December 2005). "Keeping finances on the up-and-up". *The Illinois School Board Journal*, p. 4-8.

Michael Prombo, Ares Dalianis, and Scott Metcalf (September 2009). "Identifying and Mitigating Sources of Revenue Erosion". *School Business Affairs*.

Scott Metcalf and Ares Dalianis (Winter 2015). "Capturing All of Your Revenues". *IASBO Update*, p. 31-33.

Chapter 13

Citizens Organized to Save the Tax Cap v. State Board of Elections, et al., 392 Ill. App. 3d 392, 910. Retrieved from N.E. 2d 605, 331 Ill. Dec. 196 (1st Dist. 2009)

Illinois Association of School Boards. (2018). Connecting with the Community: The Purpose and Process of Community Engagement as Part of Effective School Governance. Retrieved from http://iasb.mys1cloud.com/communityengagement.pdf

Illinois Council of School Attorneys (September 2018). Answers to FAQs Regarding Referendum Activities Conducted by School Officials. Retrieved from https://www.iasb.com/law/ref_FAQ.pdf

Chapter 14

Illinois State Board of Education. (undated). Mechanics of a School District Budget: A Guide to Understanding the Illinois School District Budget Process. Retrieved from https://www.isbe.net/Documents/mechanics.pdf

continued

William K. Poston (2011). *School Budgeting for Hard Times: Confronting Cutbacks and Critics*. Thousand Oaks, Cal.: Corwin Press.

Chapter 16

Ill. Admin. Code tit. 23, § 226.730. Retrieved from https://ilga.gov/commission/jcar/admincode/023/023002260H07300R.html

Illinois State Board of Education, Special Education (January 2024). Retrieved from https://isbe.net/specialeducation

Illinois State Board of Education-Special Education Deviations (January 2024). Retrieved from https://www.isbe.net/Pages/Special-Education-Deviation-Applications.aspx.

Chapter 18

American Physical Plant Association. *Maintenance and Custodial Staffing Standards*. Included in presentation on school maintenance by Kenneth Roiland and others. IASB/IASA/IASBO Joint Annual Conference, Chicago, November 2019.

Graves, Bill. *Going Electric; School Bus Fleets on the Road to Diesel Alternatives*. The School Administrator, October 2022.

Gallagher Insurance (April 2020). *Guidelines for Reopening School Transportation*. Retrieved from www.ajg.com.

Brad Spicer (October 23, 2013). "11 Components of a Secure School Front Entrance." Campus Safety Magazine. https://www.campussafetymagazine.com/safety/11-components-of-a-secure-school-front-entrance/#:~:text=A%20secure%20entrance%20can%20prevent,and%20implement%20intruder%20response%20plans

Brian Braun (2022). *Illinois School Law Survey, 17th edition*. Springfield, IL, IASB.

Illinois State Board of Education. *Child Nutrition Response Waivers and Other Resources*. Retrieved from ISBE.net/nutrition.

Illinois State Board of Education. *Student Transportation Reimbursement Instructions*. Retrieved from ISBE.net/transportation.

National Center for Education Statistics (February 2022). *Revenues and Expenditures for Public Elementary and Secondary Education, FY2022*, Retrieved from NCES.gov/pubs2022-301tables 3 and 4.

Gallagher Insurance. *Workshop on Cyber Insurance*. Marcus Henthorn and Tyler MacKenzie. *Illinois Association of School Business Officials, www.iasbo.org*, April 2023.

Illinois Association of School Boards PRESS Policy Service. *Sample Policies 4.170 School Safety and 4:190 Targeted School Violence Prevention Program*.

Recommendations of the Illinois Terrorism Task Force, April 2018.

National Clearing House for Educational Facilities. *Low-Cost Security Measures*. Downloaded from www.ecf.org.

North Shore School District 112 Community Newsletters, August and September 2022. *NSSD.org*.

National School Boards Association, *Recommendations on Cybersecurity*. www.nsba.org, 2023.

Chapter 19

Karen Hawley Miles, Kaitlyn Pennington and David Bloom (February 2015). *Do More, Add More, Learn More: Teacher Salary Redesign: Lessons from 10 First-Mover Districts*. Center for American Progress, American Progress.org.

Chapter 21

Illinois State Board of Education. *The School District Financial Profile*. Retrieved from https://www.isbe.net/Documents/School-District-Financial-Profile-Report.pdf

Chapter 25

Illinois Association of School Boards (2023). *Coming to Order – A Guide to Successful School Board Meetings*, Third Edition. Springfield, Ill.: IASB.

Hank Boer (July/August 2004). "Student Activity Funds Need Good Policies". *The Illinois School Board Journal*, p. 4-5, 29.

Hodges, Loizzi, Eisenhammer, Rodick and Kohn (2021). *A School Board Member's Handbook*.

Ross Hodel (November 1981-February 1982). "School Boards as Borrowers and Lenders". *The Illinois School Board Journal*, 36-40.

Appendix C / Index of Tables and Figures

Chapter 1
Figure 1: Sources of School Revenues, FY 2018, page 3
Table 1: Fiscal Year 2024 Illinois General Fund Projected Revenues and Expenditures, page 4

Chapter 2
Table 2: ISBE Budget Form, page 8
Table 3: Major Funds for Budgeting and Accounting, page 9

Chapter 3
Glossary of Terms, page 11
Figure 2: The Tax Cycle Players and What They Do, page 12
Summary of Taxpayer and School Appeal Options, Timelines, and Consequences, page 14
Figure 3: Farmland Assessment Process, page 16
Figure 4: Property Tax Appeals Overview, page 17
Figure 5: How a TIF District Works, page 18
The Seasons of the Property Tax Cycle, page 19
Figure 6: Tax Revenue Formula, page 20
Table 4: School District Tax Rate Limitations, page 21
Tort Liability Fund Levy Requires Card, page 23
Certificate of Tax Levy, page 24

Chapter 4
Sample Extension Calculation for a Tax-Capped District – North Shore SD 112, page 36
Computation for Allowable Tax Extensions in a Non-Tax-Capped District, page 27
Table 5: Year of Enactment of Property Tax Extension Limitation Law (And Levy Year for Determining Debt Service Extension Base), page 28
Table 6: History of CPIs Used in PTELL Calculations, page 29
Table 7: Formula for Computing Allowable Tax Extensions Under the Tax Cap (outside Cook County), page 30
Table 8: Worksheet for Estimating Limiting Tax Rate and Total Allowable Extension, page 31
Strategies to Reduce the Levy Without Affecting Long-Term Operating Revenue, page 32
Tax Caps and the Effects of Decreasing Property Values, page 35

Chapter 6
Figure 7: How Close is the School District to Adequacy, page 41
Table 9: The Elements of the Evidence-Based Model, page 42
Table 10: Effect Sizes of Key Evidence-Based Model Elements, page 43
Glossary of State Aid and EBF Terminology, page 45-46

Chapter 7
Table 11: FY 2024 Budget Allocations for Mandatory Categorical Grants (MCATs), page 48
Table 12: FY 2024 Budget Appropriations for Selected Grants and ISBE Programs, page 49

Chapter 8
Table 13: Federal Education Spending, FY 2023 Budget Appropriations for Selected Programs, page 53
Table 14: Selected State-Administered Federal Grants, page 54

continued

Education Grants 101, page 55

Chapter 9
Waiver of Meal and Required School Fees, page 59
Taking New Initiatives with County Sale Tax, page 62

Chapter 10
Changes in Assessments and Revenues Lag Changes in Property Values, page 65
Sample Cash Flow Worksheet – Education Fund, page 66
Notes to Sample Cash Flow Worksheet – Education Fund, page 67

Chapter 11
Table 15: Loans and Transfers, page 70
Sales Tax Can Support Alternate Revenue Bonds for Facilities, page 72

Chapter 13
Organizing Campaign Committee Work, page 81

Chapter 14
Table 16: ISBE Budget Form, page 84
ESSA Site-Based Expenditure Reporting Now Required on School Report Cards, page 87
Table 17: Budget Summary, page 88

Chapter 15
Model Expenditure Budgeting Calendar, page 91

Chapter 16
Figure 8: Total Enrollment, page 95
Figure 9: 2022 Grade Snapshot, page 95
Table 18: Five-Year Enrollment Trend, page 96
Table 19: Five-Year Projected Enrollments, page 96
Table 20: Classroom Staffing Guidelines for the Home Valley Elementary Schools
       Showing Enrollment and Number of Class Sections, page 97
Table 21: First Section Projection for Home Valley School – Next Year, page 98
Table 22: Projected Specialist Time for Home Valley School, page 99
Table 23: Illinois Evidence-Based Funding Guidelines, page 100

Chapter 17
Table 24: Historical Enrollment of One Department, page 103
Table 25: Home Valley High School Budget Summary, page 104

Chapter 18
Table 26: Cleaning Staff for a 75,000-Square-Foot Building, page 107
Table 27: System Design Life in Years, page 110
Upgrading Security and Plans to Respond to a Shooting Event, page 114
Table 28: 2023-2024 School Food Service Program Rate, page 115
Table 29: Illinois Per Pupil Expenditures by Function, FY 2020, page 117

Chapter 20
Table 30: Education Fund Expenditures, page 124

Chapter 21
Figure 10: Financial Strength Profile of Elgin U-46, page 126
Annual Financial Report – Supplemental Reports, page 127
Table 31: School District Financial Profile Ratings, Fiscal Years 2020 and 2021, page 127
Table 32: FY 2019 Education Fund Balances, page 128
Figure 11: Education Fund Balances Current Budget and Five-Year Projection, page 128
Table 33: Financial Profile Ratings Compared with EBF Tiers, page 129

Chapter 24
Fund Balance Policy Statements for the School Board to Consider, page 137

Chapter 25
Internal Controls Protect District Funds, page 142-143

Chapter 26
Table 34: Choosing a Title for the School Business Official, page 147

Index

– A –

Abatements, 18-19, 29, 77
Accounting categories, 6–9
Activity accounts, 77, 141, 142
Adequacy, 40–41, 43–44, 45, 132
Adequacy targets, 4, 43, 44
Administrative expenditures, 116
Adult education tuition, 58
Aggregate extension base (AEB), 33
Alternate bonds, 73
American Physical Plant Association (APPA), 106
American School Board Journal, 118
Annual Financial Report (AFR), 57, 127, 128
Answers to FAQs Regarding Referendum Activities Conducted by School Officials, 82
Appeal, 11, 14, 15–17, 19, 37, 76
Assessment, 11–25. *See also* Equalized assessed valuation (EAV)
Assessors, 10–13, 15–17
Association of School Business Officials International, 63, 141
Attendance, 77
Audits, 78, 141–144
Authorized maximum tax rate, 27

– B –

Backdoor referenda, 29, 31, 71–73
Balanced budget requirement, 87
Ballooned levies, 18
Banking services, 144–145
Base Funding Minimum (BFM)
    Chicago Block Grant, 46
    defined, 45
    revenue projection, 68
    Special Education grants, 45
Benefits, 115–116, 120, 123–124
Bilingual Education grants, 45
Block grants, 45
Board of Review, 12, 14
Boards of education, *See* School boards
Bond insurance, 75
Bond Issue Notification Act, 71, 73
Bond rating, 74–75
Bonds. *See also* Referenda
    cash flow use, 75
    overview, 71–72
    principal and interest payments, 25
    repayment, 74–75
    treasurer's, 144
    used to exceed debt limit, 74
Borrowing
    federal regulations, 66, 68
    interfund loans and transfers, 69
    long-term, 71–73, 123–124
    planning, 69, 73–74
    role of investments, 78
    short-term, 71, 73–74
    tax cap rules, 29, 31
Braun, Brian A., 63
Breakfast and lunch, *See* Lunch and breakfast
Budgeting
    calendar, 90–93, 139–141
    categories, 6–9
    communication, 91–92
    comparisons to other districts, 117
    development and goals, 146
    expectations, 133
    expenditure management, 118–122
    ISBE Budget Form, 6–9, 83–89
    legal steps, 90–91
    long-term, 123–124
    multi-year, 89
    performance budgeting, 89
    purpose, 83, 85
    structure, 83–89
    techniques, 87–89
Building bonds, 72
Building maintenance, 106–112
Building repairs, 109–110
Building security, 112–114
Building-based budgeting, 87, 97–98

– C –

Campaign committees, 81
Campaign finance reporting, 82
Capital Projects Fund, 9, 25, 67
Capitalized value, 13
Career and Technical Education grants, 53
Cash flow, 66–67, 71–72. *See also* Working cash fund
Cash on hand, 125–126
Categorical grants, 45, 48–50
Census data, 97
Center for American Progress, 120
Center for Tax and Budget Accountability (CTBA), 39, 40

Certificate of Excellence in Financial Reporting, 131
Charter schools, 46
Checks and balances, 78, 133, 136, 141, 142–143
Chicago Block Grant, 45, 46
Chicago Public Schools (CPS), 45, 46, 74, 94
Child find surveys, 97
Child Nutrition programs, 54, 114–115
Childhood Hunger Relief Act, 115
Children Requiring Special Education Services, 57
Chronicle of Philanthropy, 54
Circuit Court, 14–15
Civic Federation, 20
Class size, 98, 119
Cleaning and maintenance, 106–109
Cohort survival, 96–97, 102–103
Coming to Order — A Guide to Successful School Board Meetings, 139
Communications, 80, 82, 90–93, 118
Community Eligibility Process (CEP), 50
Community relations, 80, 82, 118
Comparable Wage Index (CWI), 46
Competitive grants, 48, 56
Computed tax rate, 27
Consortium for Policy Research in Education, 119
Consumer Price index (CPI), 28–29, 30, 31
Contracting labor, 121
Cook County
    assessment, 10–14
    equalization, 12–13, 17
    levy adjustments, 34
    PPRT, 38, 43
    tax billing and collection, 34–36
    tax cap, 26
Cooperative programs, 57–58
Coronavirus, *see* COVID-19 Pandemic
Coronavirus Relief Funding, 52
Cost of living (COL) adjustments, 33, 77, 120, 122
County assessors, 10–13, 15–17
County board of election commissioners, 79
County clerks, 34, 80, 91, 116, 140
County Schools Facility Occupation Tax Law, 61–62, 72, 79
County treasurers, 10, 11, 12
COVID-19 Pandemic
    budget, 9
    delay in distribution of taxes, 35
    fees, 77
    property tax appeals, 14–15
    property tax relief, 20–21
    revenue sources, 52
Credit rating, 75
Curriculum adoptions, 92
Curriculum, high school, 100
Custis, Tim, 142–143

– D –

Debt, *See* Borrowing
Debt certificates, 72
Debt service, 73, 75, 116
Debt Service Extension Base (DSEB), 28, 29, 31–32, 75, 79
Debt Service Fund, 9, 25, 116, 124
Decentralization, 130–131
Defeasance, 32
Deficit reduction plan, 87, 90
Demographics, 95–96
Do More, Add More, Earn More, 120
Driver education fees, 58

– E –

Early childhood education, 49
Education, trends in, 130–132
Education Fund, 36, 58, 66, 67, 72, 84, 123–124, 128
Education Grants, 33, 55
Education Week, 53
Effect size, 43
Election Interference Prohibition Act, 82
Elections, See Referenda
Elementary and Secondary Education Act (ESEA), 51
Elementary schools
    enrollment, 94–97
    non-personnel expenditures, 100–101
    personnel, 97–100
Employment Cost Index, 43, 46
Employment Information System, 43, 46
Energy expenditures, 109
English Language Acquisition grants, 53
English language learners, 43–44, 47, 94
Enrollment
    changes in, 94
    maintaining records, 77
    projections, 94–97, 121–122
    secondary schools, 102–103
    trends in, 94
Entitlement grants, 56
Equalization, 11, 15–17
Equalized assessed valuation (EAV)
    computing tax rate with, 26–29
    debt limits, 125
    debt service and, 73
    defined, 11
    in extension process, 26
    in levy process, 21–23
Equipment expenditures, 124
Equity, 39–40, 45, 132
Equity-based budgeting, 87–88
Ethics laws, 82
Every Student Succeeds Act (ESSA), 51–52
Evidence-Based Funding (EBF)
    accountability, 47
    adoption, 3–4
    budgeting, 88–89

calculation, 42
development and goals, 39-40
effect sizes of elements, 43
financial profile and, 129
funding elements, 39
research, 119
revenue projection, 65
Evidence-Based State Aid, 4
Expenditures. *See also* Budgeting
assumptions, 93
calendar, 91
categories, 85–86
ISBE Budget Form, 84
long-term projections, 123–124
managing, 118–122
NCES report, 117
Extension, 11, 20, 26–27

– F –

Facility Audit, 109–110
Fair market value (FMV), 10–11, 13, 15–17
Federal grants, 51–56, 66
Federal School Lunch program, 51
Fee waivers, 59
Fees, 57–60, 77
Financial administrators, 147–148
Financial consultants, 74–75
Financial policy, 135–138
Financial protection, 142–143
Financial Strength Profile, 126, 137
"Fiscal Neutrality," 40
Food services, 114–115
Foundation level, 39
Foundation support, 39
Foundations, 78
Fuel expenditures, 110–112
Functions (budgeting), 85–86
Fund accounting, 7, 9
Fund balance policy, 137
Funding bonds, 72
Fundraising events, 78
Funds (budget divisions)
balance size, 63
interfund loans and transfers, 69
list of major funds, 7, 9, 85
overview, 9
tax cap rules, 27
tax extensions, 26

– G –

General Fund, 3–5
General obligation warrants, 71
General State Aid (GSA), 39, 45, 67
Generally Accepted Accounting Principles (GAAP), 6, 75
Grants, 39–40, 44, 47, 48–50, 53–54, 55
Guaranteed energy savings contracts, 73

Guidance on Special Education Class Size for 2009–2010 and Beyond, 98
Guide to Operating and Maintaining Energy Smart Schools, 109

– H –

Health insurance, 115–116
Hodel, Ross, 144
Home rule, 27
Hospital exemption, 14

– I –

Illinois
federal grants, 51, 53–54, 55
fee waivers, 59
property tax history, 37
school funding overview, 3–4
Illinois Association of School Boards (IASB), 63, 82, 91, 109, 112, 116, 135
Illinois Association of School Business Officials, 82, 91, 109, 110, 127, 141, 147, 148
Illinois Center for Statistics, 97
Illinois Council of School Attorneys, 82
Illinois Department of Public Health, 96
Illinois Department of Revenue
assessment, 11-12, 15–17
information resources of, 19–20
PPRT, 38
tax extensions, 30-33
Illinois Energy Consortium, 109
Illinois Free Lunch/Breakfast grants, 48, 49–0, 59
Illinois Minimum Wage Law, 120
"Illinois penalty," 74
Illinois Program Accounting Manual (IPAM), 6, 25
Illinois School Board Journal, 62, 118, 143, 144
Illinois School District Liquid Asset Fund (ISDLAF), 60
Illinois School Law Survey, 63
Illinois State Board of Education (ISBE)
Budget Form, 8, 63, 84–86
categorical funding, 48–50
Certificate of Tax Levy, 24
Employment Information System, 43, 46
Evidence-Based Funding (EBF), 39–40
information resources, 116–117
School District Financial Profile, 129
Illinois Teacher Retirement System, 120
Impact aid, 53
In Search of More Productive Schools, 119
Incremental budgeting, 87
Individuals with Disabilities Education Act (IDEA), 51, 53
Inflation rates, 92
Instructional materials, 58, 92, 103
Insurance
benefits, 115–116, 120
bond, 72

property and liability, 116
Insurance reserve bonds, 72
Interest revenue, 60
Interfund loans and transfers, 69, 70, 85
Investments, 78

– L –

Levies
    backup to alternative bonds, 73
    ballooned, 18
    calendar, 29, 33–34, 140
    debt service, 73–74, 116
    defined, 11, 20
    planning, 76–77
    process, 20–25
    tax cap rules, 29, 31, 75
    tax cycle problems, 17–18
    zero increase, 32
Liability fund, 23
Liability insurance, 116
Life-Safety bonds, 72
Life-Safety funds, 77
Limited bonds, 75
Limiting tax rate, 21–23, 31, 33, 111
Line-item budgeting, 87
Local capacity targets, 40, 41, 43–44, 45
Local funding sources, 57–63, 77–78
Long-term revenue projections, 9, 93
Low Income grants, 47
Lunch and breakfast
    as effective educational practice, 122
    federal grants, 49–50, 54, 65, 114–115
    fees, 59, 77
    state demographics, 94–96
    state grants, 49–50

– M –

Maintenance and cleaning, 109
Mandated programs (MCATS), 45, 48
Mangan, Michelle Turner, 41, 43
McKibben, Jerome, 96, 102
Meals, *See* **Lunch and breakfast**
Mechanics of a School District Budget, 7, 9, 87, 90, 116
Mineral assessment, 16
Multiplier, 11, 17

– N –

Naming rights, 78
National Association of Secondary School Principals, 105
National Center for Educational Statistics (NCES), 3
National School Foundation Association, 78
New property, 19, 22, 23, 28–29, 30
No Child Left Behind Act (NCLB), 51
Non-personnel expenditures, 92–93, 100–101, 105, 118–120

Non-resident tuition, 57
North Shore School District, 114

– O –

Objects (budgeting), 86
Odden, Allan, 40
O'Neal-McElrath, Tori, 54
Operating fund tax rates (OTR), 22
Operations & Maintenance Fund, 71, 85
Operations and Maintenance Best Practices Guide, 109
"Organizing Campaign Committee Work," 81
Orphanage Act, 49
Outsourcing, *See* **Contracting labor**

– P –

Pandemic, *See* **COVID-19 Pandemic**
Participation fees, 58, 77
Personal Property Replacement Tax (PPRT), 38, 43
Personal property replacement tax notes, 71
Personnel
    administration, 116
    benefits, 115–116, 119–120, 125
    cleaning and maintenance, 106–109
    decentralizing decisions, 131
    elementary schools, 94–101
    enrollment-based estimations, 94–96
    expenditure control, 118–120
    limitations, 133
    projections, 125–127
    secondary schools, 102–103
    transportation, 110–112
Phillips, Bill, 143
Picus, Lawrence O., 40, 43, 119
Planning Guide for Maintaining School Facilities, 109
Policy Reference Education Subscription Service (PRESS), 60
Poston, William K., 88
Private Facility, 57
Private school tax credits, 45–46
Professional judgment methodology, 41
Program budgeting, 131–132
Property assessment, *See* **Assessment**
Property insurance, 116
Property tax
    correlation with school funding ability, 4
    exemptions, 14
    fund allocation, 7–8
    future of, 37
    glossary of terms, 11
Property Tax Appeal Board (PTAB), 13, 14, 15, 17
Property tax cycle
    assessments, 10–20
    calendar, 19
    information resources, 19–20
    levies and extensions, 20–25
    overview, 10

problems, 17–18
Property tax exemptions, 19
Property Tax Extension Limitation Law (PTELL), 22, 26–37, 77, 80
Property Tax Extension Limitation Law Technical Manual, 28, 37
Property tax reduction referenda, 46
Property tax relief, 20–21
Property Tax Relief Fund, 46, 47
Property values, 20, 28, 33, 35, 65. *See also* Equalized assessed valuation (EAV)
Proration, 39, 46
Public Act 94-976, 33
Public Act 96-0501, 29
Public Act 97-0542, 61–62
Public Act 100-0465, 39
Public Act 102-0519, 36
Purchasing, 120–121, 136

– R –

Referenda
    calendar, 81
    communication and campaigns, 79–82
    property tax reduction, 46
    sales tax, 61–62
    tax cap rules, 29, 31, 73, 80
Regional Office of Education (ROE), 72
Regionalization factor, 41, 46
Remediation, 119
Restricted revenues, 48
Restructuring debt, 73
Revenue anticipation notes, 71
Revenue controls, 76–78
Revenue management, 76–78, 93, 125–129. *See also* Budgeting
Revenue projections, 9, 18, 64–68, 93

– S –

Safety, 112–114
Salaries, 119–120
Salary factor, 46
Sales tax, 61–62, 72
The School Administrator, 118
A School Board Member's Handbook, 70, 139
School boards
    bank selection, 144
    calendar, 139–145
    establishing need for referenda, 79
    financial controls, 76–78
    financial policy, 135–138
    financial responsibilities, 139–141
    role in budgeting, 90–91
    role in levy process, 19–20, 25
    role in referenda, 79–82
    treasurer, 144
"School Boards as Borrowers and Lenders," 144

School Budgeting for Hard Times, 89
School Business Affairs, 63, 118
School District Financial Profile, 129
School districts
    cooperative programs, 57–58
    EBF calculations, 41, 43
    equity, 39–40
    financial health, 125–129, 139
    financial policy development, 137–138
    rural, 15
    state aid under EBF, 3–4
    tax cap rules, 26–27, 29, 31
    tax rate limitations, 21
    tiers, 46
School Facility Occupation Tax Fund, 61–62
School Funding Reform Act, 65, 77
School Lunch and Breakfast Program, 49–50
School-site budgeting, 87
Secondary schools, 102–105
Securities and Exchange Commission, 69
Security, 112–114
Special education
    alternatives, 119
    cooperatives, 57
    IDEA, 51, 57
    teachers, 98–100
    transportation, 111
Special Education grants, 47
Special subject teachers, 98–100
Staff, *See* Personnel
State aid anticipation certificates, 71
State budget, defined, 46
State Officials and Employees Ethics Act, 82
Student-based funding (SBF) budgeting, 87
Summer school tuition, 57
Superintendents, 91, 146–148. *See also* School districts
Supervisor of Assessment, 12
Surety bonds, 144
Surveys, 79

– T –

Tax anticipation notes, 71
Tax anticipation warrants, 71
Tax caps. *See also* Property Tax Extension Limitation Law (PTELL)
    borrowing under, 75
    and changes in enrollment or programs, 29
    defined, 11
    extension process, 26–27
    monitoring yearly calculations, 30–31
    property value effect on, 26–27, 29, 35
    purpose, 26–27
    referenda under, 80
    tax rate calculations, 30, 33–34
    transportation expenditures, 110–112

Tax Increment Financing (TIF) districts, 18–19, 28, 47, 64, 73, 76, 134
Tax rates
    calculations under tax caps, 30, 33–34
    defined, 11
    in extension process, 26–27
    limitations, 21
    property value effect on, 28–29
    PTELL restrictions, 80
Taxes, See Levies; Property tax; Sales tax
Tax-exempt status, 60, 63, 69, 78
Taxpayers' Federation of Illinois, 20
Teachers, 94, 97–100, 119–120, 124. See also **Personnel**
Teachers' orders, 71–72, 126
Technology expenditures, 92–93, 100–101, 116, 120–121
Textbook sales and rental, 58, 141
Theft safeguards, 141–142
Tier funding, 40, 44, 46
Title I grants, 51, 53–54
Tort Immunity and Judgment Fund, 70, 85
Tort judgment funding bonds, 72
Tort liability funds, 23, 77
Transition ratio, 96
Transportation
    criminal gang activity, 111
    expenditures, 110–112
    fees, 58
    grants, 48
Transportation Fund, 85
Treasurers, county, 12

Treasurers, school board, 144
Truth in Taxation Act, 19, 140
Tuition, 57–58

– U –

U.S. Census, 97
U.S. Department of Education, 51–54, 55, 66–68
U.S. Department of Energy, 109
U.S. Environmental Protection Agency, 109
Utilities, 109

– V –

Vehicles, 110–112
Vocational education cooperatives, 58
Vocational Transportation grants, 65
Voter registration, 81

– W –

Wealth neutrality, 46
Whole-school models, 122, 131–132
Winning Grants Step by Step, 54
Wisconsin School Adequacy Initiative, 132
Working cash bonds, 71, 137
Working Cash Fund, 25, 63, 69–72, 75, 78, 85, 125–126,

– Z –

Zero increase levy, 32
Zero-based budgeting (ZBB), 87